IMAGES
of America

FILIPINOS IN HOLLYWOOD

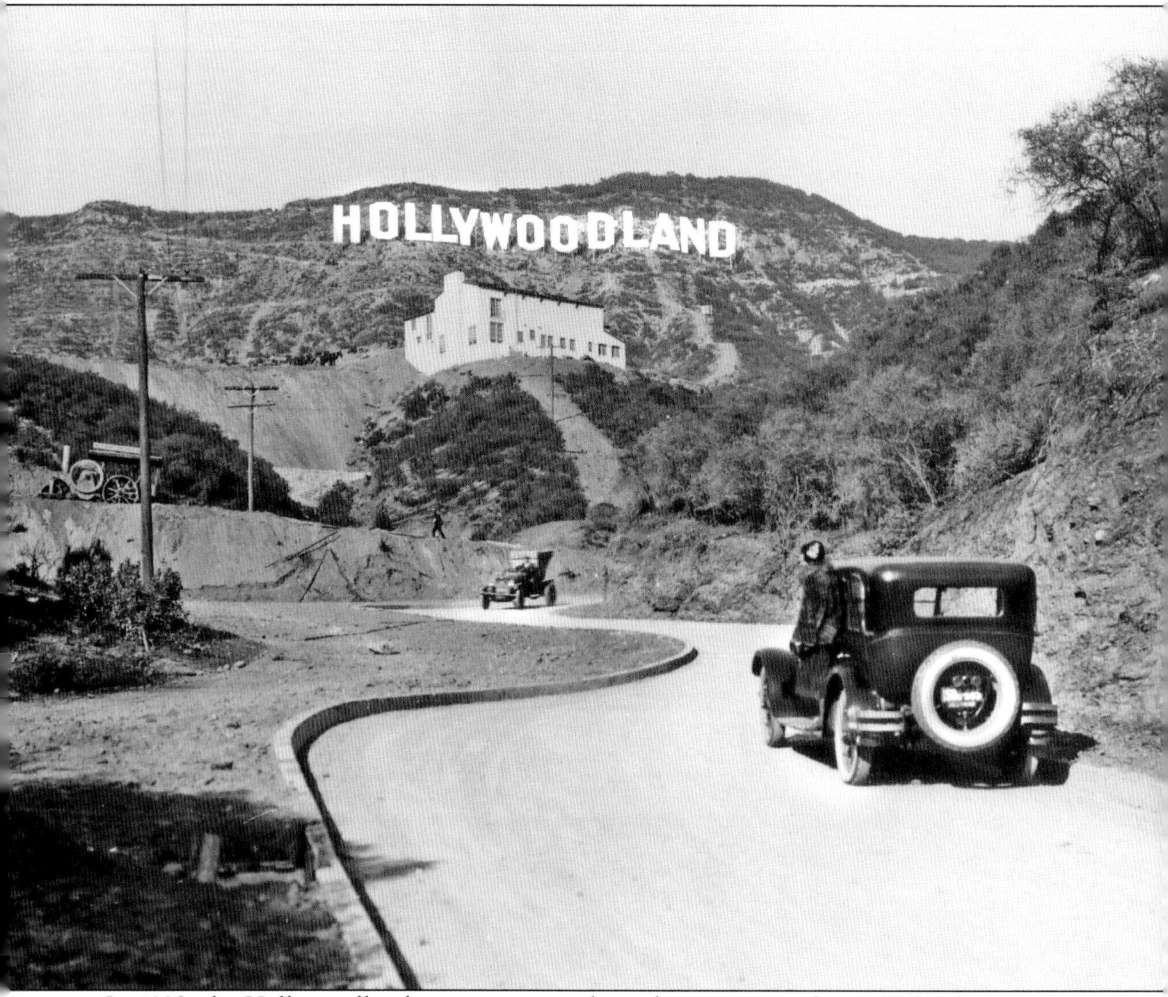

In 1923, the Hollywoodland sign was created to advertise a new housing development in a desirable area of Hollywood. The sign was constructed of 50-foot, individual, white letters that were displayed in the hills above Hollywood. The new houses became homes to the wealthy, many being affiliated with the movie industry. As the need for houseboys, cooks, and chauffeurs grew, so did the needs of the early Filipino settlers in Los Angeles to find work. Many Filipinos that sought work in Hollywood were offered only domestic positions in homes and in service-related fields as waiters and busboys at nearby restaurants. The Hollywoodland sign remained part of the Hollywood landscape long after the housing development was completed and sold, and the Filipinos continued to fill the needs in Hollywood in domestic and service-related positions for more than four decades. (Courtesy of Marc Wanamaker/Bison Archives.)

On the Cover: A crowd of Filipino men line up for a casting call at Metro-Goldwyn-Mayer Studios in 1929 to audition for the film *The Pagan*. The film was about a half–South Seas islander who fell in love with a white woman. Starring Ramon Novarro, a native of Mexico, the film was made before the infamous production code of 1934 that disallowed "scandalous" subject matter, such as interracial romance, in films. (Courtesy of Marc Wanamaker/Bison Archives.)

IMAGES
of America

FILIPINOS IN HOLLYWOOD

Carina Monica Montoya

ARCADIA
PUBLISHING

ISBN 978-0-7385-5598-0

Published by Arcadia Publishing
Charleston SC, Chicago IL, Portsmouth NH, San Francisco CA

Printed in the United States of America

Library of Congress Catalog Card Number: 2007934131

For all general information contact Arcadia Publishing at:
Telephone 843-853-2070
Fax 843-853-0044
E-mail sales@arcadiapublishing.com
For customer service and orders:
Toll-Free 1-888-313-2665

Visit us on the Internet at www.arcadiapublishing.com

To my family, who shares my desire in keeping our heritage alive, and to Steven De La Vega, who was the most supportive one of all in helping me accomplish this project.

Contents

ACKNOWLEDGMENTS

The most difficult task in telling a history that spans more than 80 years of a particular people in a specific place and area through photographs is finding the right photographs. There was no one source that could provide me with all of the photographs and information I desired. But I was fortunate in that each source I met led me to the next. It was much like being on a scavenger hunt, finding bits and pieces of information and photographs here and there, sometimes finding more, often finding less, and more often finding nothing. But in the end, all the bits and pieces magically came together and collectively a picture of the history of the Filipinos in Hollywood emerged.

I want to especially thank my editor at Arcadia Publishing, Jerry Roberts, for his professional guidance and support in making this book possible.

I also want to thank Carolyn Kozo Cole, senior librarian, Photograph Collection/History and Genealogy Department of the Los Angeles Public Library, for her generosity, assistance, and support of this book, and the use of the images from the Shades of L.A. Archives.

I am indebted to the family of Numeriano D. Lagmay, professional photographer, Los Angeles press agent, and longtime Angeleno, for providing many of the photographs of the Filipinos in Los Angeles during the early years; and Sthanlee B. Mirador, Filipino American Hollywood celebrity photographer, for his generosity in providing most of the new generation Filipino photographs.

My deepest appreciation goes to all who shared my vision of this book and generously contributed to it: Jennifer Aquino, actress; Faustino "Peping" Baclig, World War II veteran and Filipino American Service Group, Inc., volunteer; Jeff "Beach Bum" Berry, author; Alyse Bertenthal, Esq.; Mike Buhen, owner of Tiki Ti in Hollywood and son of legendary Ray Buhen, founder of the Tiki Ti; Gene Cajayon, writer, director, and Filipino American filmmaker; Liza Del Mundo, actress; Steven De La Vega; the Everett Collection; Joselyn Geaga-Rosenthal, founder and owner of Remy's on Temple; Patricio Ginelsa, filmmaker; Robert P. Gordon, Esq.; chef Andre Guerrero, restaurateur; John Hermann, technical guidance and Web site designer; Benita Q. Lagmay; Juliet Lagmay-Akiaten; Eileen Akiaten; Jonathan Lorenzo, administrator of the Filipino American Library; Camille Mana, actress; Joanne Mallillin, choreographer and dancer; Eric G. Montoya; Mary Lou Montoya; Ernie Pena, freelance photographer; Rosario Quitiviz; Maria Quiban, actress and weather/news reporter for Fox 11 and My 13 News; Caroline Salvador; John Herman Shaner, acclaimed screenwriter, playwright, director, and producer; Celina Taganas-Duffy, artist and founder/owner of Tagline Communications; Marilyn Tokuda, arts education director of East West Players; and Marc Wanamaker of Bison Archives, historian, filmmaker, and author.

Introduction

This book is about the role of the Filipinos in Hollywood from the 1920s to present in both the Hollywood community and the Hollywood film industry. Two historical events occurred in Los Angeles during the 1920s—the film industry settled and grew roots in Hollywood and the first wave of Filipinos arrived in Los Angeles. That first wave brought in mostly unmarried young adult men who were solicited by American agribusiness companies on the West Coast. Many of these young men worked in the California fields, while others remained in Los Angeles and sought work in the city. As the film industry blossomed over the next decade so did the community. New housing developments, restaurants, bars, and clubs proliferated around Hollywood, resulting in a growing need for service-related workers. The Filipinos that sought work in the city gravitated to Hollywood because of its need for workers. The studios hired Filipinos as assistants, chauffeurs, and cooks. As well, the studios cast Filipinos in films, often as uncredited extras. Some filled domestic positions as houseboys in the new housing developments, and others found work in Hollywood's restaurants, bars, and clubs as waiters, bartenders, and cooks.

The film industry and the community became synonymous, and both continued to grow throughout the decades, providing steady work for the Filipinos. In the early years, the role of the Filipinos was to help Hollywood fill its needs. These young men without families, forced to live under restrictive laws and among discriminating peers, created a new way of life for themselves. This was a life complete with stylish clothes, new cars, and a sense of pride in being the best at their trade. Bartenders invented many of the tropical drinks that made Hollywood restaurants and bars popular for their exotic libations, some of which are still popular today, such as the Zombie. One Filipino bartender, Ray Buhen, is credited with inventing many tropical mixed drinks, which helped the Hollywood restaurants and bars where he worked become popular, especially among celebrities during the heyday of Polynesian-style nightclubs. In the 1960s, Ray opened his own bar, the Tiki Ti, in Hollywood. Although Ray Buhen is no longer here, his son and grandsons keep Ray's spirit alive by maintaining the bar and only serving tropical drinks.

When U.S. immigration opened its doors to allow Filipino women to immigrate, the Filipino American family was born. The Filipino culture is rich in spirit and pride, and to a Filipino, to start a family means to save money, buy a home, and send the children to private schools. Filipino values are made up in equal parts of family, religion, education, and home ownership. These values are what keep the Filipino family strong and together. As families grew, so did the Filipino community. A large Filipino enclave was established in an area in nearby downtown Los Angeles, now officially designated as Historic Filipinotown. This section of Los Angeles is where many of the early Filipino immigrants bought homes. Others bought homes in the valleys of Los Angeles and in pocket areas of Hollywood. As the first generation of American-born Filipinos began to flourish, old customs were kept alive and remained a big part of the Filipino community.

Grand celebrations were given on certain occasions that marked an event in a child's life. Catholic baptisms, christenings, birthdays, First Holy Communions, musical recitals, graduations, debutant balls, weddings, and beauty pageants were all recognized and were celebrated events.

They were events interwoven within the fabric of the Filipino family. Talents that may have been ignored or gone unnoticed outside of the Filipino community were highly recognized and celebrated within the community. The recognition the community gave its children widened the door for others to see and enter the world of the Filipino American.

The early Miss Philippines pageants were fund-raising events. Proceeds helped raise enough money to build the Filipino American Community Center in Los Angeles (FACLA). The FACLA was the first of its kind that was planned, built, and designated as a Filipino American community center in the United States. Club meetings, events, celebrations, and youth dances were often held at the center. The center greatly helped the Filipino community become visible within Los Angeles. As the community center grew, Filipino Americans began taking more active roles within the community, which greatly enhanced their political position as one of the fastest-growing minorities in the city. Dignitaries from the Philippines began visiting Los Angeles and were graciously received by Los Angeles's city leaders, such as the mayor and the city council. The involvement of the city's political leaders began to extend into the Filipino community on a more personal level. They began to attend many Filipino events, and Filipino Americans began to run for and hold public offices.

With the obstacles of discrimination against minorities in general having waned, the Filipino Americans became fully assimilated, and the first generation of American-born Filipinos who reached adulthood were now mostly educated and in a position to realize their potential in becoming anything they desired. Institutions that once discriminated against Filipinos were now soliciting them for their talents and skills. With the population of Filipinos in Southern California being one of the highest concentrations of Filipinos in America, the Filipinos in Los Angeles in general, and Hollywood in particular, have evolved into becoming highly acknowledged for their contributions not only to the city and America, but also internationally through business, academic accomplishments, specialized skills, and talent.

The new generation of Filipinos today are the products of the hard work and sacrifice of the Filipinos of yesteryear. Beginning as one of the least recognized and least documented Asian ethnic groups in Hollywood, Filipinos today shine in Hollywood's limelight as a big part of the business community, industry, and glamour. The earlier generations of Filipinos laid the groundwork, mostly behind the scenes, for today's Filipino American success.

One

EARLY YEARS IN HOLLYWOOD

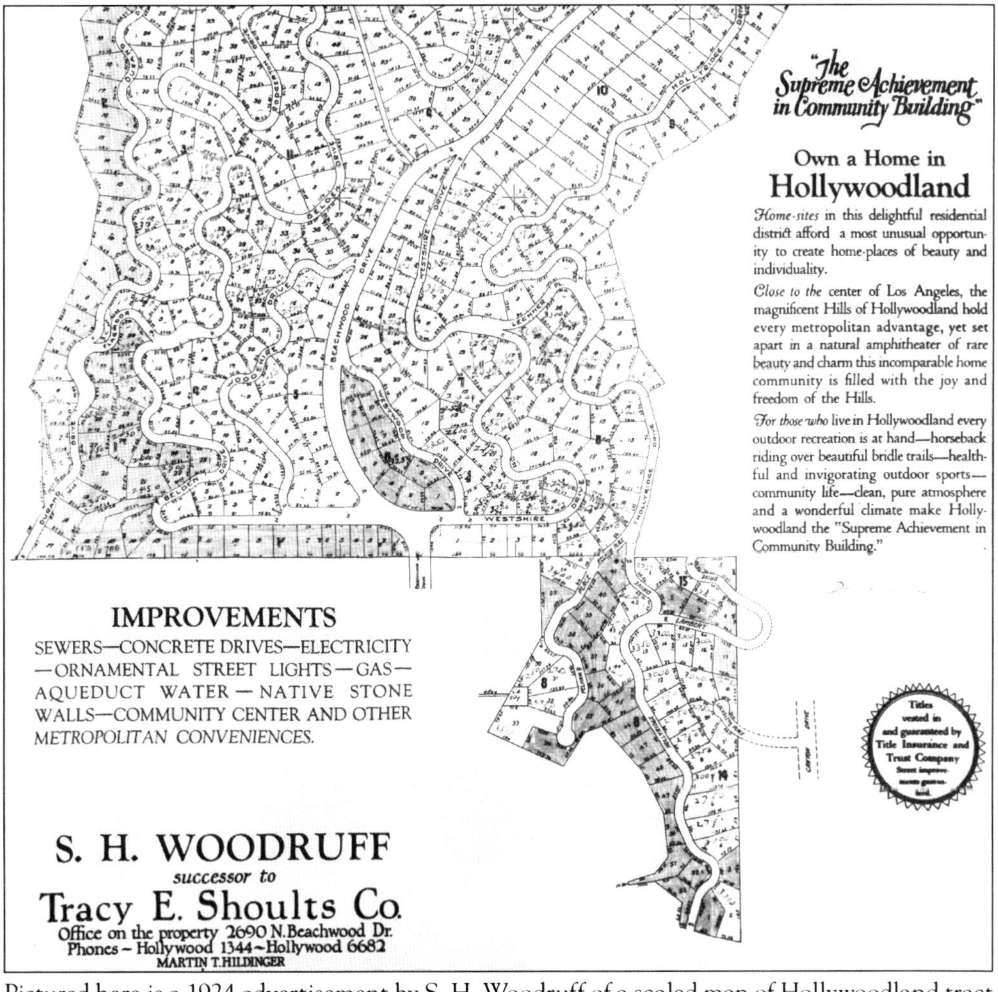

Pictured here is a 1924 advertisement by S. H. Woodruff of a scaled map of Hollywoodland tract No. 6450. The bottom half of the photograph is an engineer's map showing available properties and roads. After its completion, this new housing development created an abundance of domestic and service-related positions, many of which the Filipinos filled. (Courtesy of Security Pacific National Bank (SPNB) Collection/Los Angeles Public Library.)

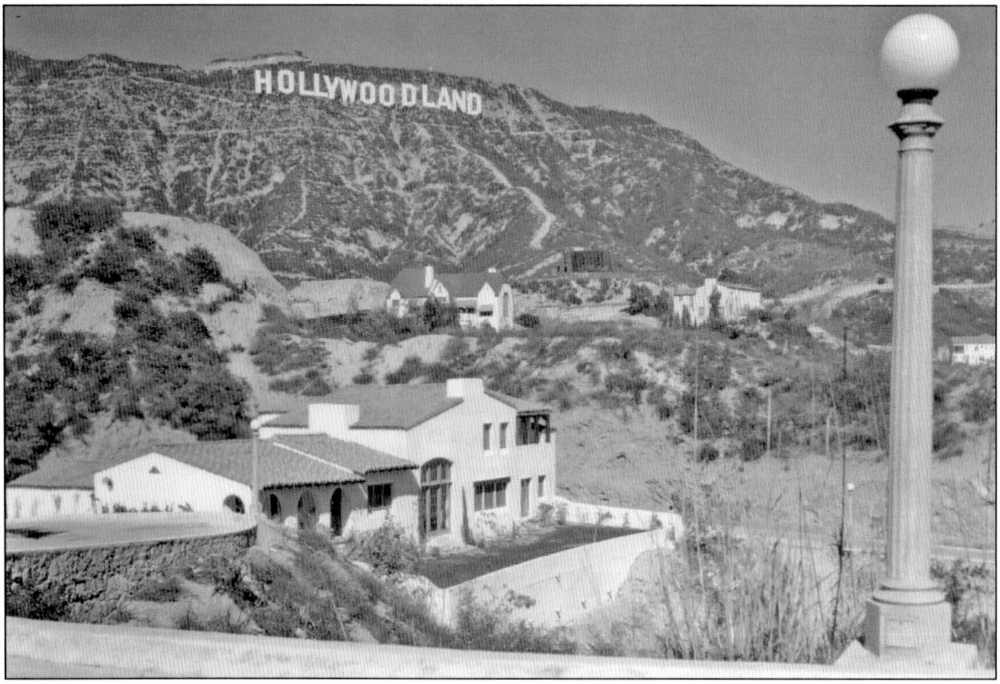

This 1930s photograph was taken from one of the winding streets leading up to the Hollywood hills. A few of the luxury homes built for Hollywoodland can be seen. Far above in the background are the 50-foot, individual, white letters that displayed the Hollywoodland sign. Not only did Hollywoodland become a desirable place in Los Angeles to live, but among the Filipinos who sought domestic work, Hollywoodland was a desirable place to be employed. (Courtesy of SPNB Collection/Los Angeles Public Library.)

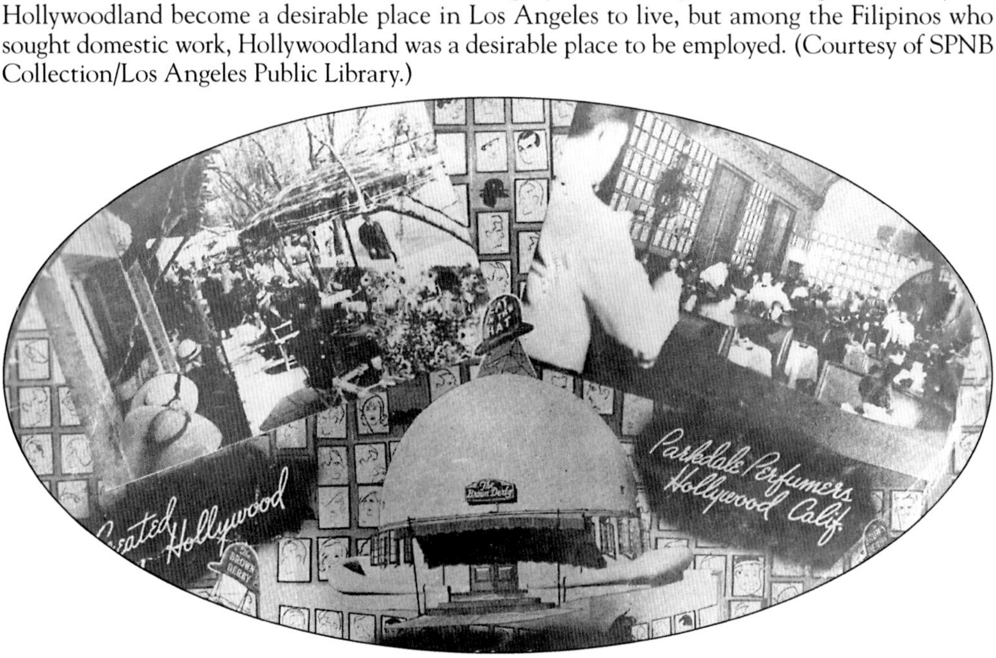

Pictured here is a 1926 collage advertisement of the Brown Derby restaurants. There were four Brown Derby restaurants: Beverly Hills, Los Feliz, Wilshire at Alexandria, and on Vine Street in Hollywood. Many Filipinos worked in these restaurants as busboys, waiters, and dishwashers. (Courtesy of SPNB Collection/Los Angeles Public Library.)

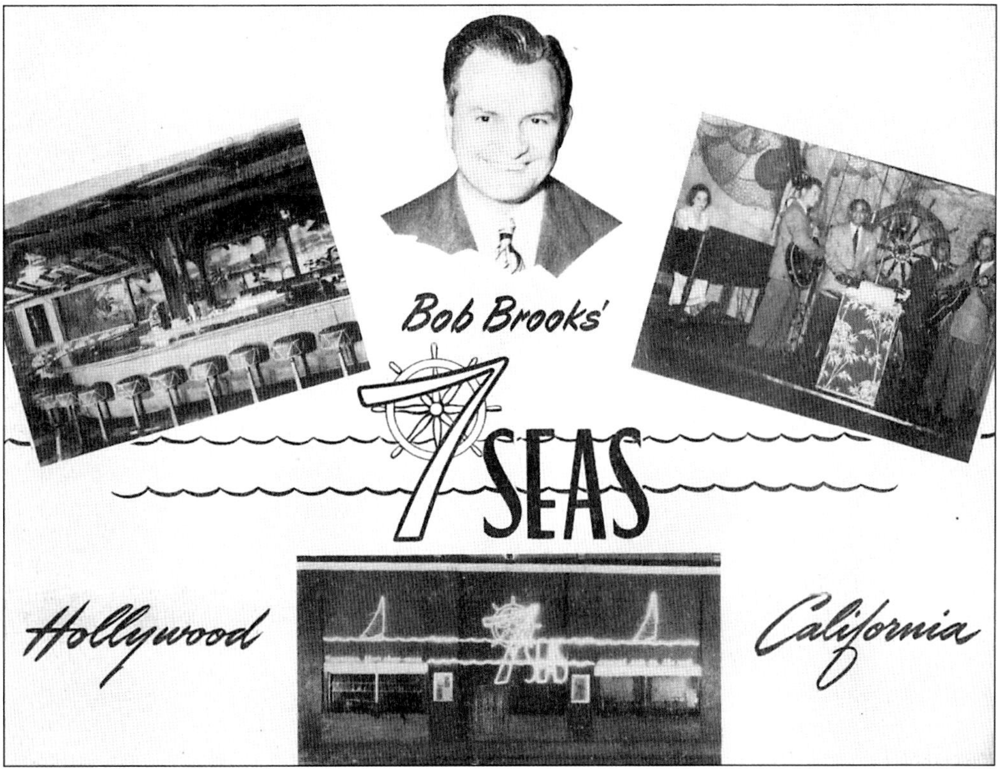

A photograph of the menu cover from Bob Brooks' Seven Seas Polynesian-style restaurant and bar that opened in the 1930s. Its competitors included Don the Beachcomber; Sugie's Tropics on Rodeo Drive in Beverly Hills; the Dresden Room; Ching Hau in Studio City; the Tropics, later renamed the Luau; and the China Trader; all known as tropic Polynesian-type restaurants and bars and all popular celebrity choices for the tropical mixed drinks that Filipinos created. These establishments employed many Filipinos as bartenders, waiters, and busboys. (Courtesy of Juliet Lagmay-Akiaten.)

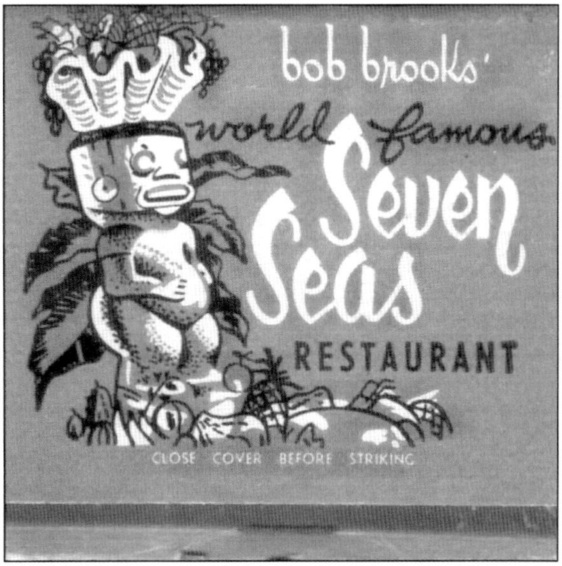

Pictured here is a matchbook cover from Bob Brooks' world famous Seven Seas bar. Some Filipinos were lured away to competitive restaurants and bars by being offered more money, especially the bartenders who became well known for making and creating new tropical drinks. (Courtesy of Juliet Lagmay-Akiaten.)

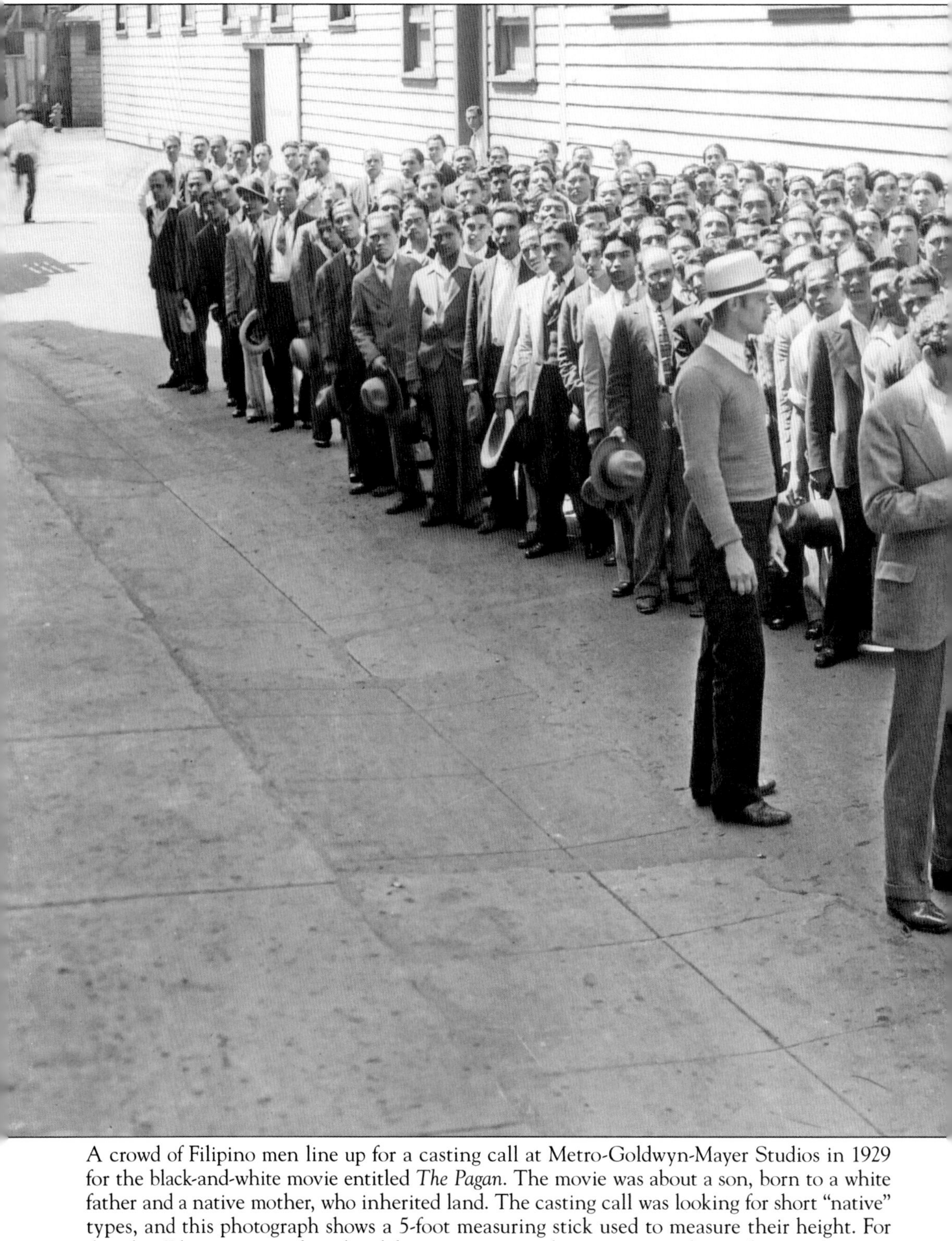

A crowd of Filipino men line up for a casting call at Metro-Goldwyn-Mayer Studios in 1929 for the black-and-white movie entitled *The Pagan*. The movie was about a son, born to a white father and a native mother, who inherited land. The casting call was looking for short "native" types, and this photograph shows a 5-foot measuring stick used to measure their height. For decades, Filipinos were often slated for native-type and service-type roles, and were often cast

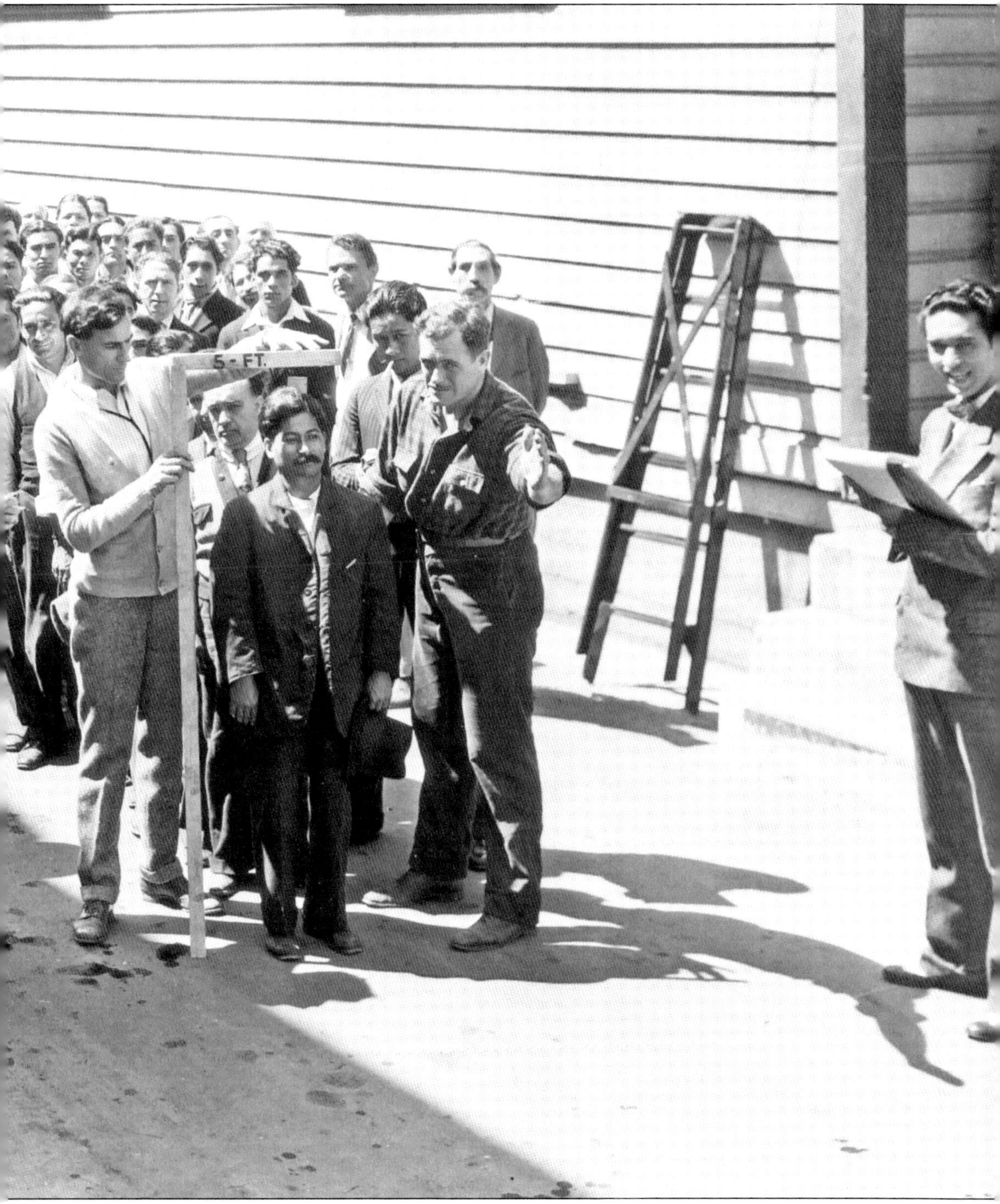

as uncredited extras despite some actors being widely known in the film community. One such actor was Leon Lontoc, who was cast in more than 50 roles (Chinese boatman, butler, steward, native, and slave) during his acting career, beginning in 1943. In the 1970s, Lontoc was cast in some popular television shows in credited roles but still as a native, aide, assistant, houseboy, and servant. (Courtesy of Marc Wanamaker/Bison Archives.)

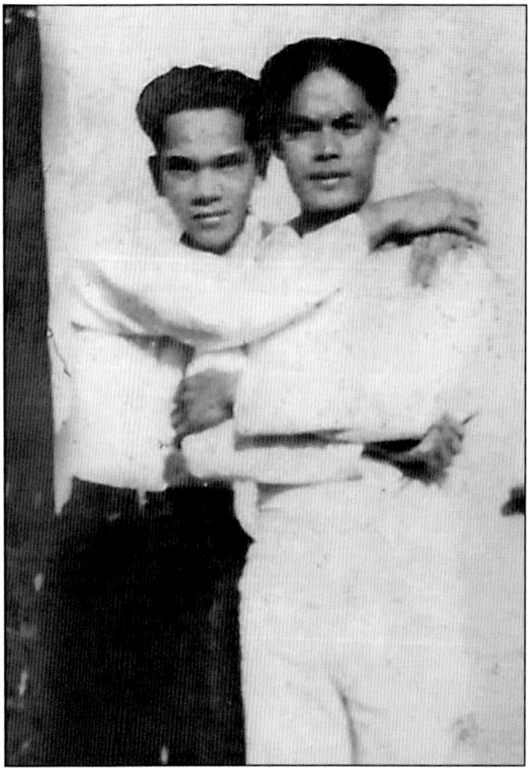

Tommy Montoya (left) poses with a friend in the 1920s. Many of the early settlers came from different areas of the Philippines and spoke different dialects, but they all shared a common dream of finding work and beginning a new life in the United States. Strong bonds formed among these single men, and jobs were typically found through each other, especially in Hollywood restaurants and bars. (Courtesy of Eric G. Montoya.)

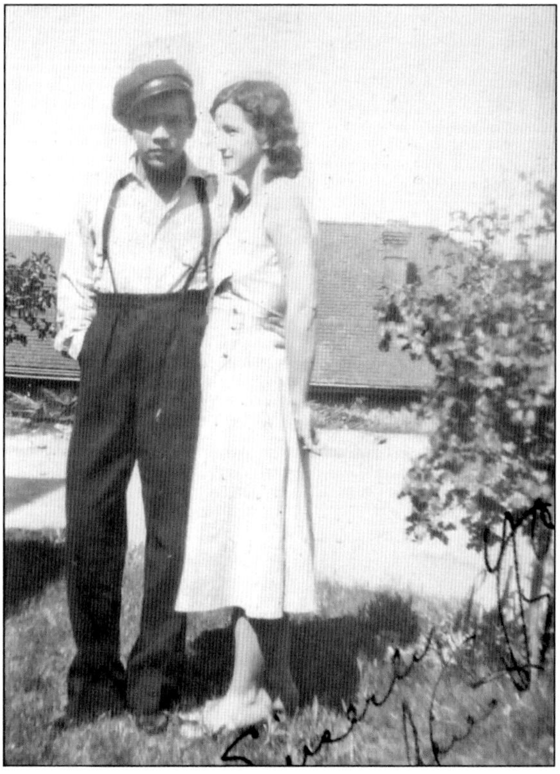

Tommy Montoya poses in this photograph with a white woman in the 1920s. Prior to the 1940s, laws prohibited interracial marriage with whites. Filipino men that arrived in Los Angeles in the 1920s were mostly unmarried, alone, forced to live in an impoverished section of downtown Los Angeles, and discriminated against by the whites in Los Angeles. Many racial confrontations occurred between Filipinos and whites, usually over a Filipino man associating with a white woman. Discrimination against Filipinos and racial tension greatly limited their freedom within a "free country." It took decades before the Filipinos in Los Angeles took an active political stance to further their rights, became acknowledged for their skills and talents, and began to be an active part of the country in general and the community in particular in which they played a big role in its early development to its success today. (Courtesy of Eric G. Montoya.)

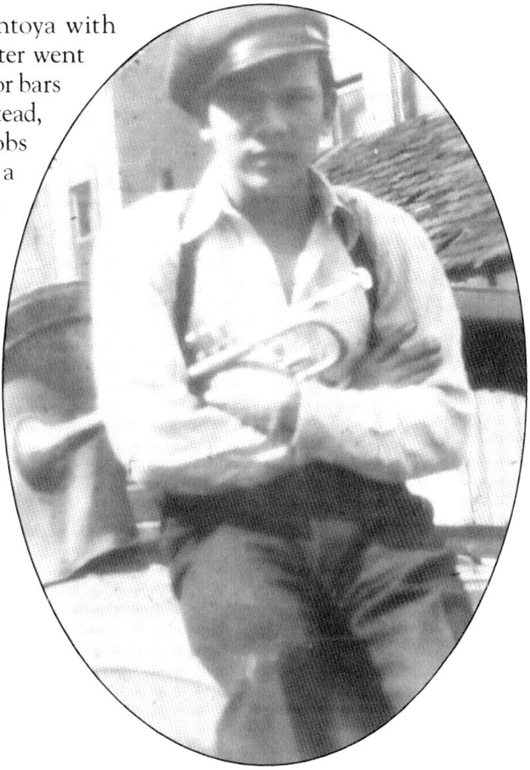

Pictured here in the 1920s is Tommy Montoya with his trumpet. His musical talent as a trumpeter went unsung, unable to sell his talent in any clubs or bars in Hollywood during the 1920s and 1930s. Instead, he was offered one of the most popular jobs available to Filipinos in the 1920s—work as a busboy in one of several Hollywood restaurants. (Courtesy of Eric G. Montoya.)

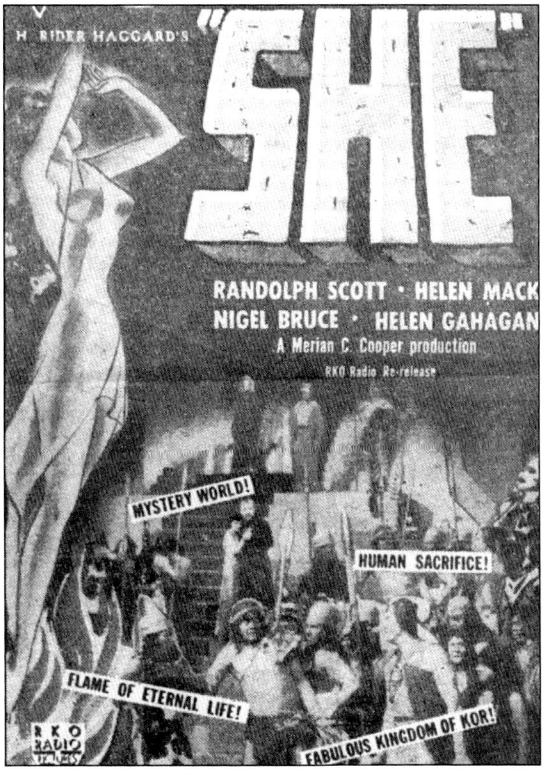

Pictured here is a movie poster of the black-and-white film *She*, released by RKO Radio Pictures in 1935. The movie, about a lost land with beautiful women, cast many Filipinos as uncredited extras to play savage-type native roles. Many Filipinos who attended casting calls were the waiters and busboys of Hollywood's restaurants and bars. Working late hours, they not only became acquainted with Hollywood's industry figures and crews who spread the word on upcoming casting calls, but they were free during the day to attend those casting calls and auditions. (Courtesy of Eric G. Montoya.)

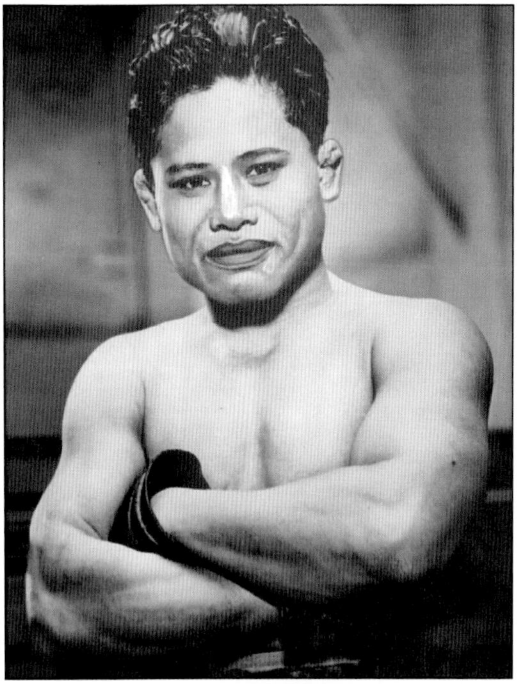

Filipino American boxer Pablo Dano is pictured in 1934. The photograph was an advertisement that read "Boxer Pablo Dano will fight at the Olympic tonight." A few Filipino American fighters, such as Dano, gained national recognition. (Courtesy of the *Herald-Examiner* Collection/Los Angeles Public Library.)

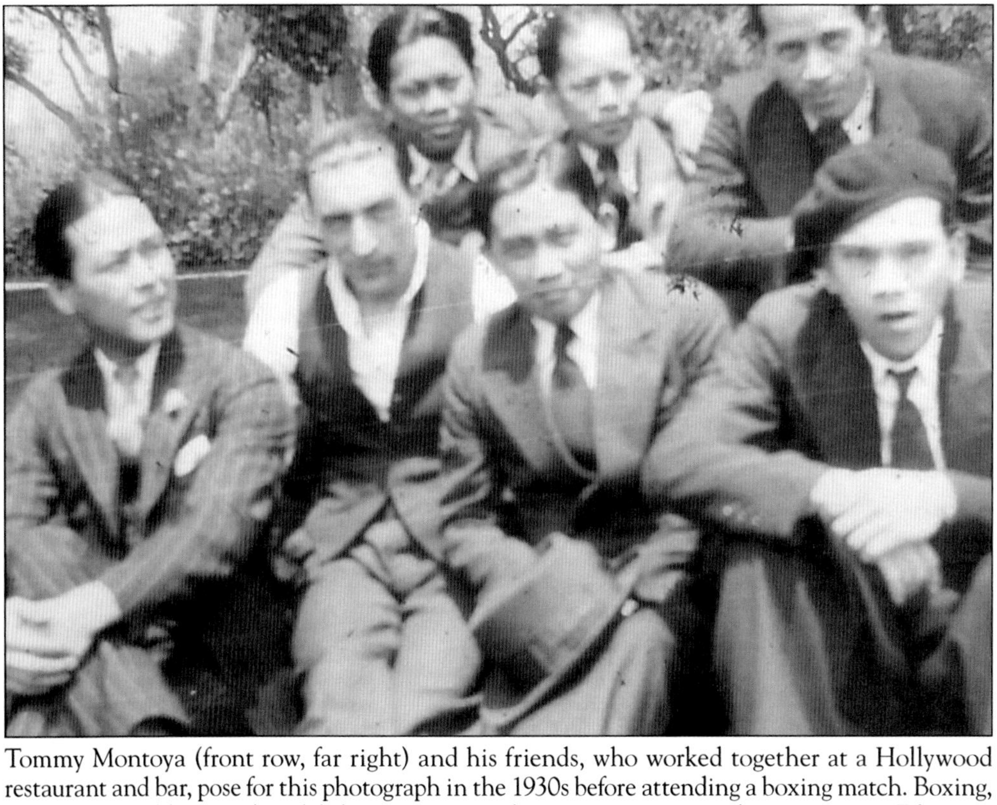

Tommy Montoya (front row, far right) and his friends, who worked together at a Hollywood restaurant and bar, pose for this photograph in the 1930s before attending a boxing match. Boxing, wrestling, gambling, and cockfighting were popular entertainment and sports among Filipinos. (Courtesy of Eric G. Montoya.)

Ray Buhen (far right) is pictured here in 1935 with members of the cast of *Mutiny on the Bounty* in front of Christian's Hut on Catalina Island. Christian's Hut, a bar named after Clark Gable's character in the film, was built on the island to serve the cast and crew who were there filming *Mutiny on the Bounty.* The six-paned window above the bar was Clark Gable's private room while he was on the island. Buhen was hired to bartend during the filming. After filming of the movie was completed, Christian's Hut was removed and relocated to Hollywood where it became a popular bar among celebrities and servicemen. It burned down in 1963. (Courtesy of Mike Buhen.)

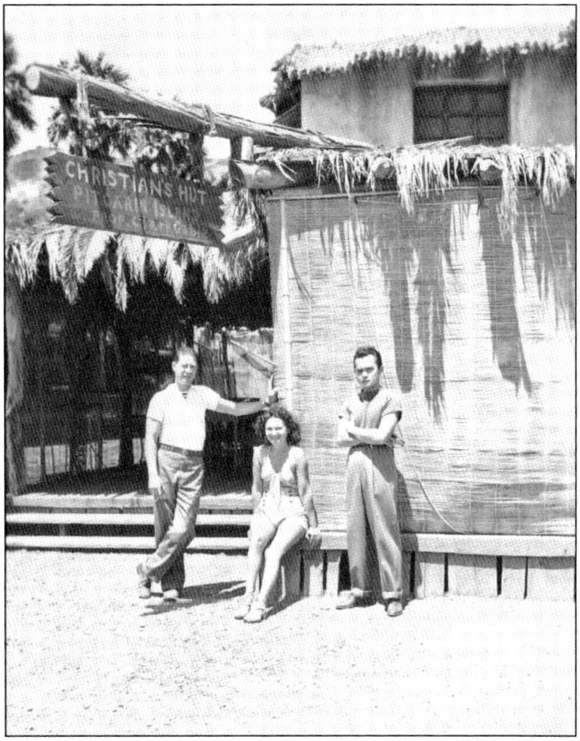

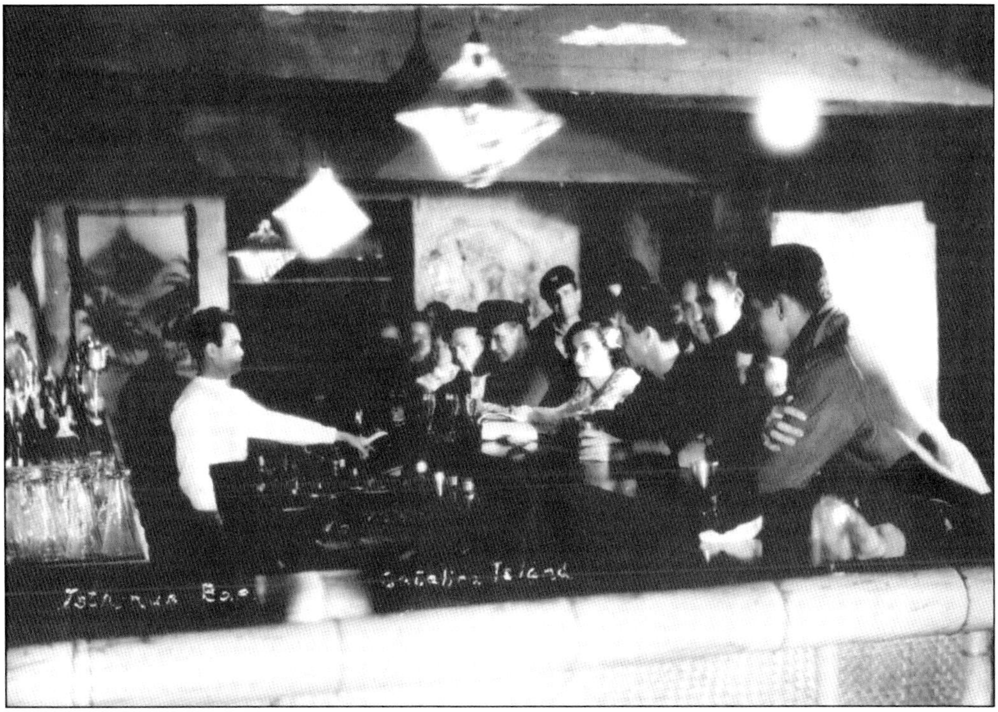

Ray Buhen (left) serves drinks to the cast and crew of *Mutiny on the Bounty* at Christian's Hut on Catalina Island in 1935. The film won the Academy Award for best picture and co-starred Charles Laughton and Franchot Tone. (Courtesy of Mike Buhen.)

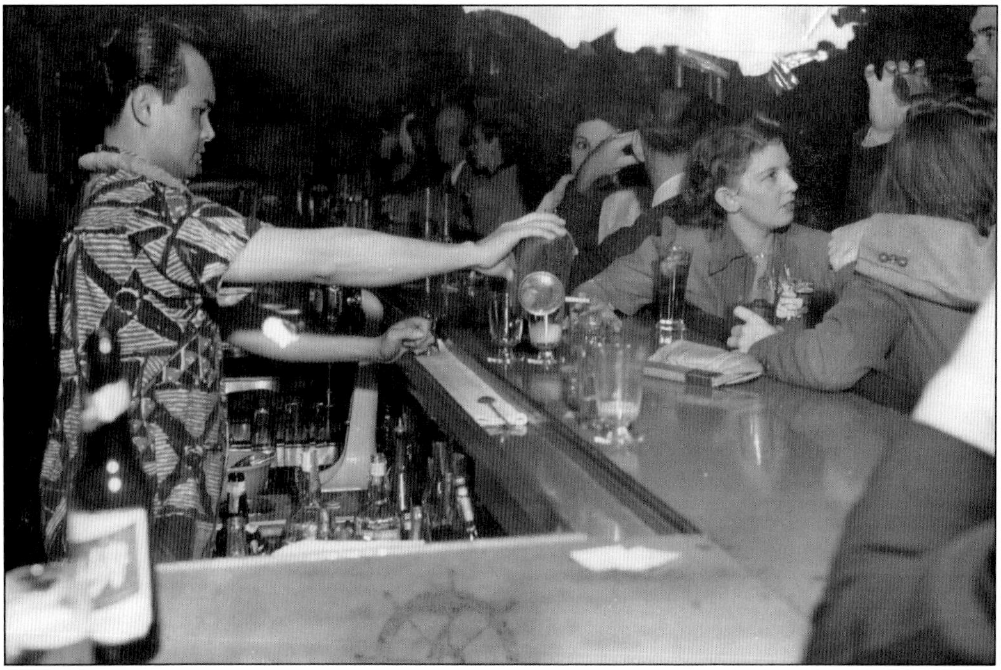

Ray Buhen (left) serves tropical mixed drinks at Bob Brooks' Seven Seas in the 1930s. Some bartenders had a loyal following of patrons, which included celebrities. Throughout his bartending career, Buhan served regulars such as Charlie Chaplin, Joan Crawford, Clark Gable, Howard Hughes, Buster Keaton, and many others. (Courtesy of Mike Buhen.)

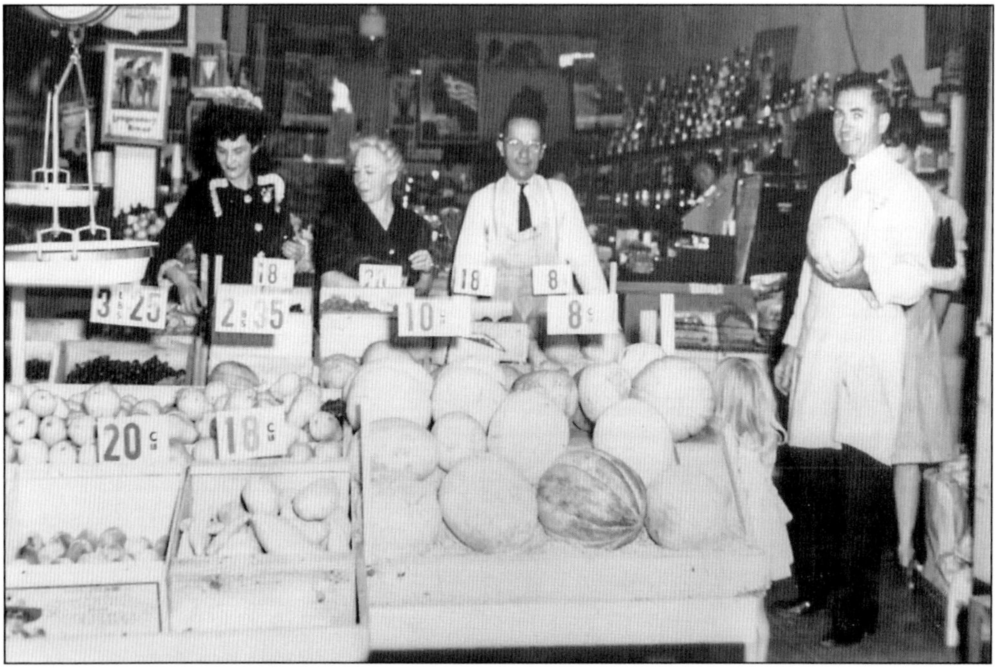

Beachwood Market in Hollywood is seen here in 1938. Filipinos found work in local grocery markets and stores as stock boys and janitors. (Courtesy of Shades of L.A. Archives/Los Angeles Public Library.)

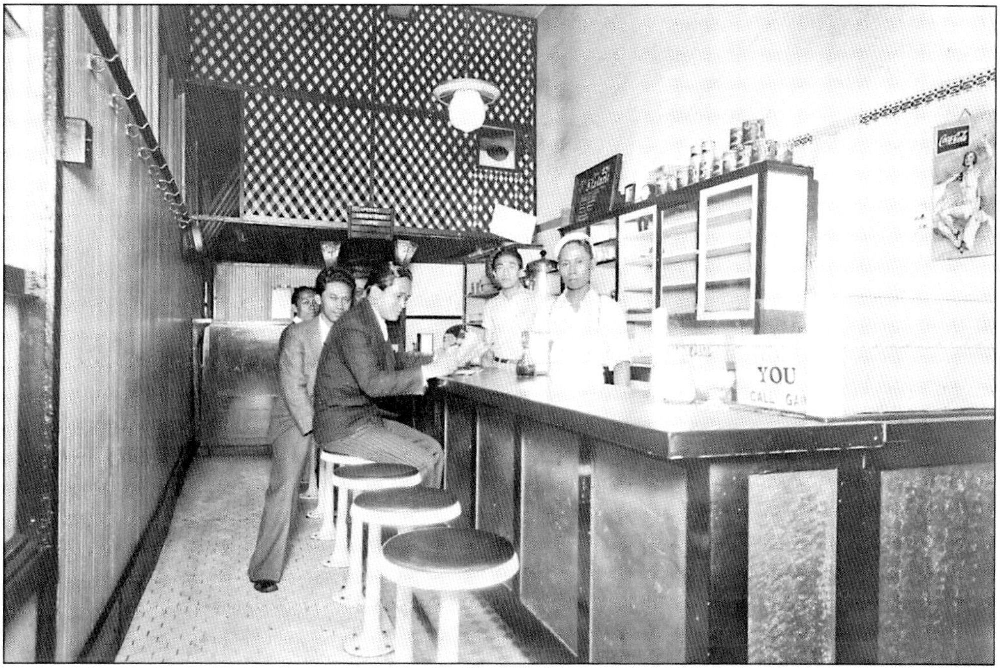

Felix Taganas (front right) opened one of the first Filipino diners in Los Angeles during the 1930s Depression. Filipinos who worked in the glamorous restaurants and bars in Hollywood, as well as those living in the mansions of the wealthy in the Hollywood Hills, were still discriminated against and were often refused service in restaurants. Taganas's diner provided a place for Filipinos to dine without being confronted or refused service. (Courtesy of Jenny Ochale and Celina Taganas-Duffy.)

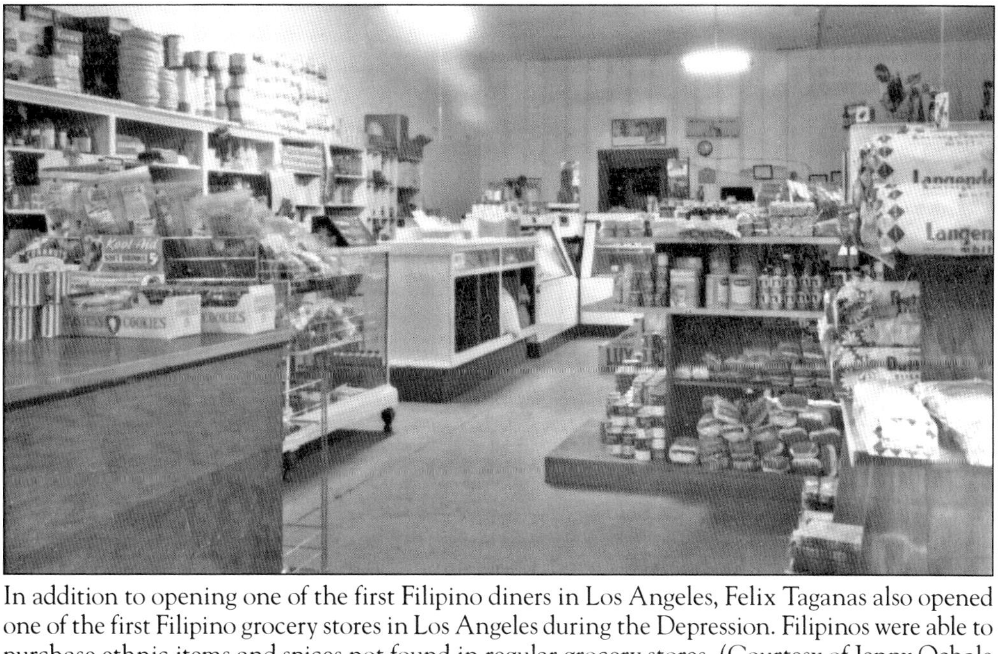

In addition to opening one of the first Filipino diners in Los Angeles, Felix Taganas also opened one of the first Filipino grocery stores in Los Angeles during the Depression. Filipinos were able to purchase ethnic items and spices not found in regular grocery stores. (Courtesy of Jenny Ochale and Celina Taganas-Duffy.)

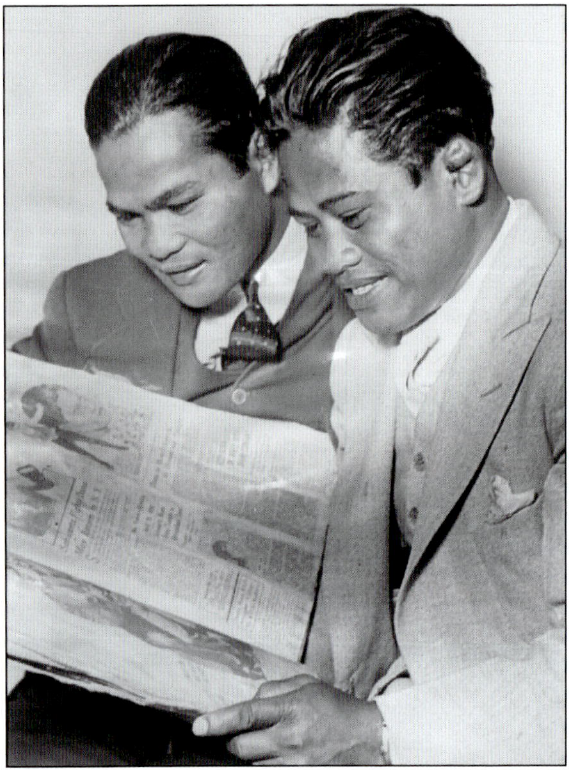

Prizefighters Pete Sarmiento (left) and Pablo Dano are pictured here in 1938. Regarded as one of the greatest Filipino fighters of all time, Sarmiento gained national recognition in newspapers and radio. (Courtesy of *Herald-Examiner* Collection/ Los Angeles Public Library.)

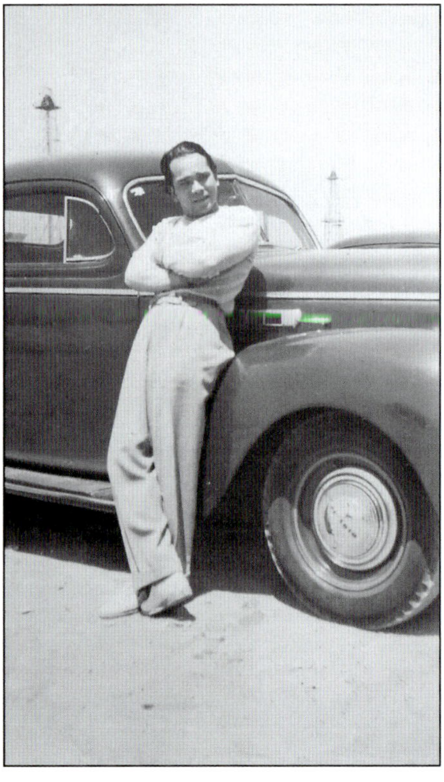

In the 1940s, Tommy Montoya poses in front of his 1939 Desoto sedan. Without families to support, many lonely Filipino men worked long hours and spent their money on fine clothes and cars, and in taxi dance halls. White women were employed at these dance halls and, for 10¢ a dance, a Filipino man dressed in a fine McIntosh suit could look like a movie star and dance with a white woman all night. San Francisco artist Carlos Villa once remarked on a Filipino man's transformation that occurred in the dance halls: "[T]his transforms you overnight from Joe Schmoe [to] . . . Clark Gable, you know. And so you're that for a couple of minutes. And so there'd be those incredible transformation of guys working for fifteen hours a day . . . and then going home to pomade their hair . . . and putting these McIntosh suits on . . . I mean, they dress like crazy." (Courtesy of Eric G. Montoya.)

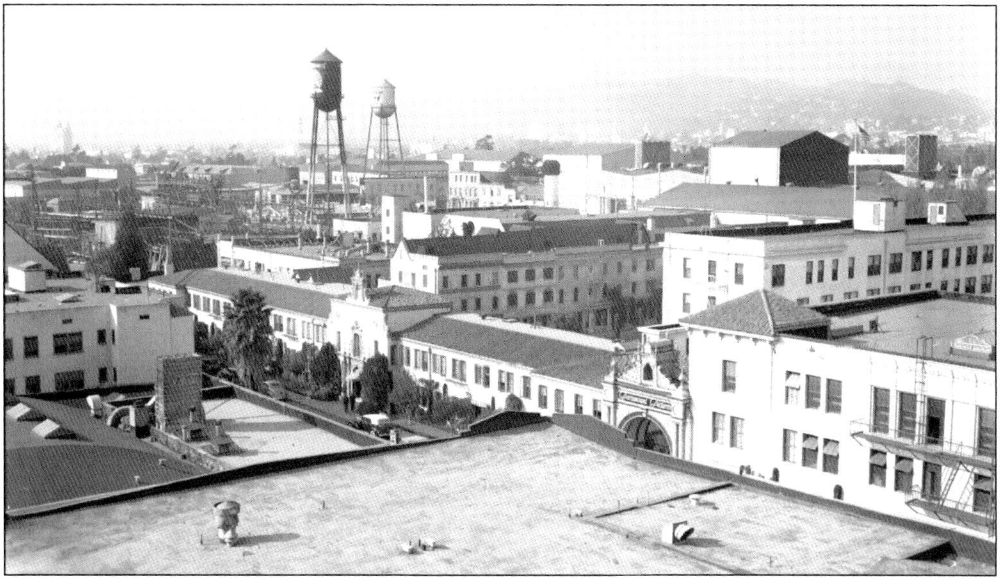

Taken from the top of the Western Costume Company building in Hollywood, this panoramic view of Paramount Pictures studios dates to 1937. The studios employed Filipinos as cooks, chauffeurs, and assistants. (Courtesy of Work Progress Administration/Los Angeles Public Library.)

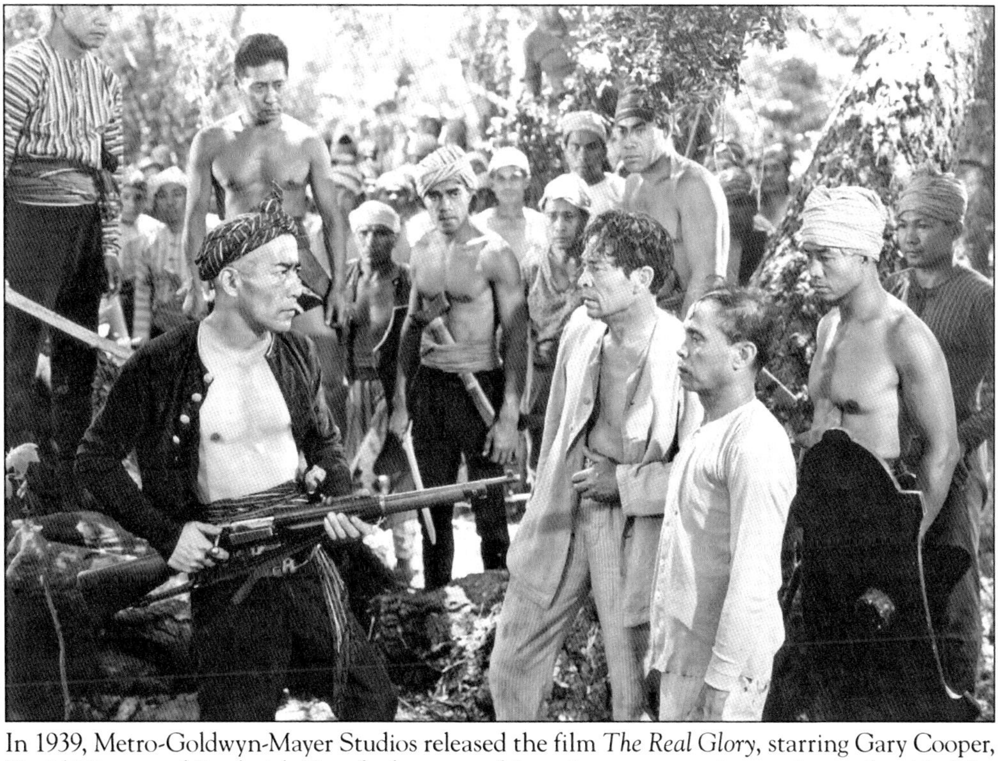

In 1939, Metro-Goldwyn-Mayer Studios released the film *The Real Glory*, starring Gary Cooper, David Niven, and Broderick Crawford, a story of American mercenaries coming to the aid of the U.S. Army in the Philippines amid several crises just after the Spanish-American War. Many Filipinos were cast in the movie but mostly as unpaid extras. (Courtesy of Marc Wanamaker/Bison Archives.)

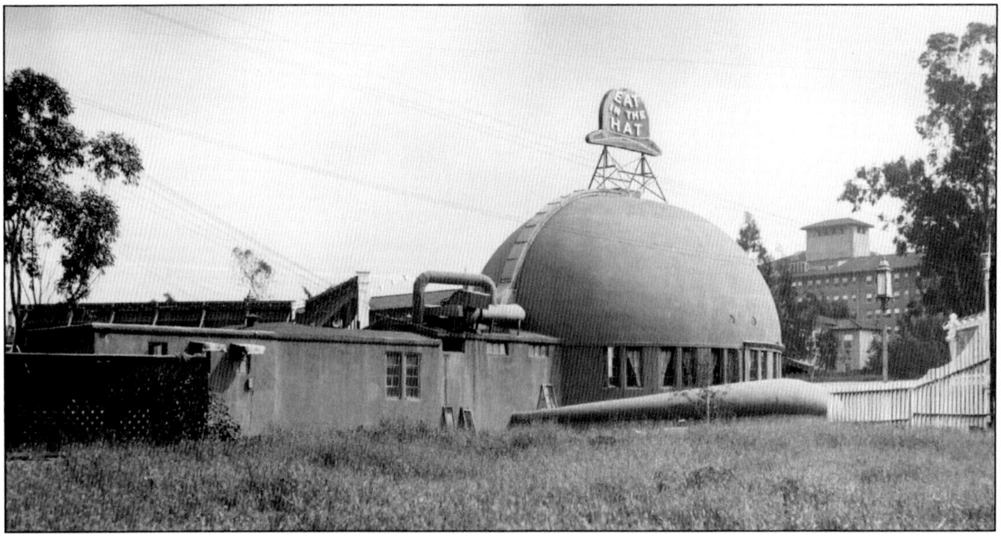

A 1937 rear shot shows one of the four famous Brown Derby restaurants in Hollywood. (Courtesy of Security Pacific Collection/Los Angeles Public Library.)

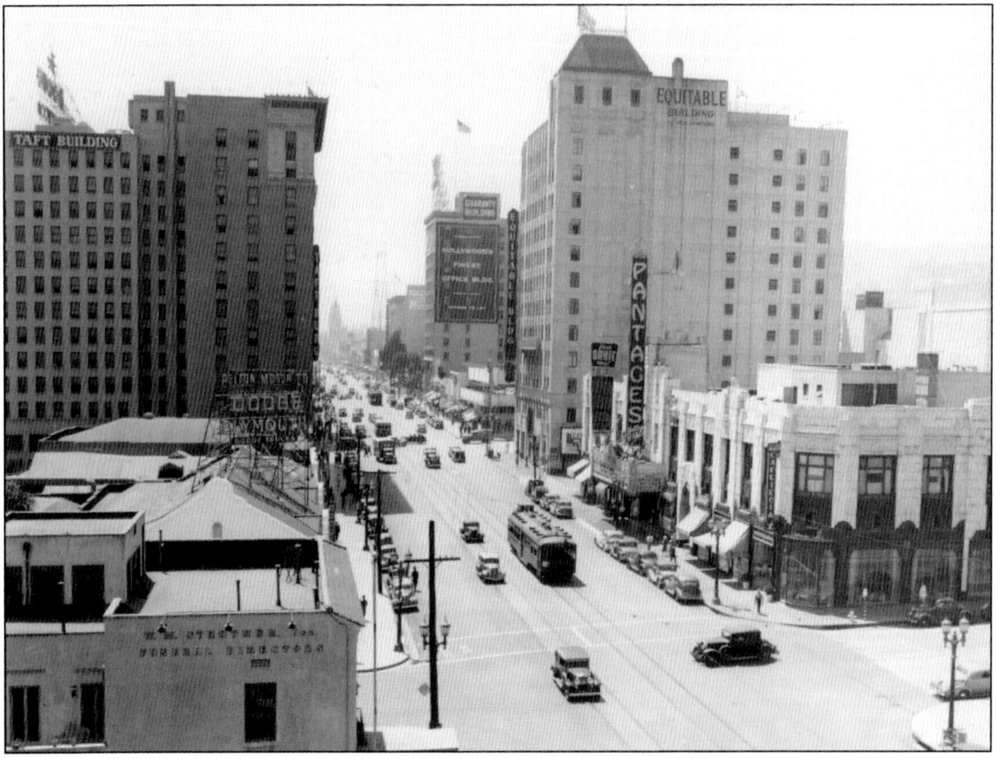

Hollywood Boulevard is seen here in 1937. The photograph was taken looking west from the top of the Regent Hotel toward the intersection of Hollywood and Vine Street. There are a few cars on the street, as well as a streetcar. The Taft Building is at left, and the Equitable Building and the Pantages Theater are on the right. Filipinos were employed in each building shown in the photograph as doormen, theater ushers, and in service-related fields at the Taft and Equitable Buildings. (Courtesy of Work Progress Administration/Los Angeles Public Library.)

This 1938 photograph shows the marquee at Hollywood Theater on Hollywood Boulevard. Filipinos filled usher positions in many popular Hollywood theaters for decades. Streetcar tracks are visible in the foreground. (Courtesy of Work Progress Administration/Los Angeles Public Library.)

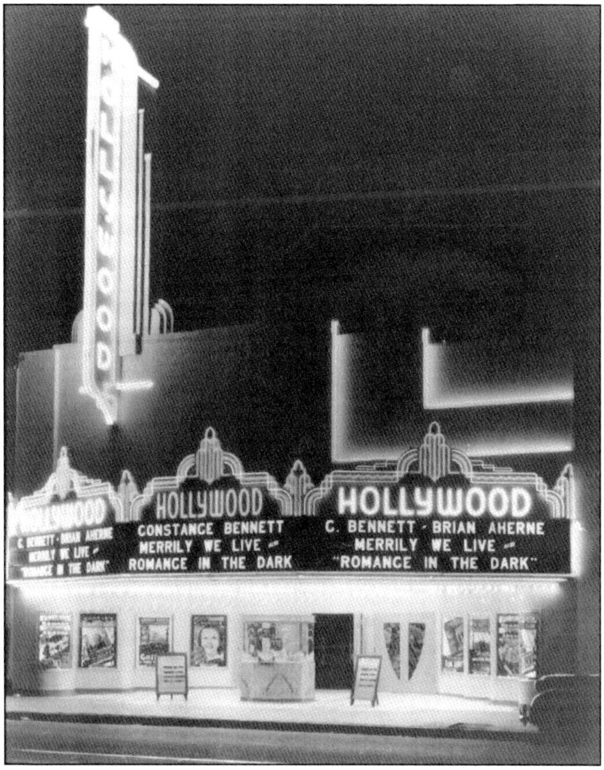

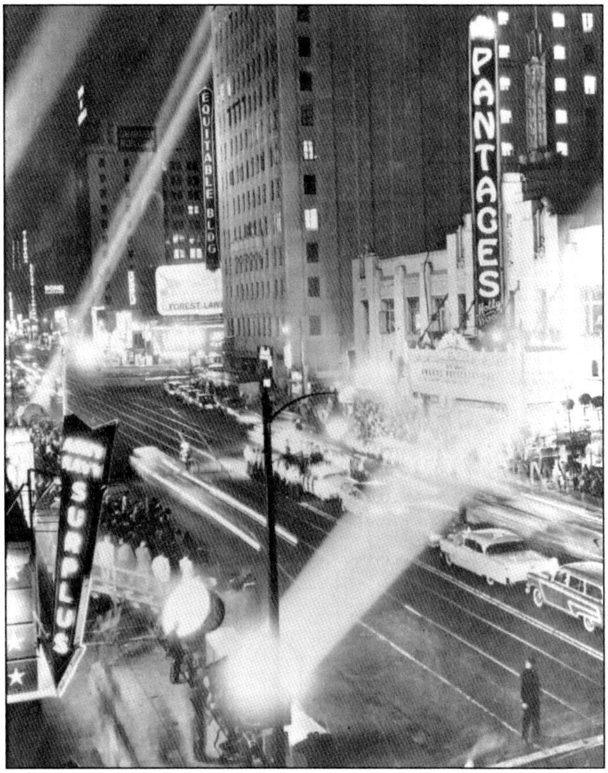

This exterior view of the Pantages Theater was taken in 1948 during the 20th Annual Academy Awards. Crowds of people are seated in bleachers directly outside the theater and on the south side of Hollywood Boulevard, and a line of cars is seen in the middle of the boulevard. Streetcar tracks are visible on the street. Various signs identify neighboring buildings and businesses: the army/navy surplus store, the Equitable Building, Bond Clothiers, the Bank of America, Cinerama, and the Guaranty Building. Filipinos catered these glamorous events as bartenders, servers, and ushers. (Courtesy of Los Angeles Public Library.)

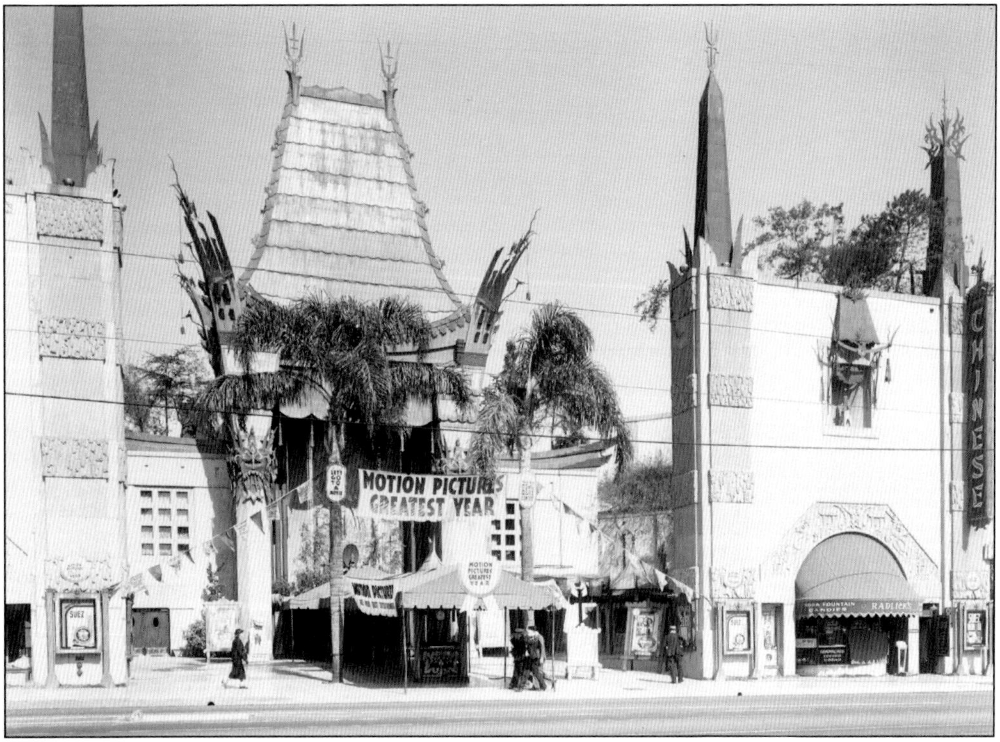

Hollywood's Grauman's Chinese Theater is pictured here in 1939. Filipinos were hired as janitors and ushers throughout the years. (Courtesy of Work Progress Administration/Los Angeles Public Library.)

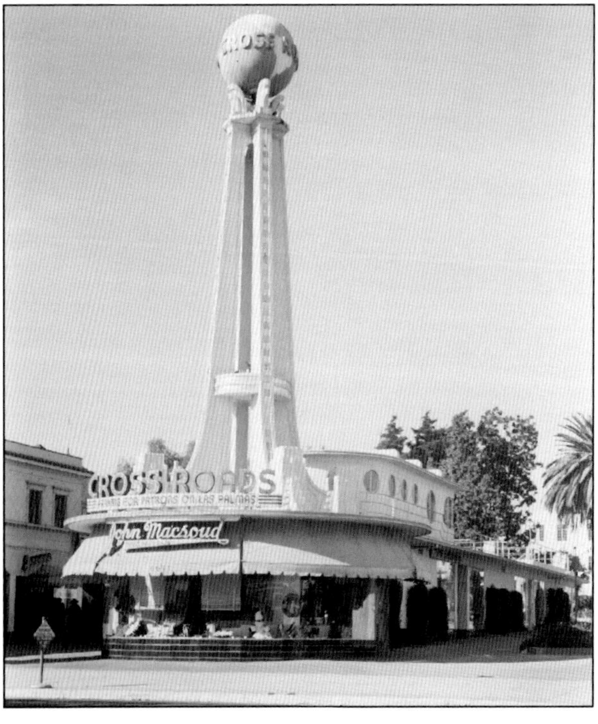

The Crossroads of the World shopping center is seen here in 1939. The center was designed to resemble a Streamline Moderne ship and has a tall, open tower topped with a lighted globe. Throughout the years, the shopping center has housed different businesses, and later it became a residence for Hollywood artists and writers. Throughout the years, Filipinos have worked in this center in service-related positions. (Courtesy of Work Progress Administration/Los Angeles Public Library.)

Two

FAMILY LIFE

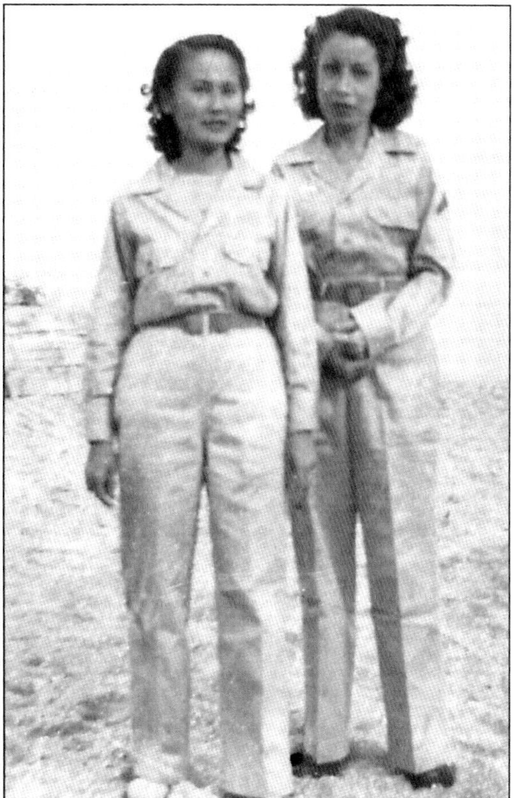

Rosario Quitiviz (left) is pictured with a friend in the 1940s. Filipina women began to arrive in the United States in significant numbers during the post–World War II years of 1946 through 1965. Many Filipina women immigrated as war brides, dependents of U.S. servicemen in the Philippines. Some immigrated to join their Filipino husbands who were already in the United States. Others were single Filipinas who came as students. The immigration of Filipinas marked a significant beginning of the Filipino American family throughout the United States, with a higher concentration of families settling in California. (Courtesy of Rosario Quitiviz.)

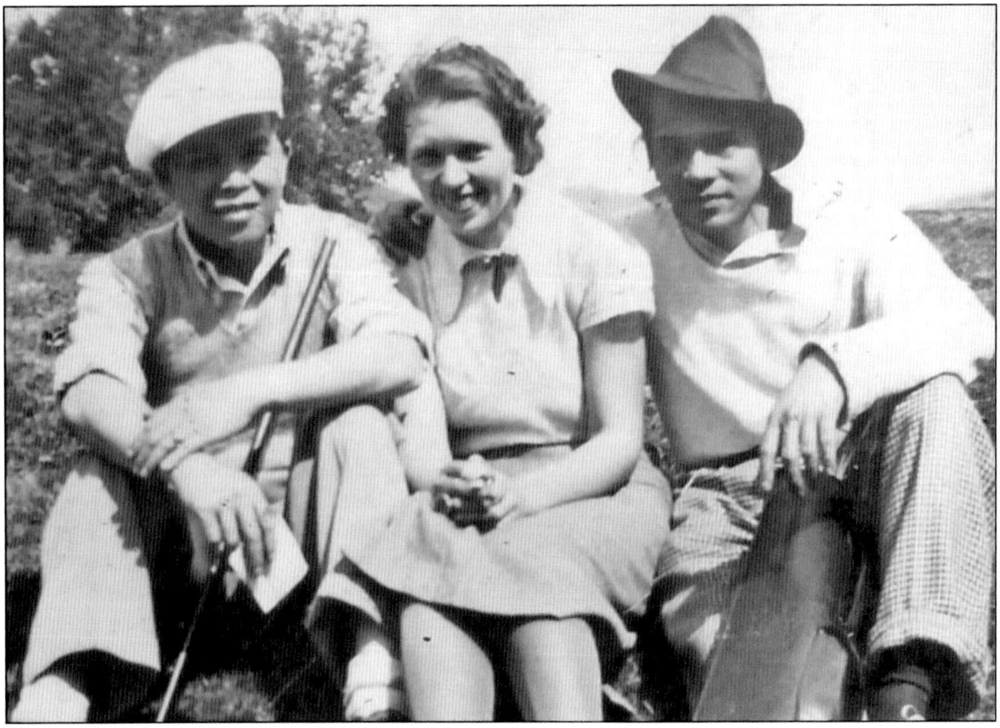

Pictured in the 1940s are three friends after a day of golf in Griffith Park. In 1933, the California State Legislature amended the antimiscegenation laws to allow Filipinos to marry whites. A couple of years later, in 1935, the Welch Bill was established to purchase one-way tickets for Filipinos to voluntarily return to the Philippines on the condition that they never return to the United States. (Courtesy of Eric G. Montoya.)

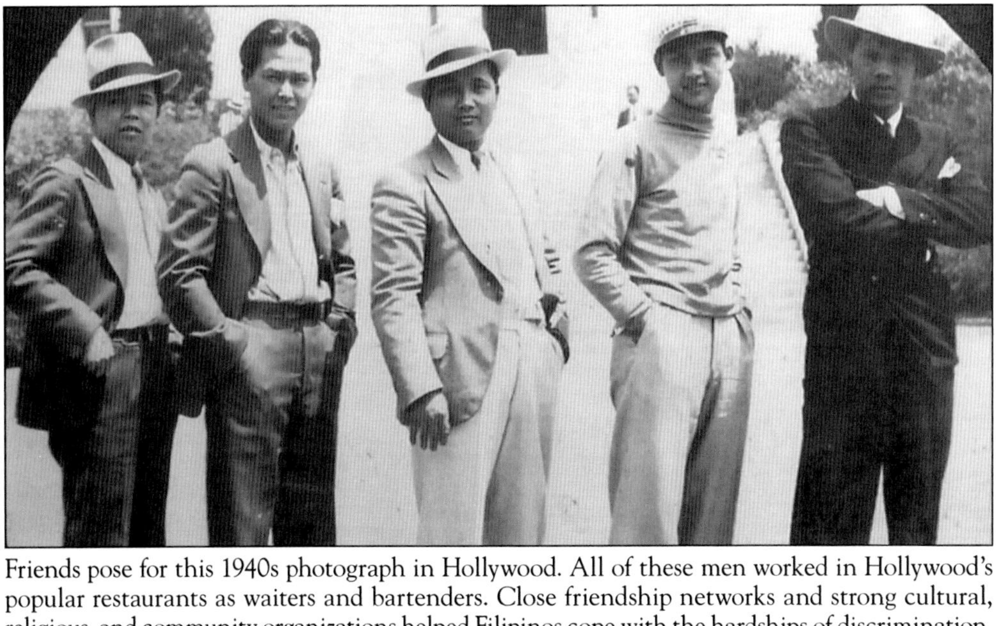

Friends pose for this 1940s photograph in Hollywood. All of these men worked in Hollywood's popular restaurants as waiters and bartenders. Close friendship networks and strong cultural, religious, and community organizations helped Filipinos cope with the hardships of discrimination. (Courtesy of Eric G. Montoya.)

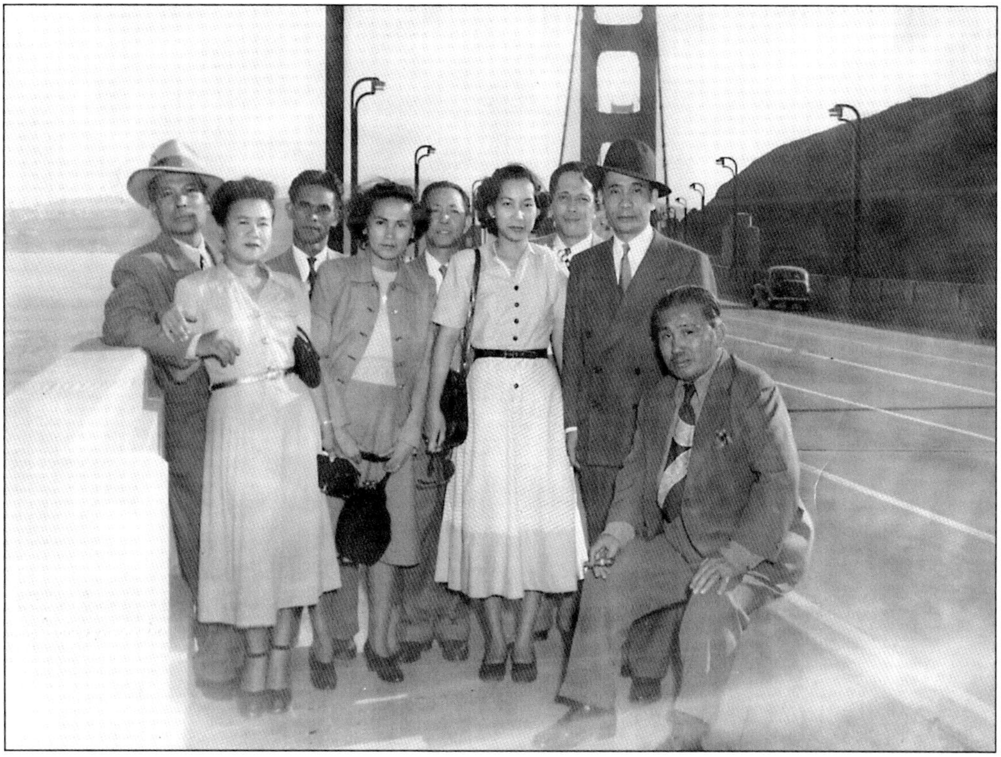

A group of Filipinos poses for this 1940s photograph (above) in front of San Francisco's Golden Gate Bridge to memorialize their arrival to the United States. A reception was given in their honor at a home in San Francisco to bid them farewell and good luck before they travelled south to Los Angeles to settle (below). (Both, courtesy of Rosario Quitiviz.)

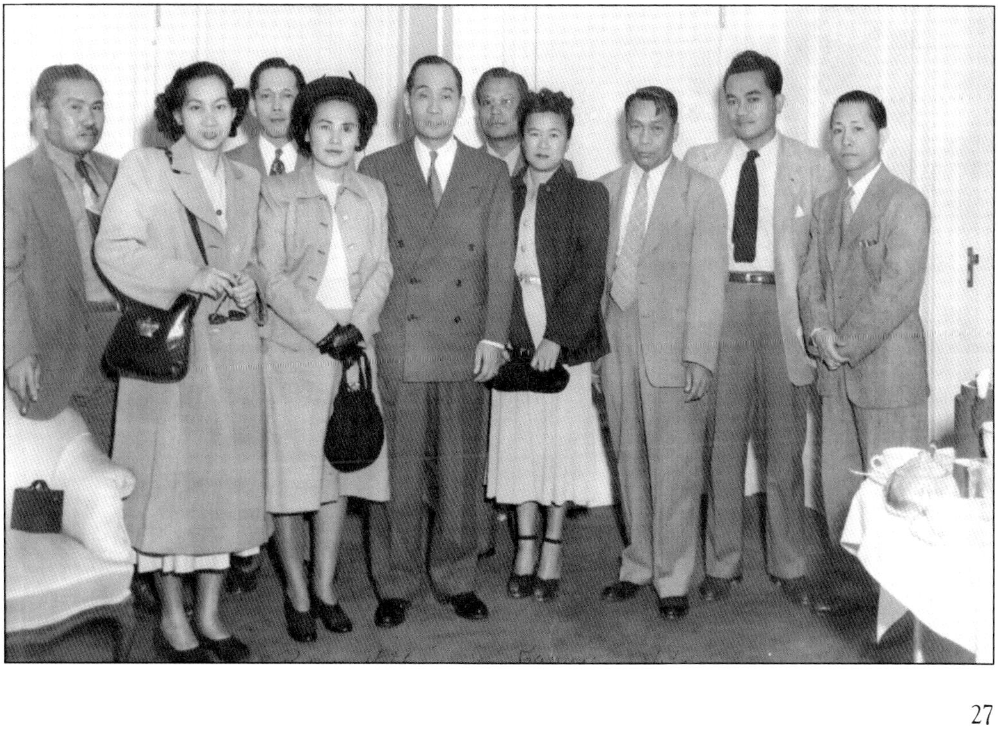

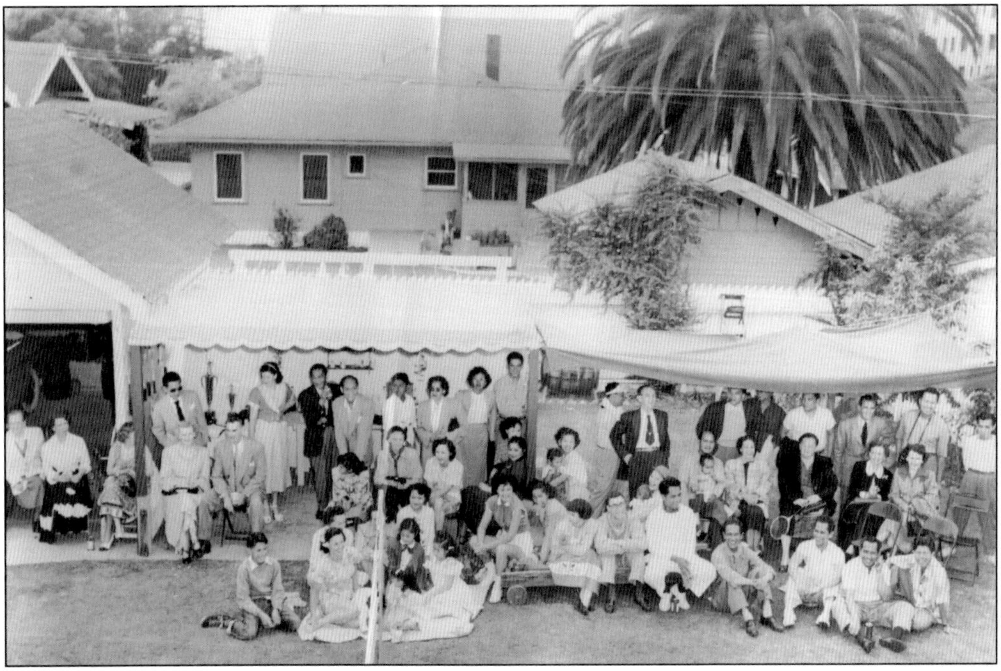

Some waiters who worked at Don the Beachcomber in Hollywood in the 1950s also were members of a tennis club. Here they attend a get together at a Hollywood home with the families of other Beachcomber staff. (Courtesy of Rosario Quitiviz.)

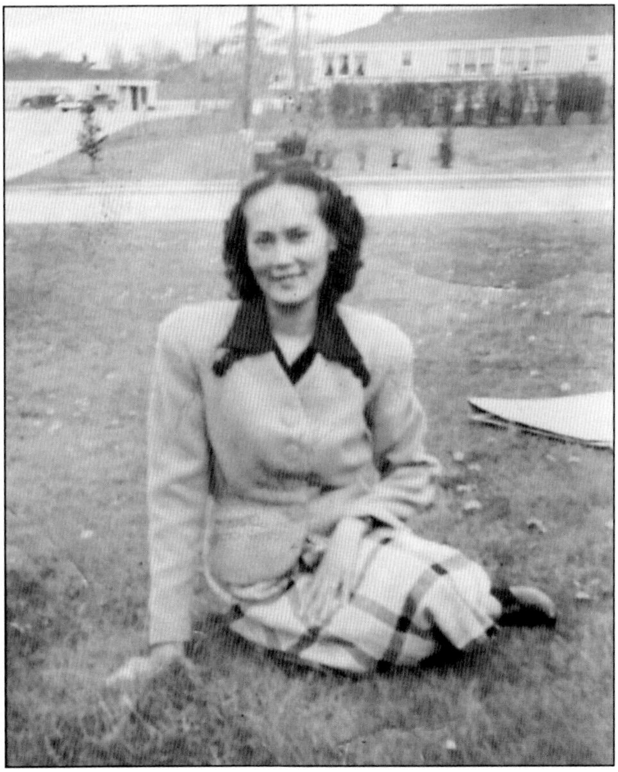

Pictured here is Rosario Quitiviz in the 1940s shortly after her arrival in the United States. Many women who arrived in the 1940s were happy to immigrate, but shortly after they were faced with some of the same obstacles of discrimination that the earlier settlers met upon their arrival. (Courtesy of Rosario Quitiviz.)

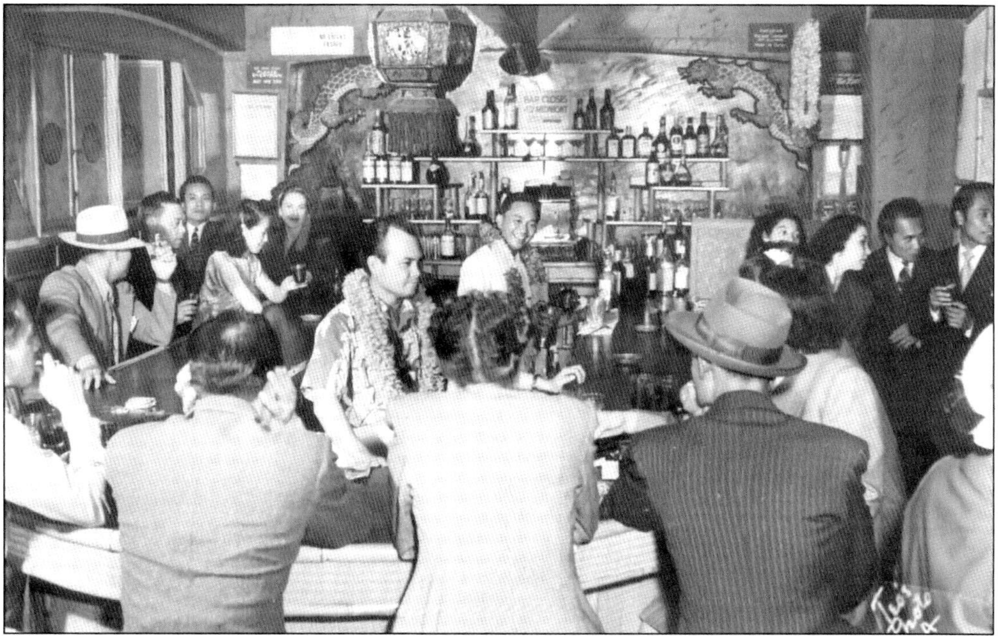

In the 1930s, Ray Buhen (center) serves drinks at a bar in Los Angeles to patrons who are predominately Filipinos. (Courtesy of Mike Buhen.)

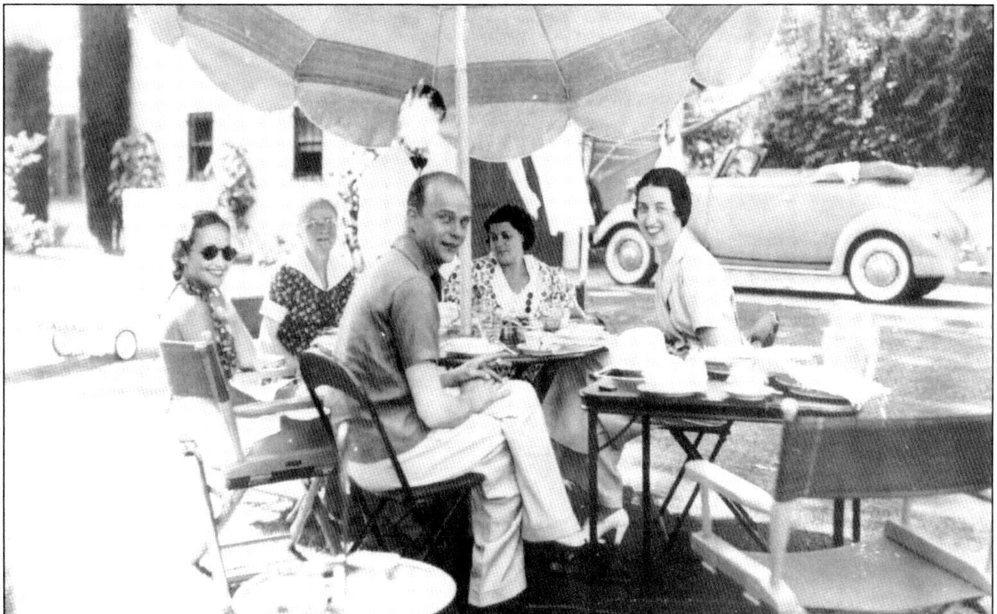

An outdoor luncheon is depicted at the home of actress Dorothy Lamour (far left). Filipino American Genaro Manantan (standing, face scratched out) was employed as her houseboy and chauffeur in the early 1940s. This is a popular and widely used photograph accompanying some Filipino writings to describe the discrimination against Filipinos. The scratched-out face of Manantan symbolizes the low status of the Filipino in Los Angeles from the 1920s to 1960s. A brown face among a white group of people with a famous celebrity may not have been desirable to some. (Courtesy of Shades of L.A. Archives/Los Angeles Public Library.)

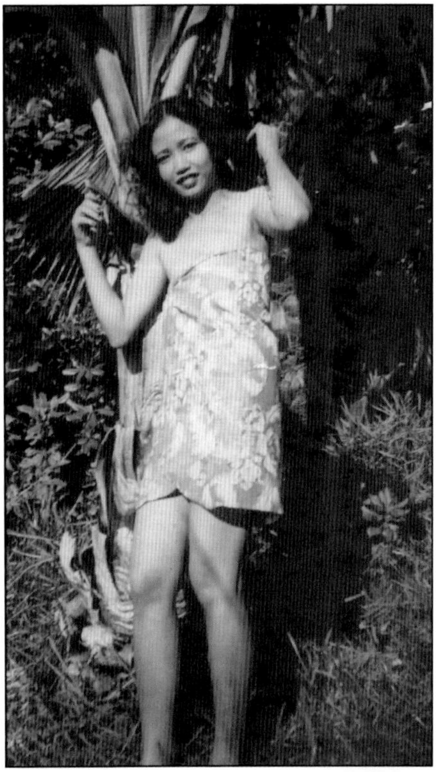

Amparo Q. Domingo poses in a sarong in the 1940s. She was a stand-in double for actress Dorothy Lamour. (Courtesy of Toni Thomas and Juliet Lagmay-Akiaten.)

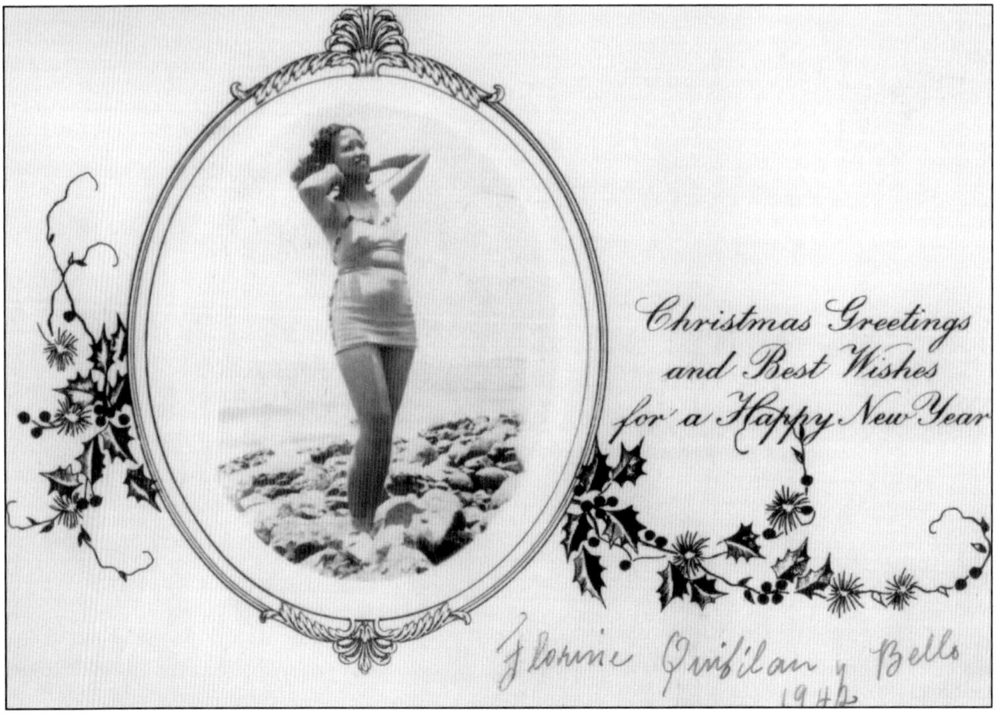

This is a Christmas greeting created from a Hollywood photograph of Amparo Q. Domingo on the beach in 1942. (Courtesy of Toni Thomas and Juliet Lagmay-Akiaten.)

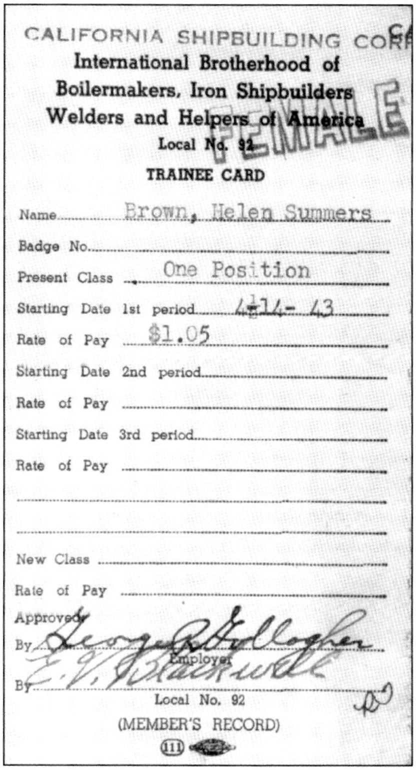
CALIFORNIA SHIPBUILDING CORP
International Brotherhood of
Boilermakers, Iron Shipbuilders
Welders and Helpers of America
Local No. 92
TRAINEE CARD
FEMALE

Name Brown, Helen Summers
Badge No.
Present Class One Position
Starting Date 1st period 4-14-43
Rate of Pay $1.05
Starting Date 2nd period
Rate of Pay
Starting Date 3rd period
Rate of Pay
New Class
Rate of Pay
Approved By George R. Gallagher Employer
By E. V. Blackwell Local No. 92
(MEMBER'S RECORD)

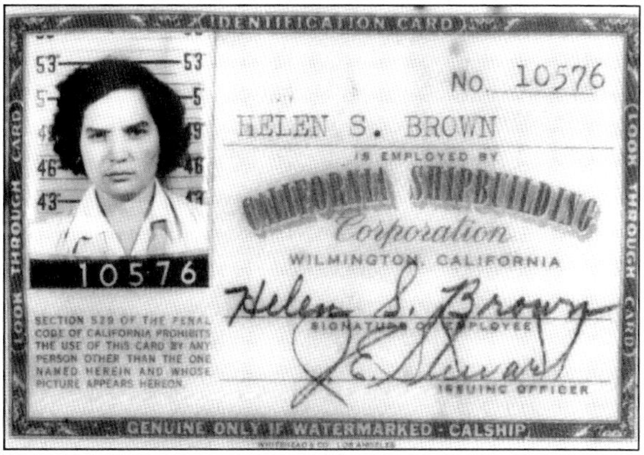
IDENTIFICATION CARD
No. 10576
HELEN S. BROWN
IS EMPLOYED BY
CALIFORNIA SHIPBUILDING Corporation
WILMINGTON, CALIFORNIA
Helen S. Brown
SIGNATURE OF EMPLOYEE
ISSUING OFFICER
10576
SECTION 529 OF THE PENAL CODE OF CALIFORNIA PROHIBITS THE USE OF THIS CARD BY ANY PERSON OTHER THAN THE ONE NAMED HEREIN AND WHOSE PICTURE APPEARS HEREON
LOOK THROUGH CARD
GENUINE ONLY IF WATERMARKED - CALSHIP

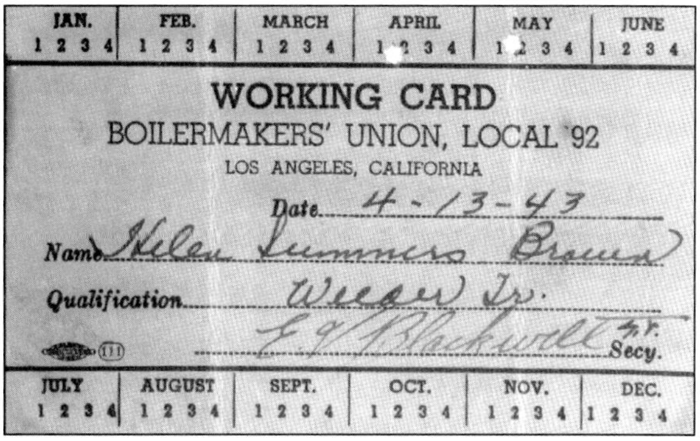
JAN.	FEB.	MARCH	APRIL	MAY	JUNE
1 2 3 4	1 2 3 4	1 2 3 4	1 2 3 4	1 2 3 4	1 2 3 4

WORKING CARD
BOILERMAKERS' UNION, LOCAL 92
LOS ANGELES, CALIFORNIA
Date 4-13-43
Name Helen Summers Brown
Qualification Welder Tr.
E. V. Blackwell Sr. Secy.

JULY	AUGUST	SEPT.	OCT.	NOV.	DEC.
1 2 3 4	1 2 3 4	1 2 3 4	1 2 3 4	1 2 3 4	1 2 3 4

Pictured from 1943 are several identification cards carried by Helen Summers Brown, a Filipino American woman who was employed as a welder during World War II. The immigration of Filipina women to the United States included both skilled and unskilled workers. (Courtesy of Shades of L.A. Archives/Los Angeles Public Library.)

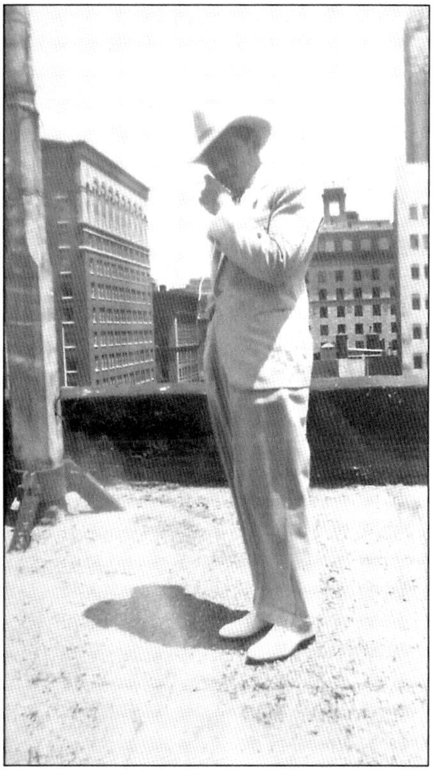

In the 1940s, Tommy Montoya poses on a Los Angeles rooftop sporting a McIntosh suit. Many white women who worked at taxi dance halls were looked down upon by white men because of their association with Filipinos, who frequented the dance halls dressed like movie stars. Women found them attractive not only for their looks, but for the respect and lavish gifts they gave the women in return for their company. (Courtesy of Eric G. Montoya.)

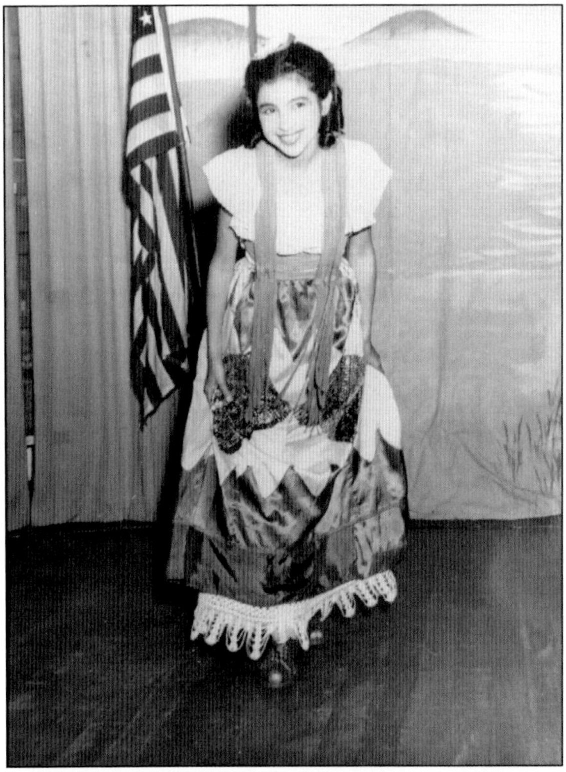

This 1948 photograph depicts a Filipino American woman performing a Mexican dance in a talent show. (Courtesy of Shades of L.A. Archives /Los Angeles Public Library.)

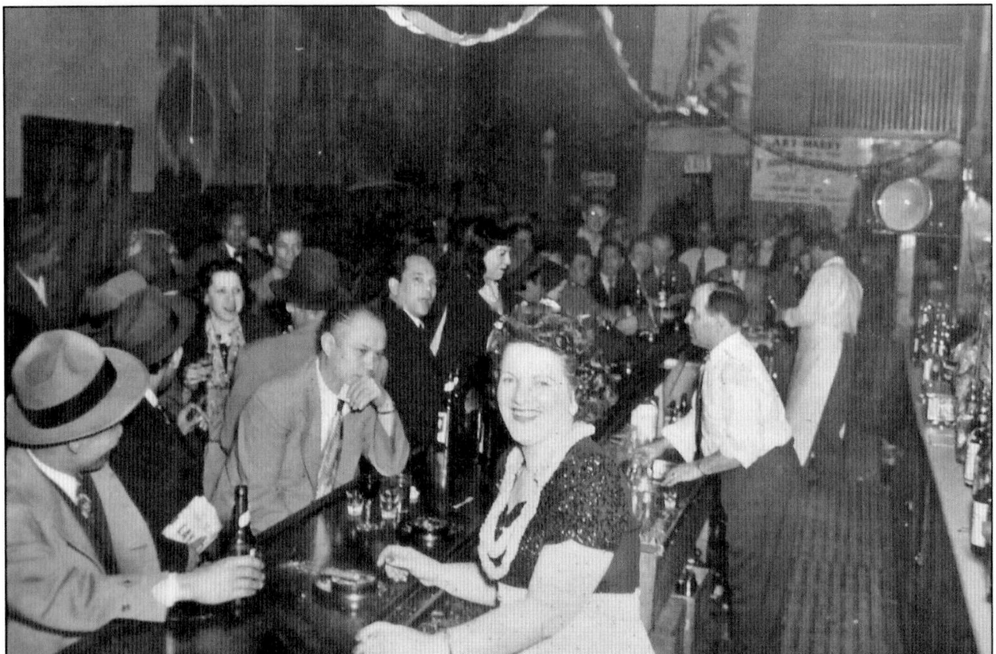

Filipino Americans gathered for drinks and socializing at a Los Angeles bar/taxi dance hall in the 1940s. Taxi dance halls employed women to dance with men for 10¢ a dance. The women dancers were known as "dime-a-dance girls" or "nickel hoppers." (Courtesy of Eric G. Montoya.)

Tommy Montoya, pictured here in the 1950s, makes his way home from working a 12-hour shift as a waiter at Don the Beachcomber in Hollywood. He attended most casting calls open to Filipinos but never received a role higher than an uncredited extra. (Courtesy of Eric G. Montoya.)

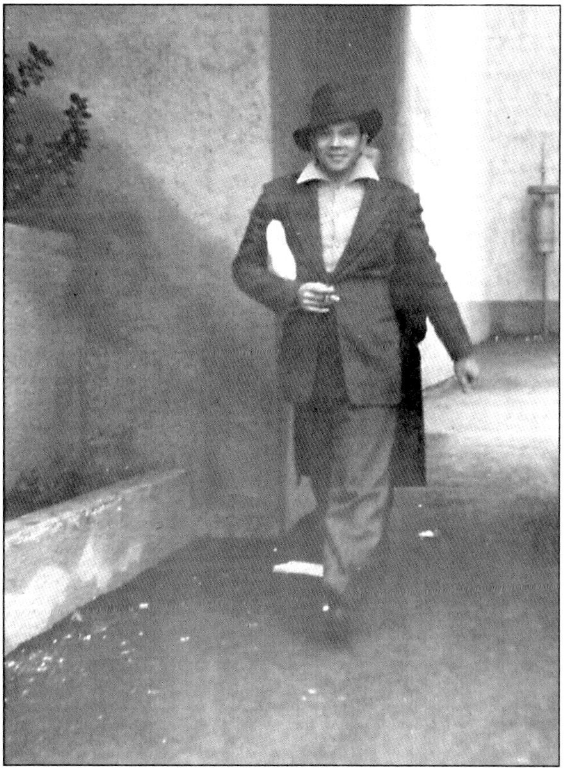

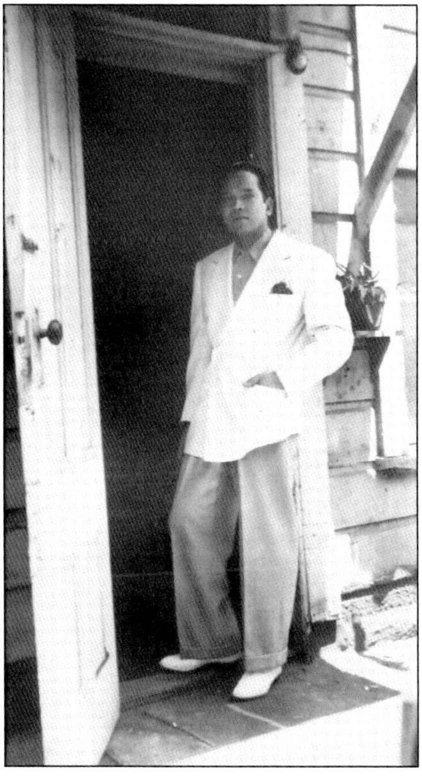

During the 1950s, Tommy Montoya, in a McIntosh suit, poses in front of his rented house in an impoverished section of downtown Los Angeles. Many single Filipino men spent most of their paychecks on clothes and cars in an attempt to be accepted among the Hollywood-types for whom they worked. (Courtesy of Eric G. Montoya.)

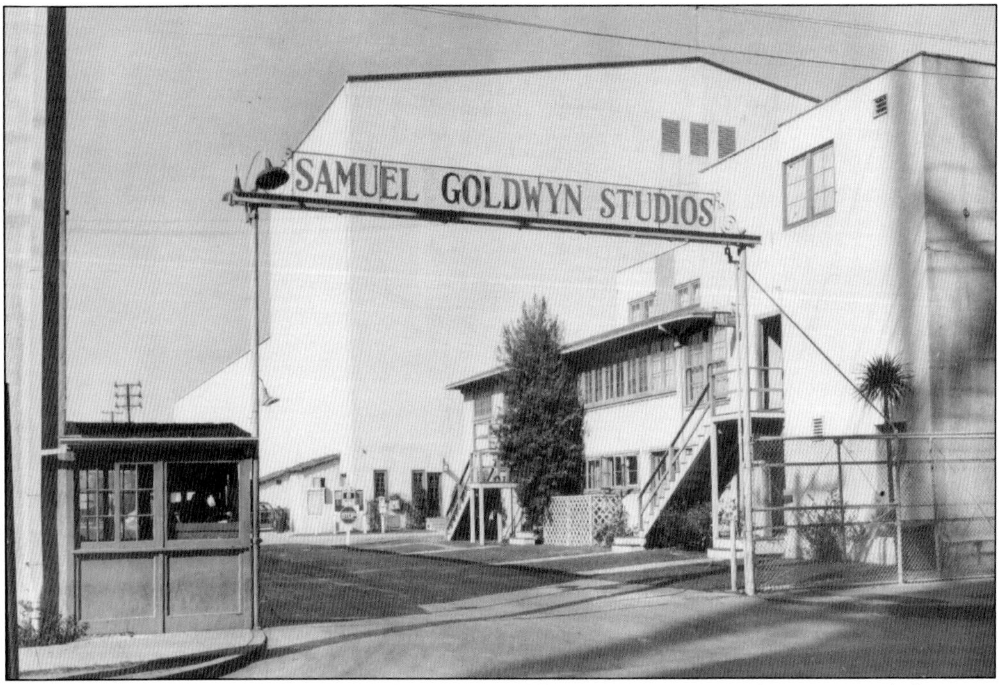

The entrance to Samuel Goldwyn Studios is pictured here in 1948. Many Filipinos attended casting calls that were held outside on the grounds of the studios. (Courtesy of SPNB Collection/Los Angeles Public Library.)

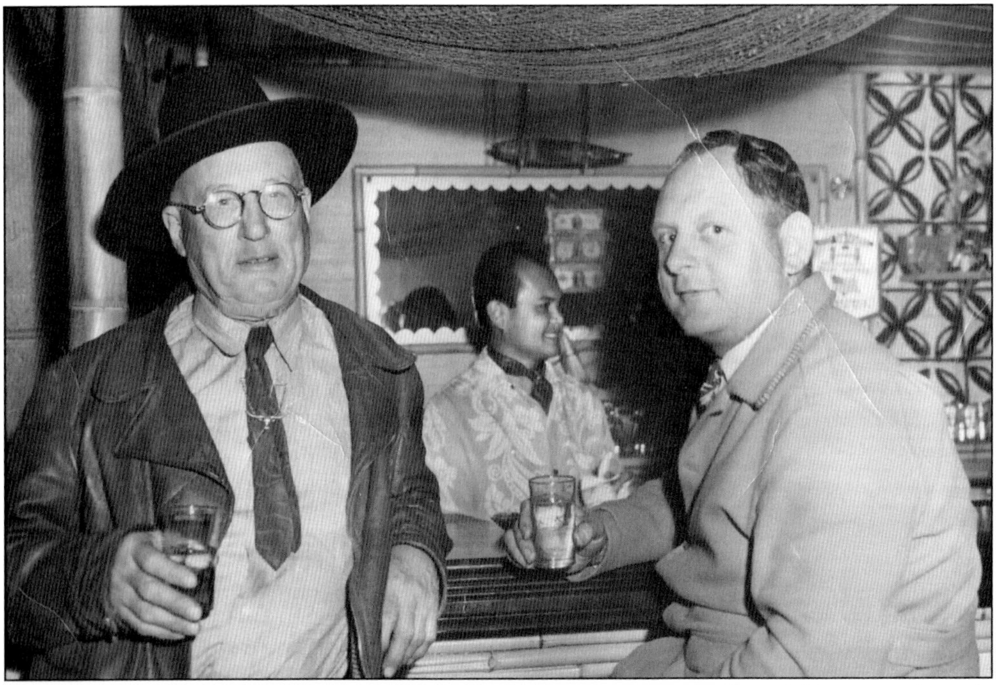

Ray Buhen (back) tends bar for many Hollywood industry patrons at Sugie's Tropics in Beverly Hills during the 1940s. By this time, Buhen was in demand for his bartending skills, having worked in most of Hollywood's Polynesian-style restaurants and bars. (Courtesy of Mike Buhen.)

Pictured here is the front cover from one of Don the Beachcomber restaurant's bar menus. Donn Beach, owner of Don the Beachcomber, is regarded as being the founder of Tiki-style restaurants, bars, and nightclubs. Don the Beachcomber has employed many Filipinos in its Hollywood location since its opening in 1934. (Courtesy of Mike Buhen.)

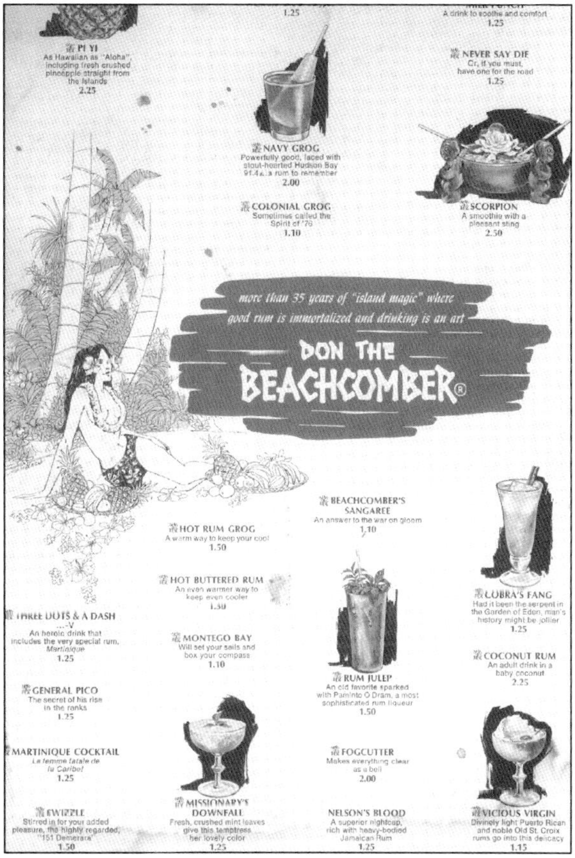

In 1953, Tommy Montoya (right) and a coworker bartend at Don the Beachcomber in Hollywood. (Courtesy of Eric G. Montoya.)

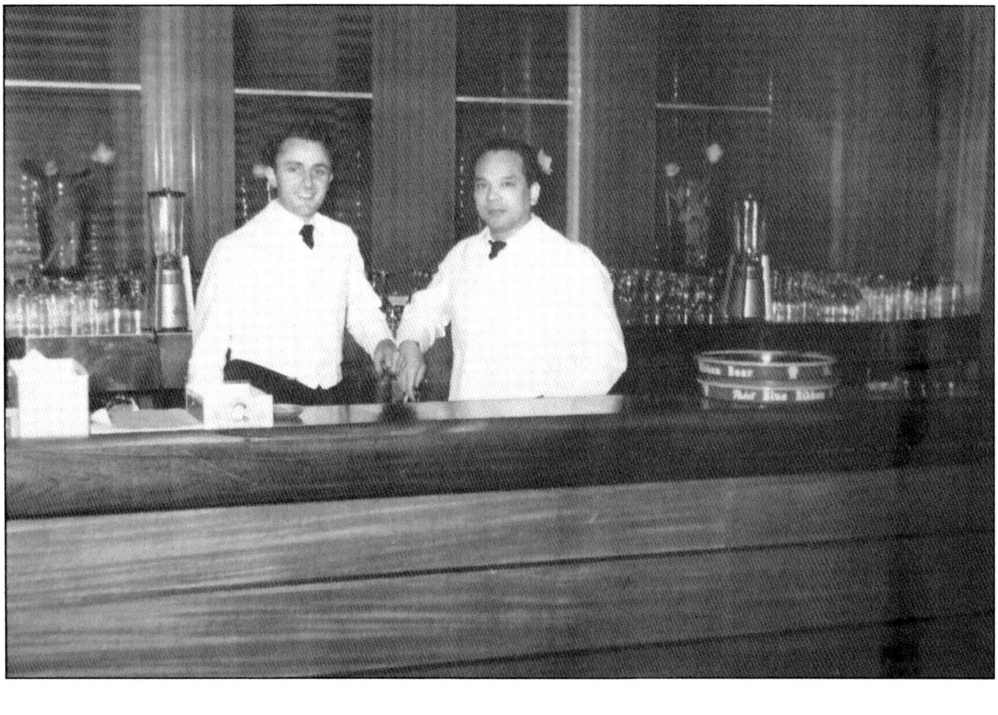

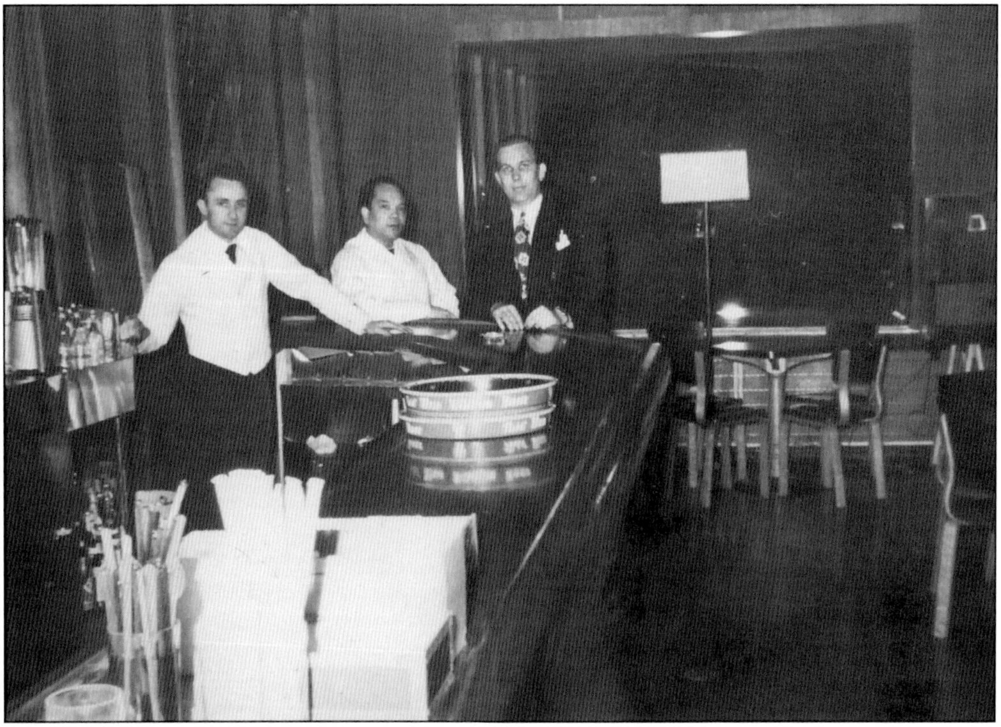

This 1953 photograph of Tommy Montoya (center) with a coworker (left) and the manager of Don the Beachcomber restaurant in Hollywood shows a portion of the seating area in the bar. (Courtesy of Eric G. Montoya.)

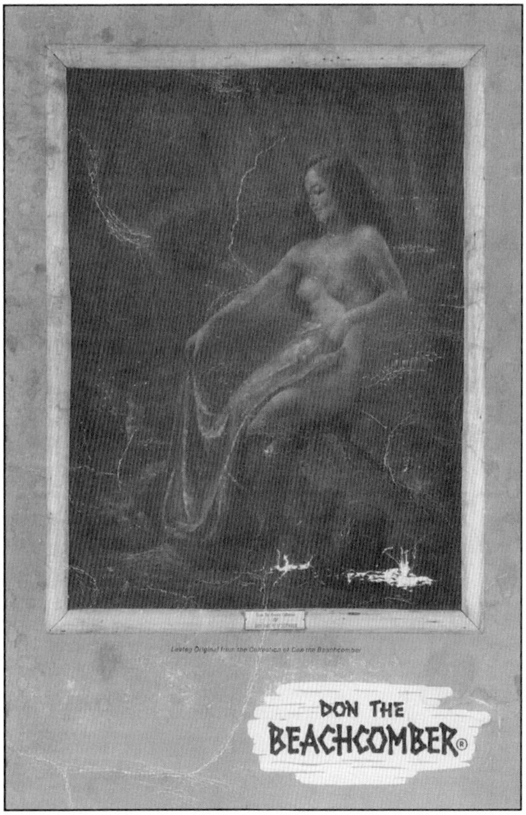

This is the front cover from one of Don the Beachcomber's menus. The restaurant was a Polynesian-style restaurant that was famous for its steaks, seafood, and tropical drinks. (Courtesy of Eric G. Montoya.)

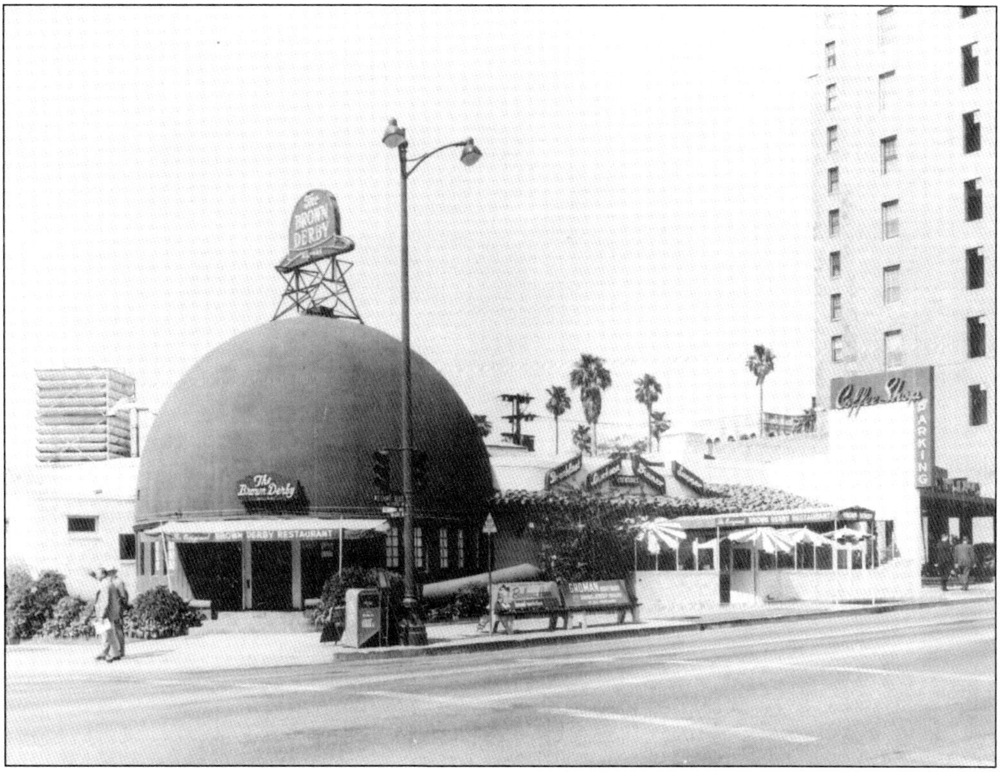

The Brown Derby on Wilshire Boulevard, shown here in 1957, was one of the restaurants that employed many Filipinos throughout the years as waiters, busboys, and dishwashers. No records can be located that indicate a Filipino chef worked at any of the four Brown Derby restaurants. (Courtesy of SPNB Collection/Los Angeles Public Library.)

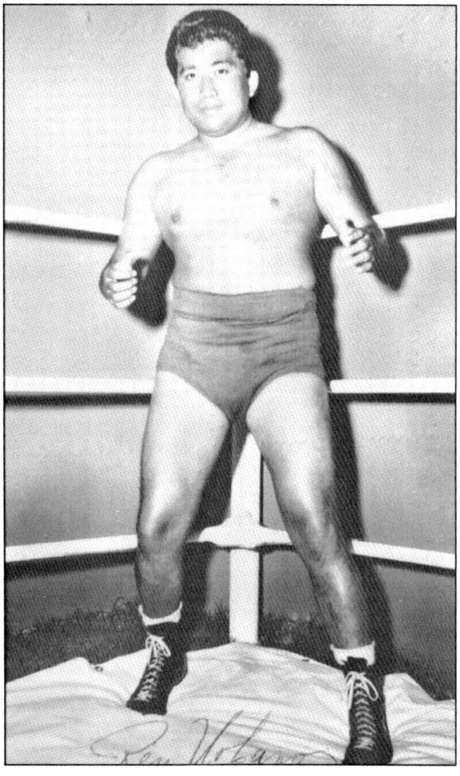

Pictured here in a 1950 photograph is Filipino wrestler Ray Urbano, whose real name was Rey Urbano. He often went by the nickname "Kabooki." Urbano was an international wrestling figure and is best remembered as the first to use the painted-face look of the Great Kabuki. One of his notable matches was with Los Angeles' famed wrestler Bobo Brazil in the 1960s. (Courtesy of Shades of L.A. Archives /Los Angeles Public Library.)

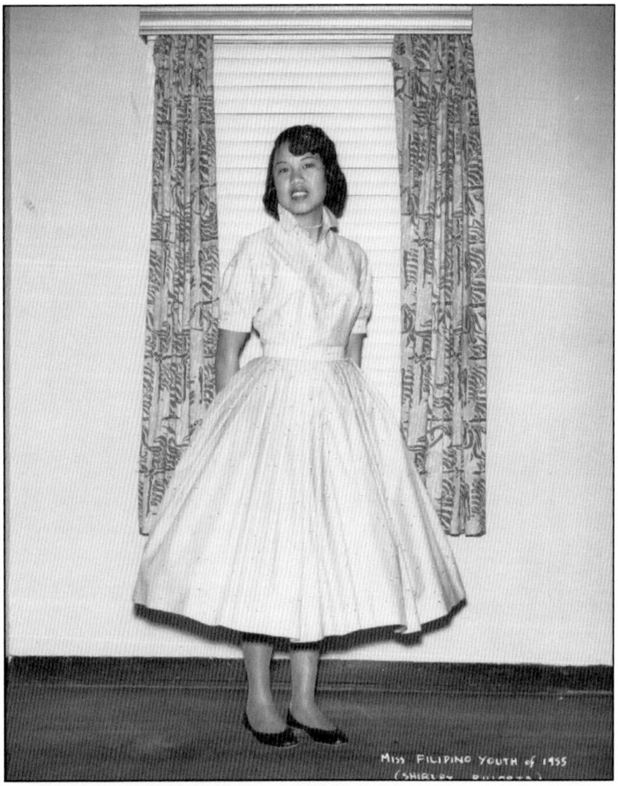

Shirley Rillorta was crowned Miss Filipino Youth of 1955. Pageants are a significant part of the Filipino culture. Every Filipino community in America has their own beauty pageants, and they include prizes for Miss Sampaguita, Miss Teenage Filipino, Miss Filipino Youth, Miss Philippines, and Mrs. Philippines. (Courtesy of Benita Q. Lagmay and Numeriano D. Lagmay.)

Miss Philippines candidates are being presented at an event in Los Angeles in the 1950s. (Courtesy of Benita Q. Lagmay and Numeriano D. Lagmay.)

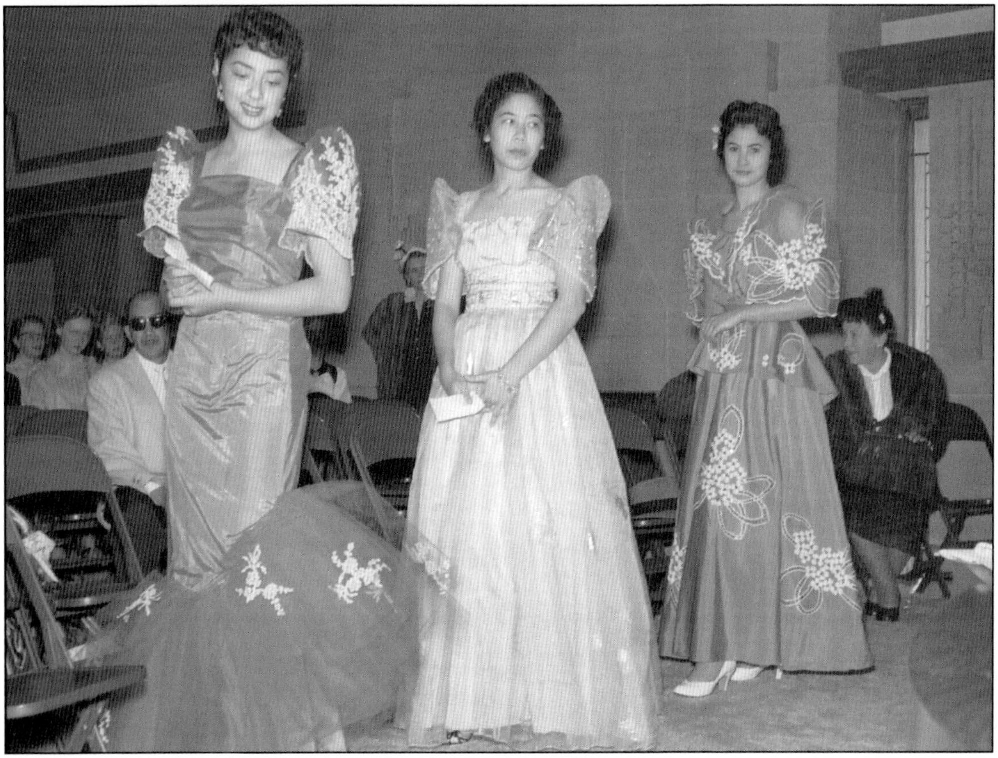

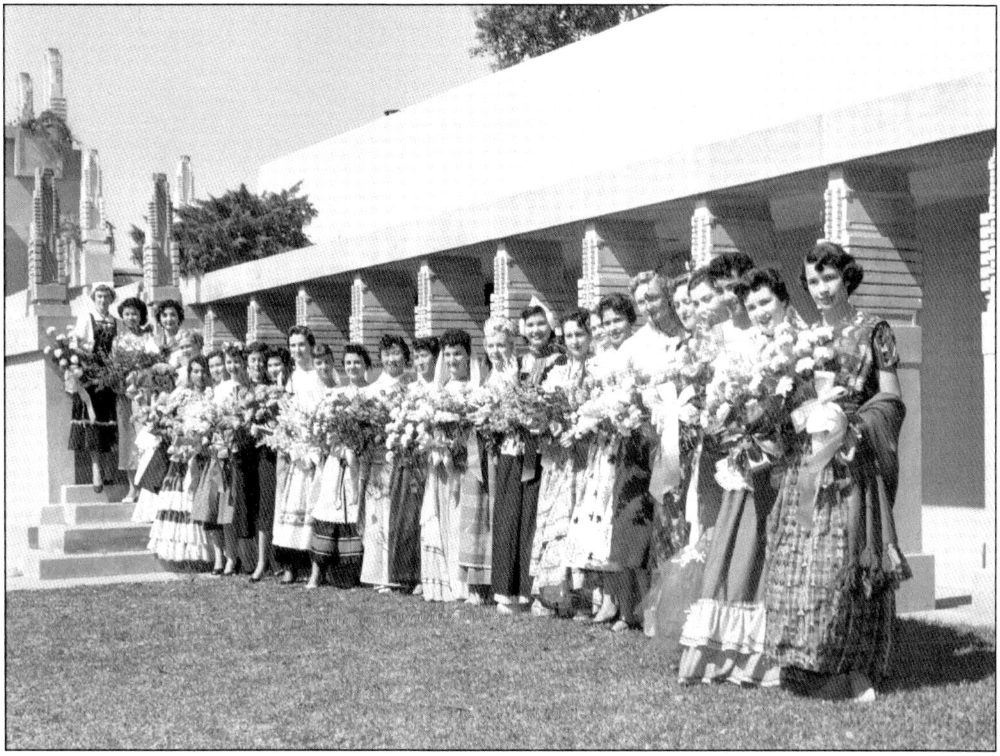

In the 1960s, young Filipina women compete for the crown in the Miss Philippines pageant in Los Angeles. These pageants are considered important social functions because beauty is admired and respected. Those who are crowned are regarded as celebrities. (Courtesy of Benita Q. Lagmay and Numeriano D. Lagmay.)

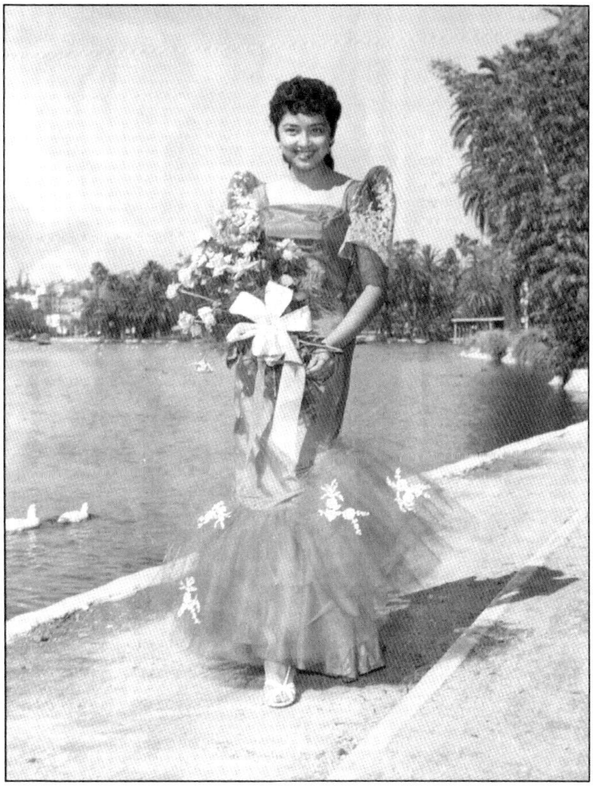

A 1960s winner of a Miss Philippines pageant poses with her bouquet at Echo Park. Miss Philippines beauty pageants were held each year with the coronation of the winners taking place at annual, grand ball events in Hollywood. They were newsworthy events drawing coverage from the *Los Angeles Times* and *Herald-Examiner*. (Courtesy of Benita Q. Lagmay and Numeriano D. Lagmay.)

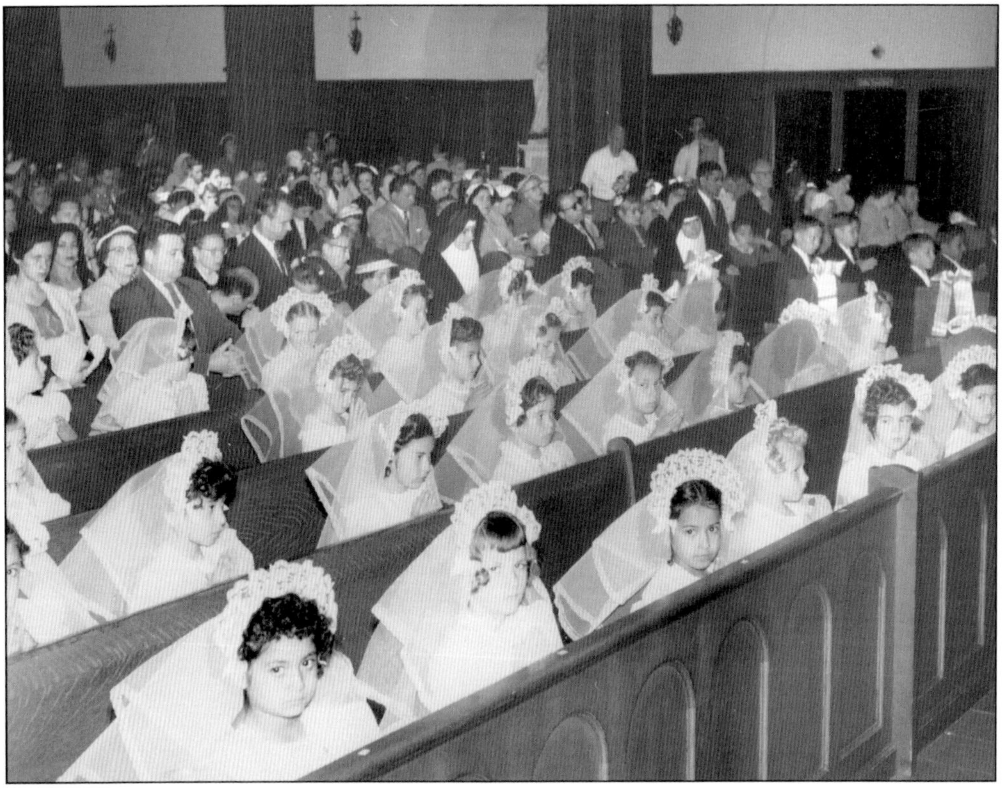

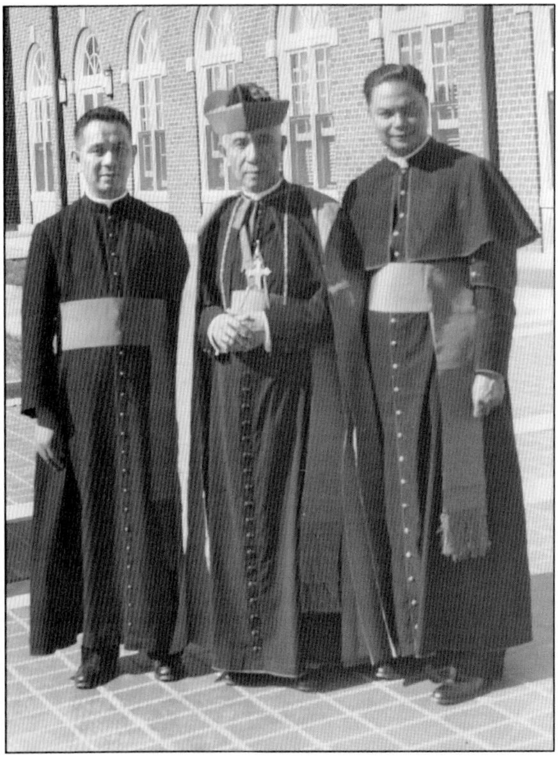

Pictured (above) are young girls and boys, including Filipino American children, receiving their First Holy Communion in the 1950s. To understand Filipino culture, it is important to know that the core Filipino values are family, religion, and education. The Philippines is a Christian country, the result of Spanish colonization, and most Filipinos are Christians, predominantly Roman Catholics. With a substantial arrival of Filipino women in the 1940s and the lifting of the law that once prohibited mixed racial marriages, the Filipino American family began to flourish. Filipino Catholic clergy (left) visit the Filipino community in Los Angeles in the 1950s. Such visits were always met with grand receptions followed by personal invitations to homes for dinner and blessings. (Both, courtesy of Juliet Lagmay-Akiaten.)

Eric G. Montoya (left) and his neighbor Jacqueline Nolan celebrate their First Holy Communion in the 1960s. Both attended Immaculate Heart of Mary Catholic School in Hollywood. (Courtesy of Rosario Quitiviz.)

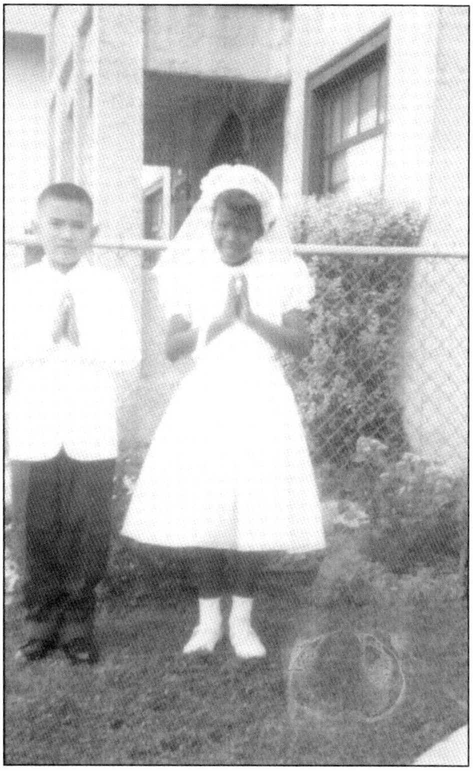

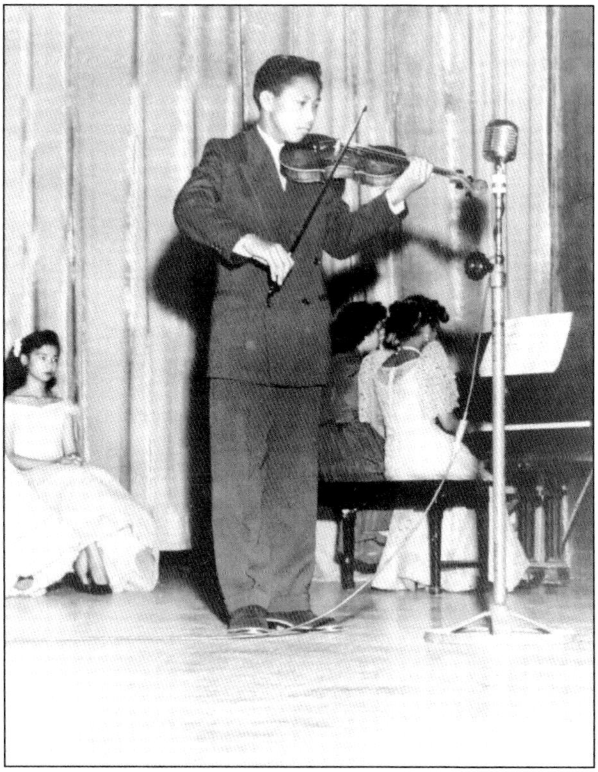

Vicente Noble performs on stage with his violin in this 1953 photograph; Anita Noble is at far right on the piano. Many talented Filipinos performed in Filipino events and for Filipino organizations. Within Filipino circles, one's talents for music, song, dance, and acting were recognized, acknowledged, and celebrated. (Courtesy of Shades of L.A. Archives/Los Angeles Public Library.)

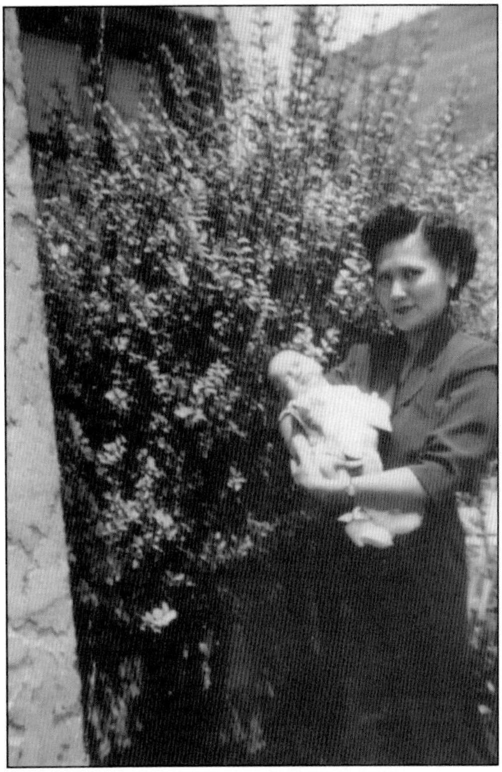

Some Filipino families elected not to teach their American-born children Tagalog or other Filipino dialects and steered them away from certain customs in order for them to not appear different among their American peers. Rosario Quitiviz is seen (left) with her newborn son in 1952 and (below) with her son and her daughter, who was born in 1956. (Both, courtesy of Rosario Quitiviz.)

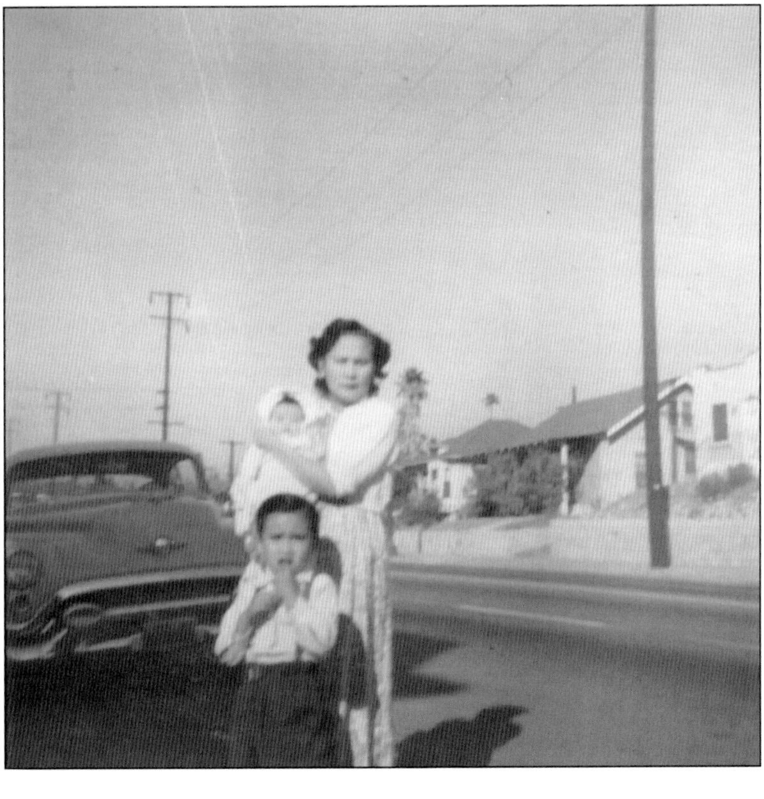

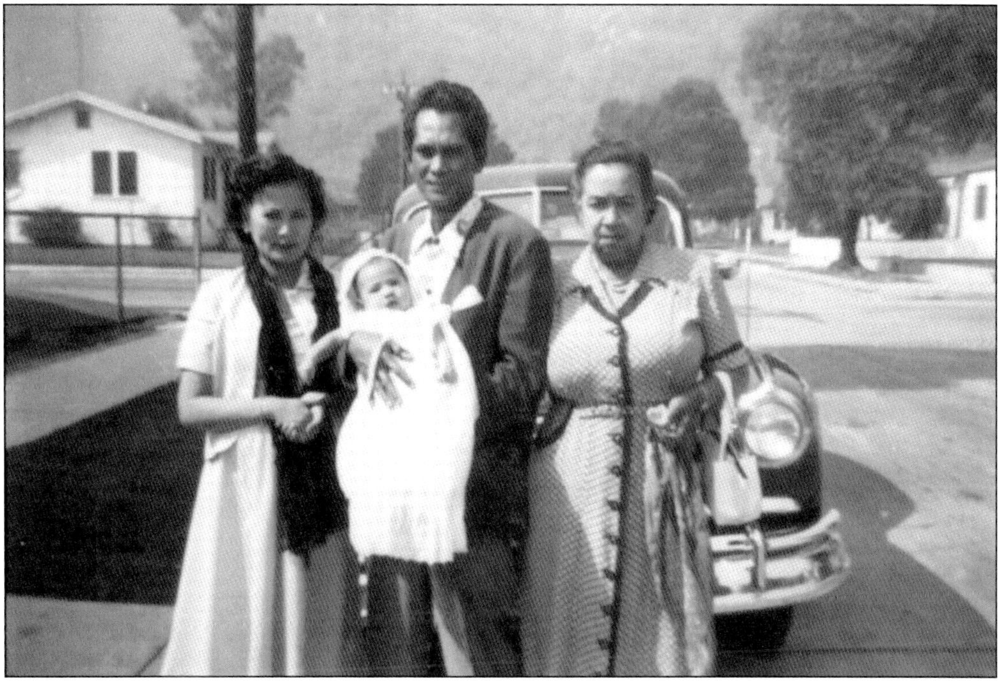

Rosario Quitiviz attends the baptism of a newborn first-generation Filipino American in the 1950s. Pictured from left to right are Quitiviz, Henry Tupas (holding the baby), and Albertha Estopinal-Andersen. (Courtesy of Rosario Quitiviz.)

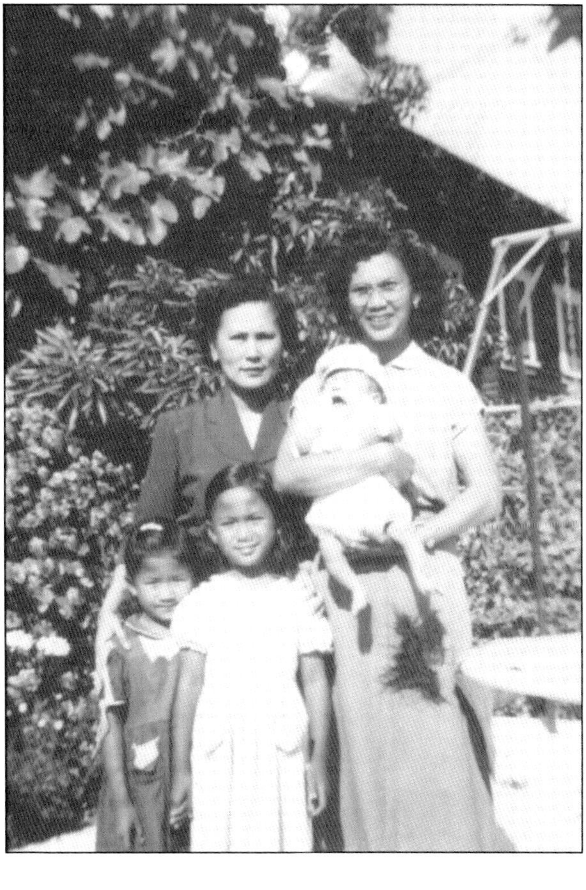

First-generation Filipino American children are seen here in the 1950s. Pictured from left to right are (first row) Tina Peralta and Stephanie Peralta; (second row) Rosario Quitiviz and Lucille Peralta holding Eric G. Montoya. This photograph was taken in front of a house Lucille Peralta and her husband purchased in an area of Los Angeles now officially designated as Historic Filipinotown. (Courtesy of Rosario Quitiviz.)

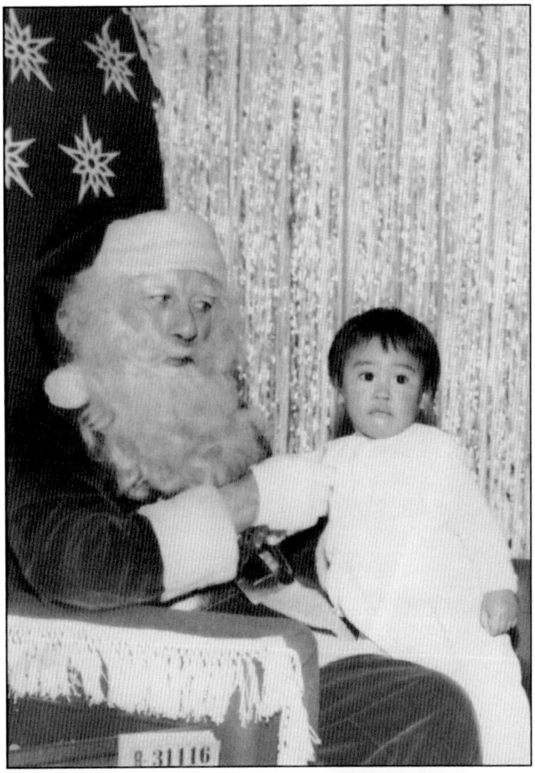

Eric G. Montoya is pictured here with Santa Claus during the annual Hollywood Christmas Parade on Hollywood Boulevard in the early 1950s. (Courtesy of Rosario Quitiviz.)

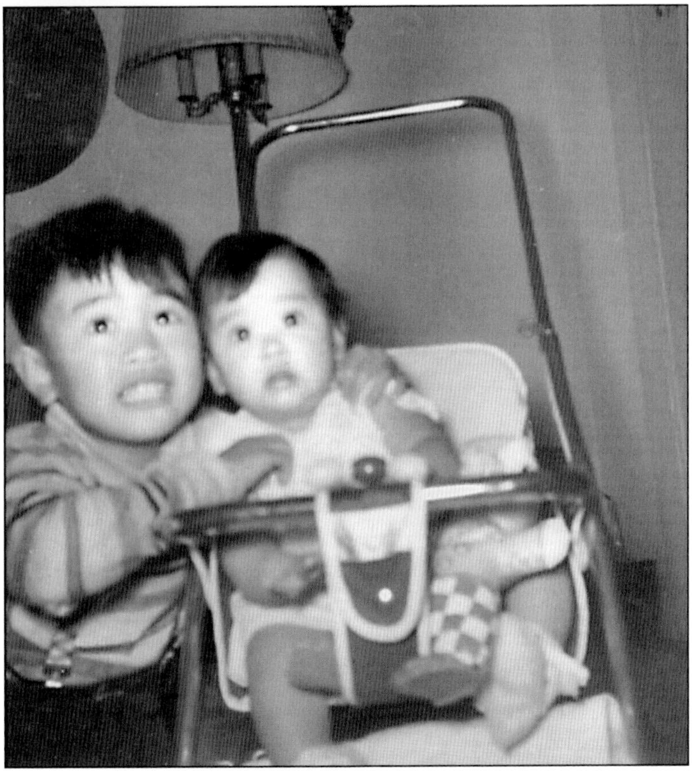

Eric G. Montoya and his new baby sister are seen in the 1950s. Filipino families in the early 1950s and 1960s typically had two or more children. (Courtesy of Rosario Quitiviz.)

Rosario Quitiviz (center) is shown among friends who all immigrated to the United States between 1949 and 1952 in a Hollywood neighborhood in the 1950s. (Courtesy of Rosario Quitiviz.)

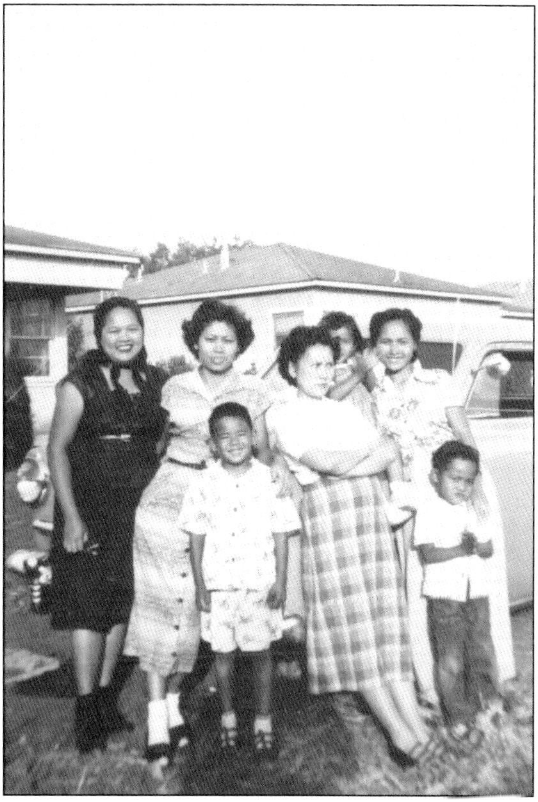

Carina Montoya (first row, far right) celebrates her sixth birthday with friends and neighbors in the backyard of her home in a Hollywood neighborhood in the 1960s. (Courtesy of Rosario Quitiviz.)

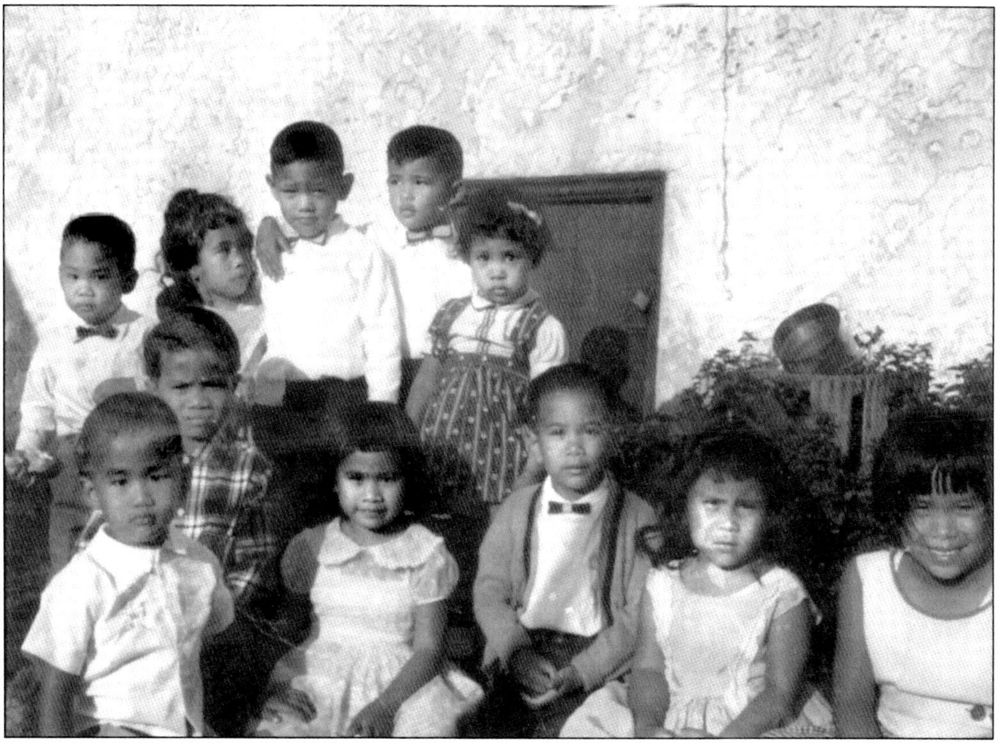

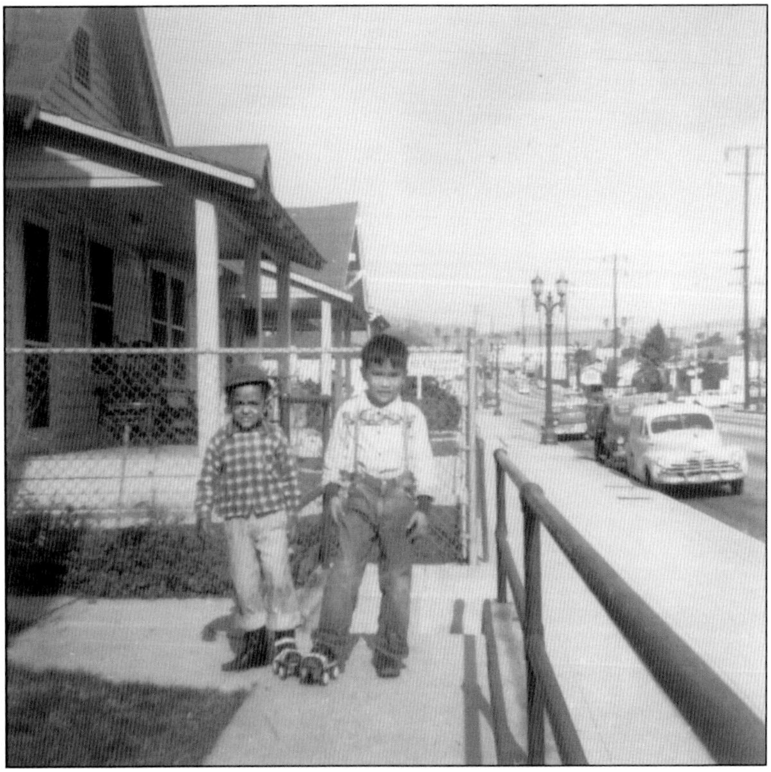

Eric G. Montoya (right) and a friend share skates in a Hollywood neighborhood in the 1950s. (Courtesy of Rosario Quitiviz.)

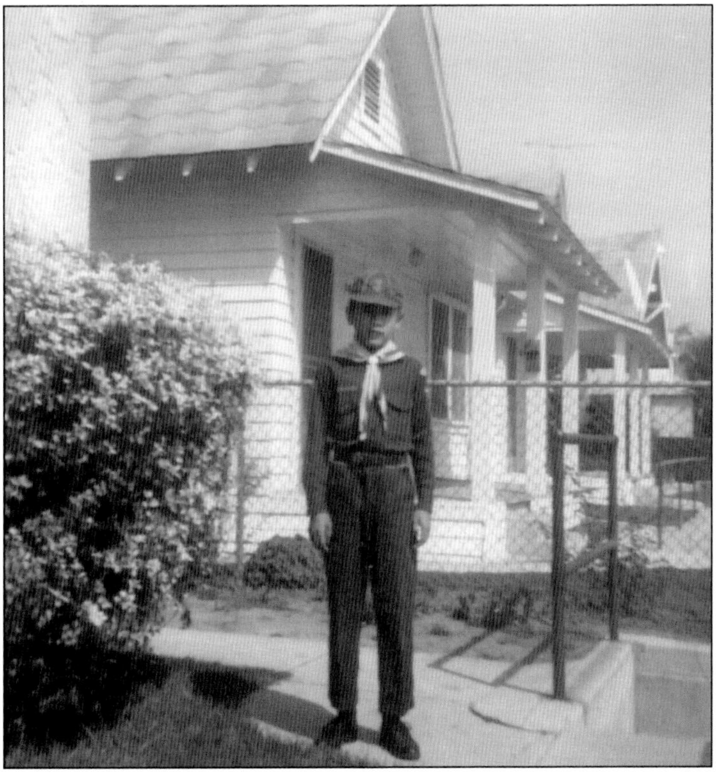

First-generation Filipino American Eric G. Montoya is pictured in his Cub Scout uniform in the 1960s. First-generation children did not suffer the hardships of discrimination encountered by the early arrivals; assimilation into mainstream society was easier for succeeding generations. (Courtesy of Rosario Quitiviz.)

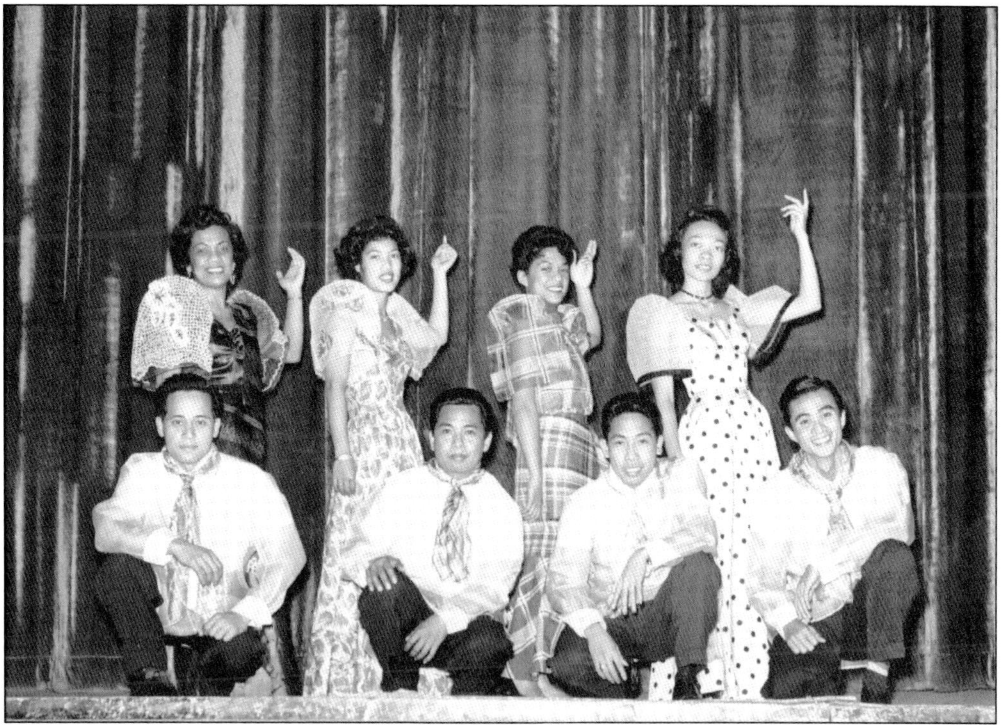

Filipino folk dancers continued to be one of the main sources of entertainment at functions and events in the 1950s. (Courtesy of Rosario Quitiviz.)

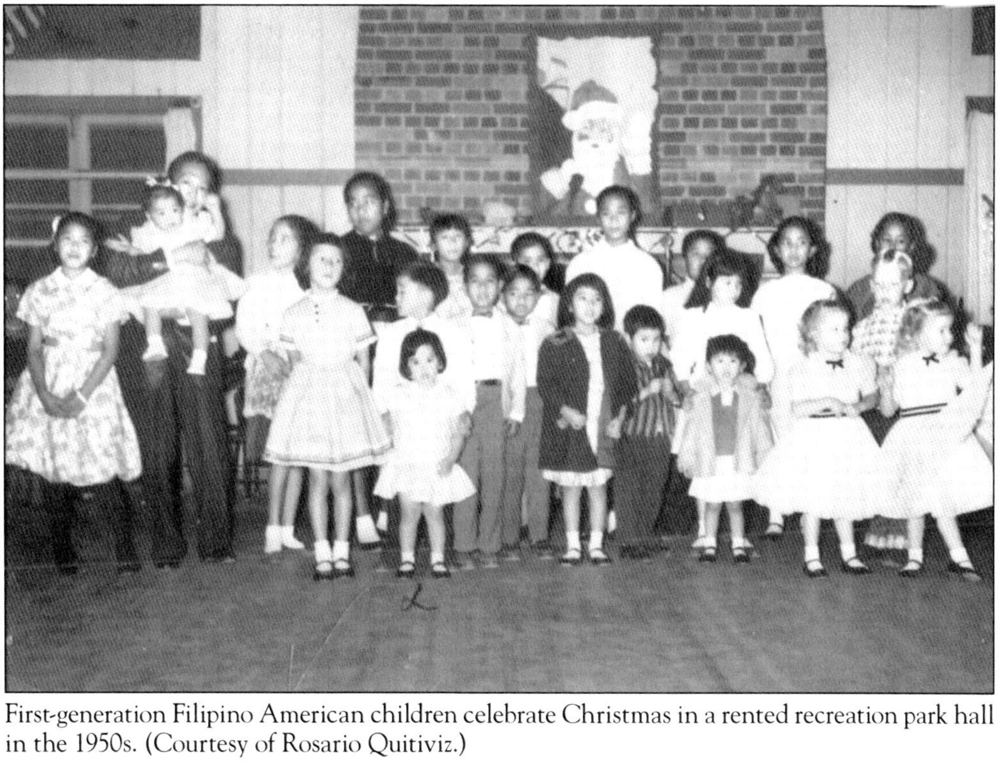

First-generation Filipino American children celebrate Christmas in a rented recreation park hall in the 1950s. (Courtesy of Rosario Quitiviz.)

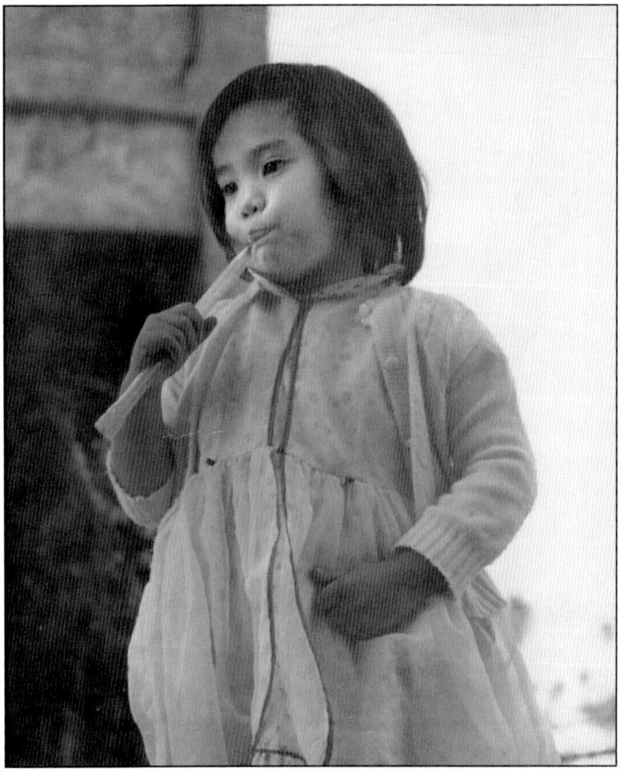

This 1950s photograph was taken surreptitiously by a professional photographer. The photographer later offered money to the child's family to use the photograph in an advertisement depicting impoverished children. Poor but proud, the parents were insulted and closed the door on the photographer. (Courtesy of Rosario Quitiviz.)

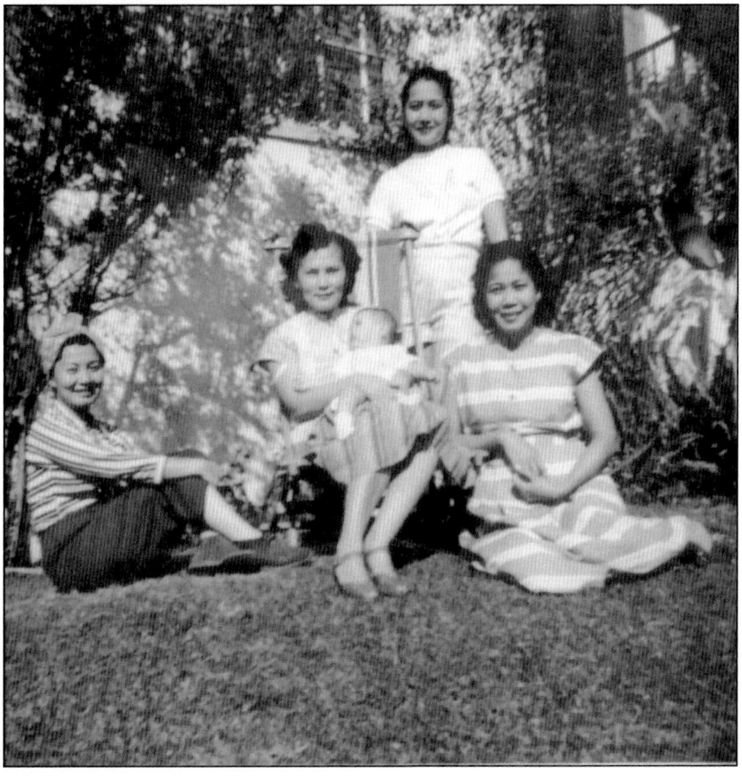

Many first-generation Filipino American children were born in the 1950s. The mothers, some who were war brides, were able to immigrate to the United States in the 1940s and 1950s. (Courtesy of Rosario Quitiviz.)

Three

A Growing Community

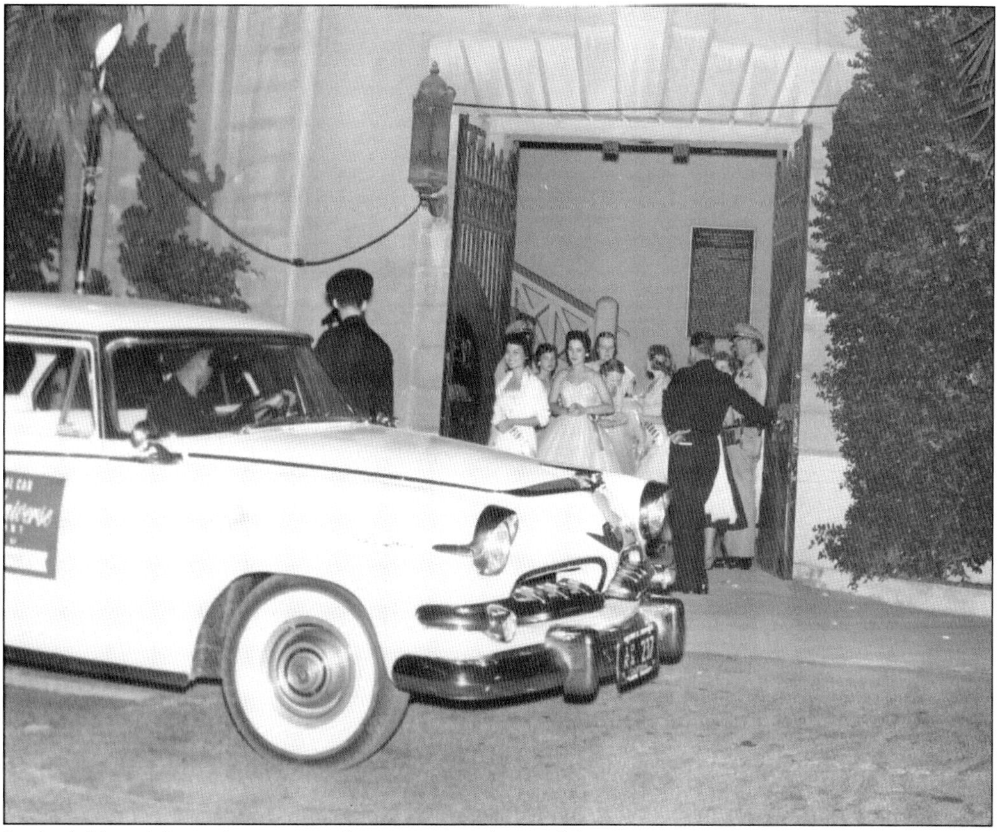

In the lobby of the Lafayette Hotel in Long Beach, candidates competing in the Miss International Beauty Pageant, get ready for a limousine ride. Established in Long Beach in 1960, the pageant was founded upon the concept of candidates possessing passion and energy to spread friendship and goodwill around the world. (Courtesy of Benita Q. Lagmay and Numeriano D. Lagmay.)

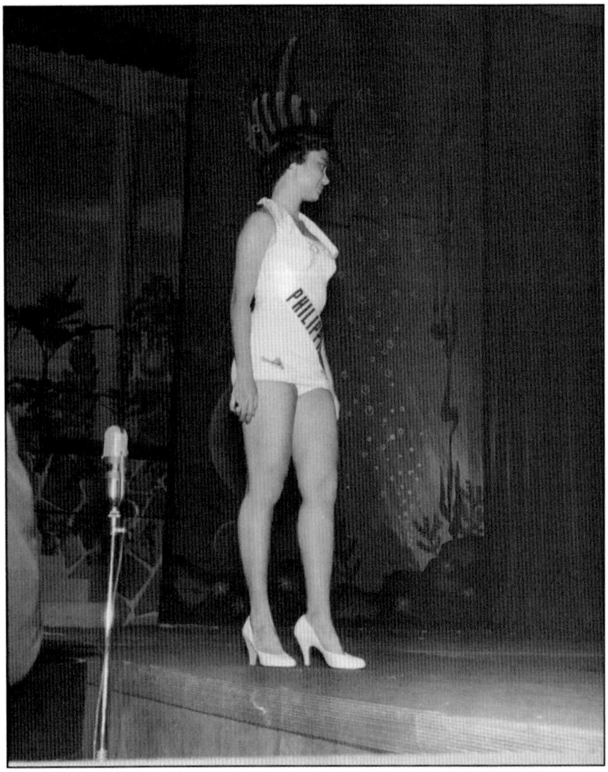

Miss Philippines is being judged on stage in 1960 at the first Miss International Beauty Pageant, held in Long Beach, California. The ultimate goal of the Miss International Beauty Pageant is to promote world peace, goodwill, and understanding, and the winners serve as ambassadors of peace and beauty. The pageant was given extensive press coverage; the *Los Angeles Times* covered the contest, and television station KTTV broadcasted all of the pageant's major festivities from the contestants' arrivals, to the crowning of the first Miss International. Thirteen years later, Filipina Margarita Moran would be crowned Miss Universe in 1973. (Courtesy of Benita Q. Lagmay and Numeriano D. Lagmay.)

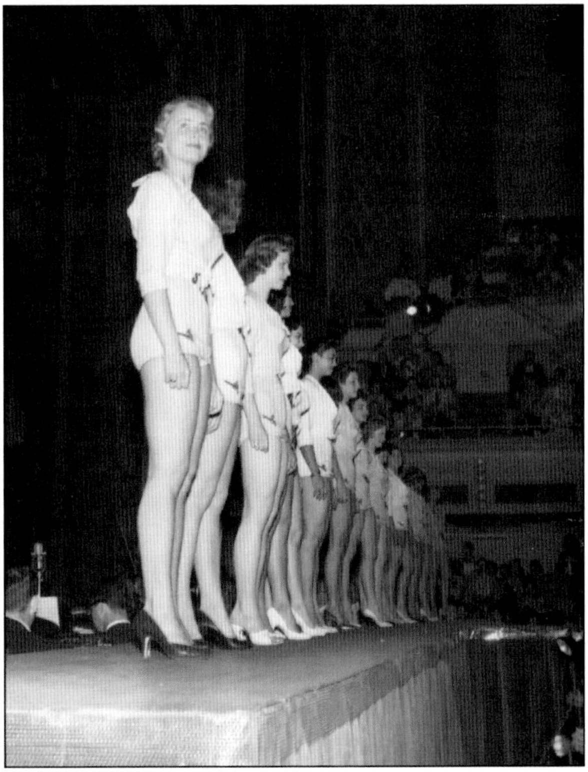

Pictured here are all the representatives of the participating countries in the Miss International Beauty Pageant held in Long Beach, California. The candidates are chosen as representatives of international society, and each is judged by their intelligence and ability to take action. (Courtesy of Benita Q. Lagmay and Numeriano D. Lagmay.)

Two generations of Filipino American couples dance at a 1960s event. By the 1960s, taxi dance halls no longer existed in Los Angeles, but today there are establishments known as hostess clubs that employ women to entertain men with drinks and conversation. (Courtesy of Benita Q. Lagmay and Numeriano D. Lagmay.)

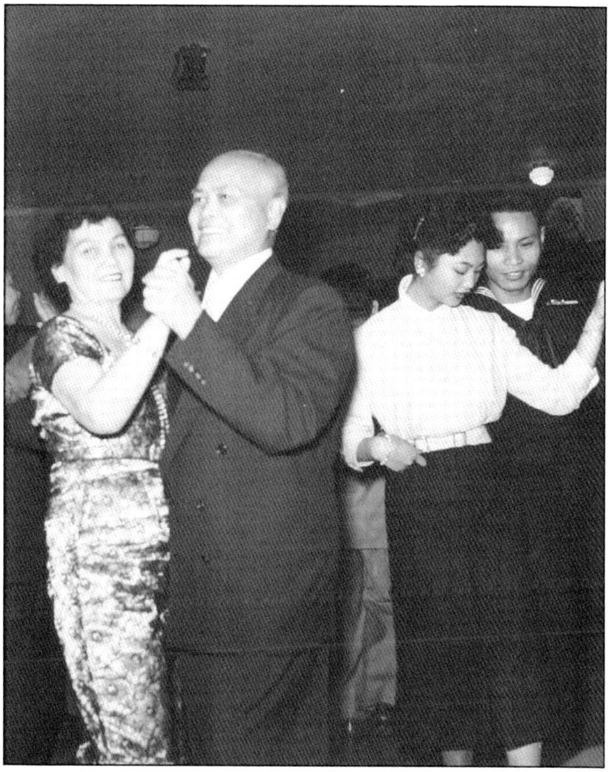

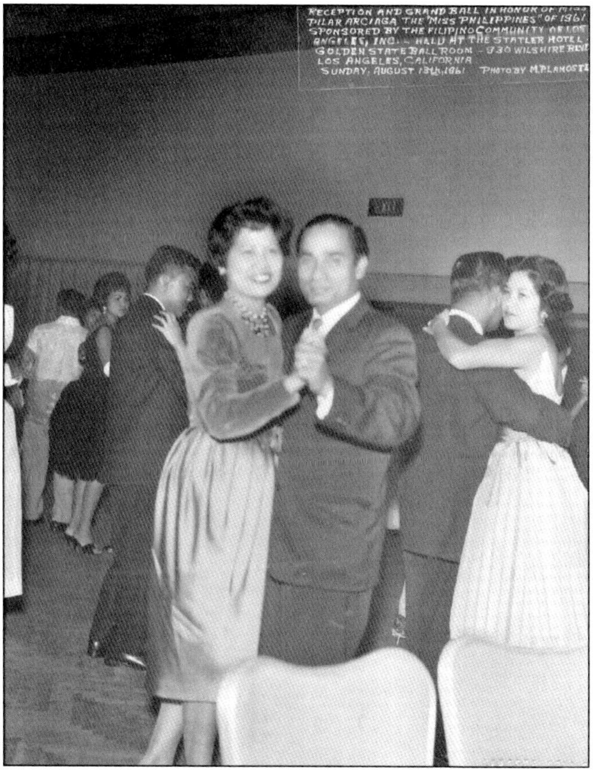

Benita Q. Lagmay and Numeriano D. Lagmay (center) dance at a reception and grand ball in honor of Miss Philippines, Pilar Arciaga, in the Statler Hotel's Golden State Ballroom on Wilshire Boulevard in 1961. The grand ball was sponsored by the Filipino Community of Los Angeles. (Courtesy of Benita Q. Lagmay and Numeriano D. Lagmay.)

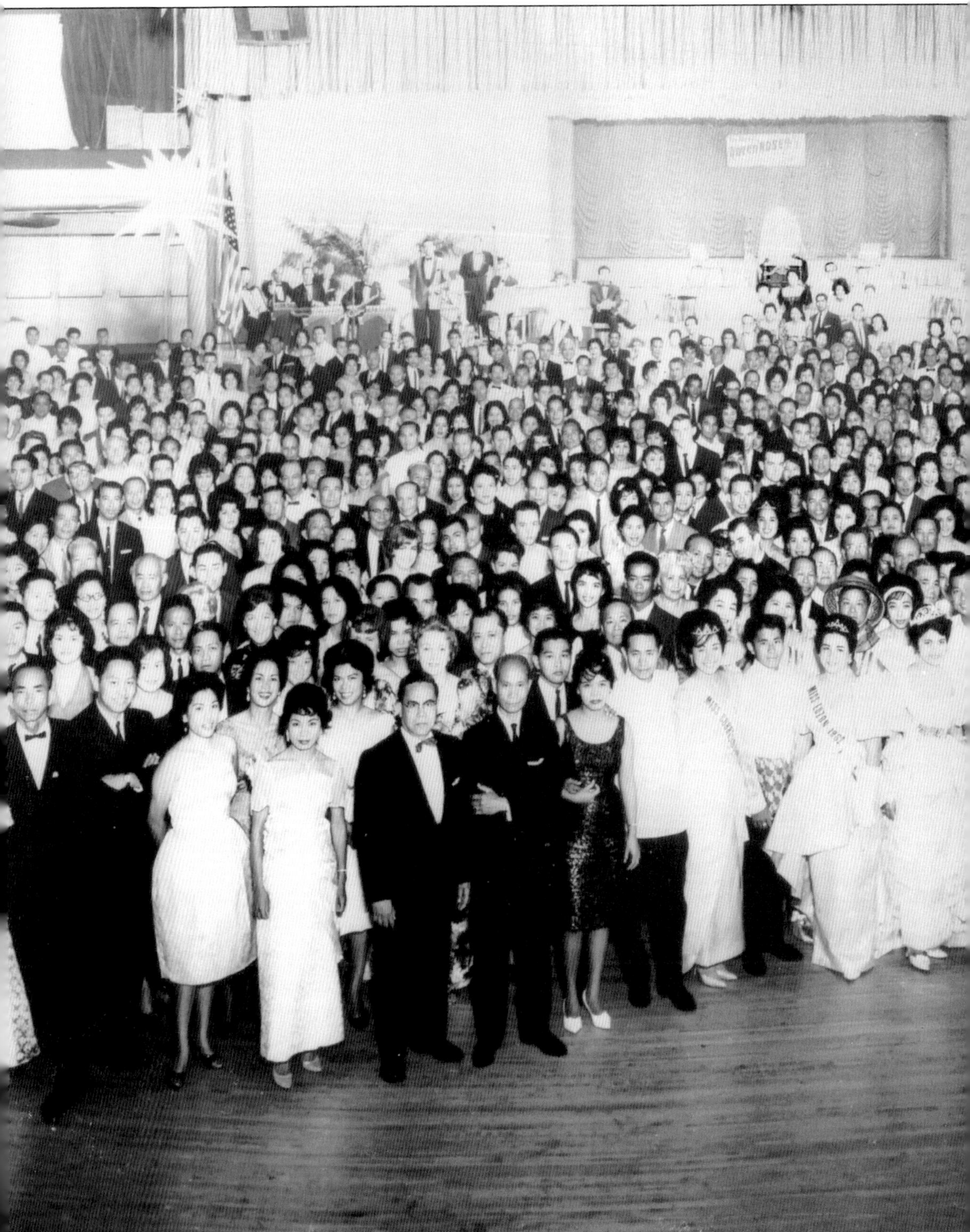

Pictured is the July 4, 1962, Grand Independence Day Ball and coronation of the queen at the Hollywood Palladium. The grand ball was sponsored by the Filipino American Community of

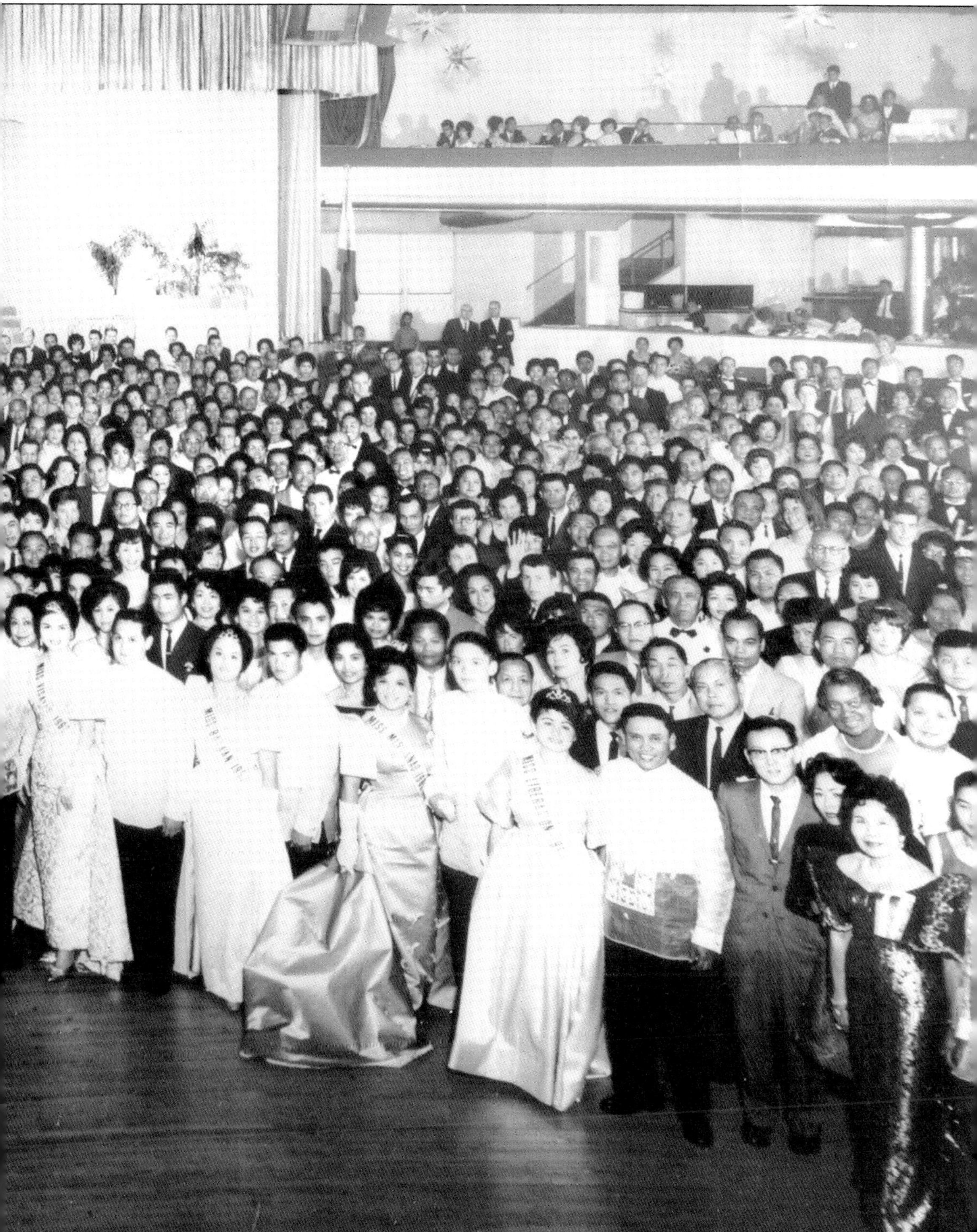

Los Angeles and was a huge event that received local news recognition. (Courtesy of Shades of L.A. Archives/Los Angeles Public Library.)

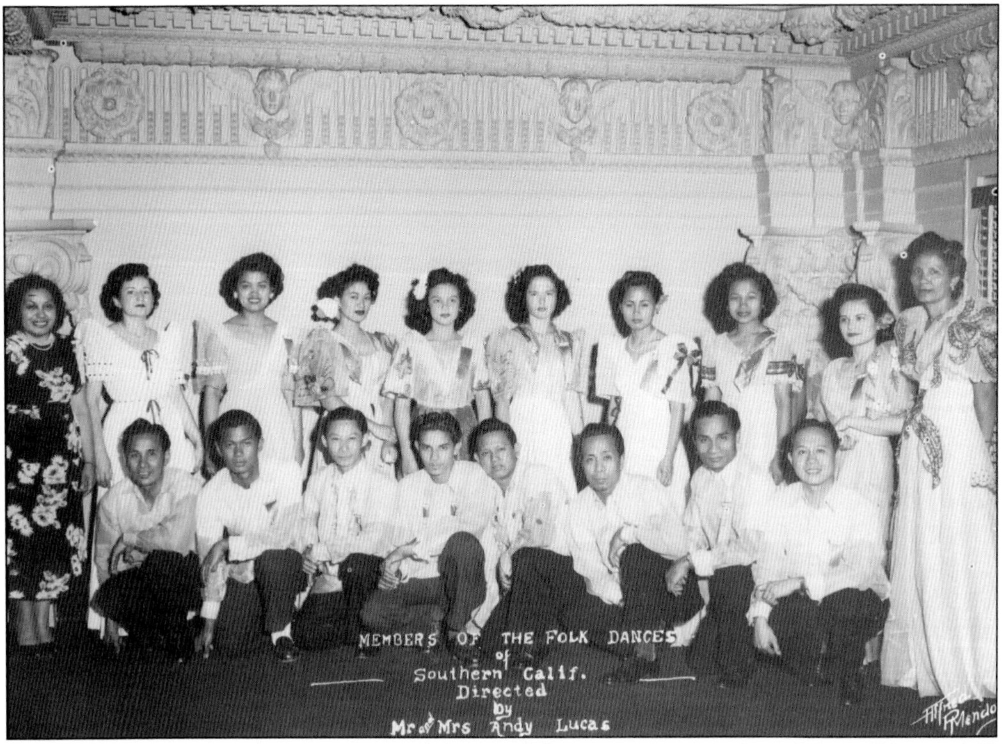

Numeriano D. Lagmay (first row, second from right) is seen as a member of these Filipino folk dancers of Southern California. (Courtesy of Benita Q. Lagmay and Numeriano D. Lagmay.)

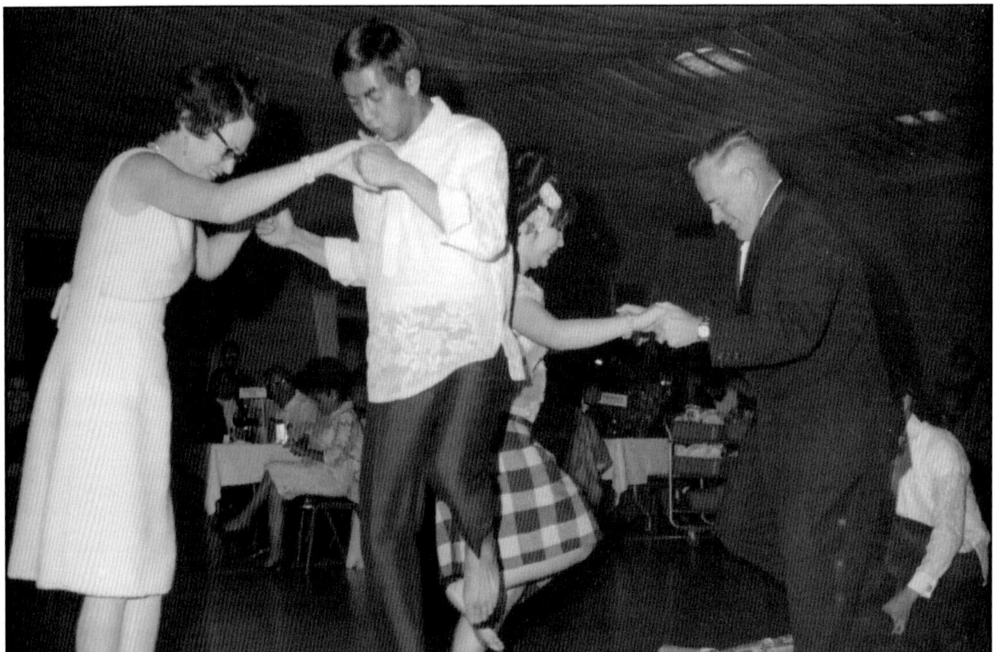

Non-Filipino Americans attended Filipino events in the 1960s and joined in the entertainment to learn traditional folk dances. (Courtesy of Benita Q. Lagmay and Numeriano D. Lagmay.)

Numeriano D. Lagmay (right), a photographer and Filipino American activist and leader, presents a photograph he created to a Los Angeles councilman as a gift in the 1960s. (Courtesy of Benita Q. Lagmay and Numeriano D. Lagmay.)

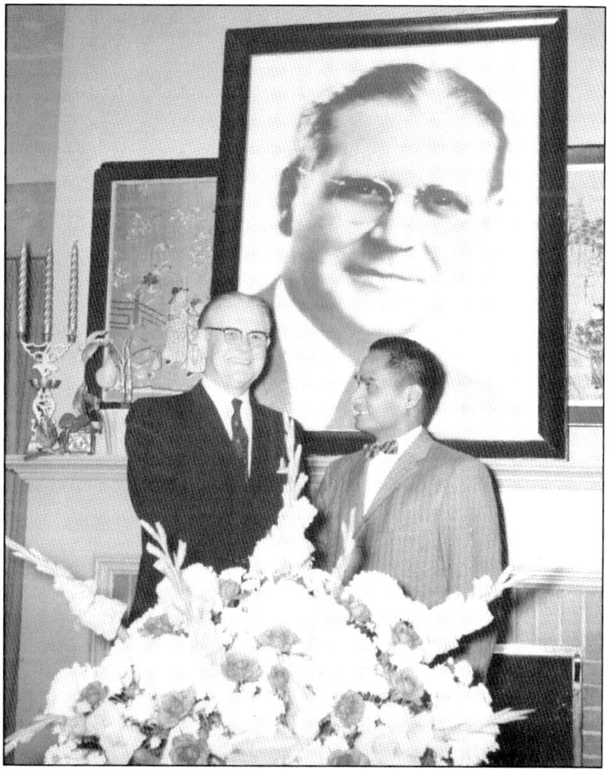

In the 1960s, Filipino Americans and non-Filipino Americans gathered at a grand event in one of Hollywood's or downtown Los Angeles's grand hotels. (Courtesy of Benita Q. Lagmay and Numeriano D. Lagmay.)

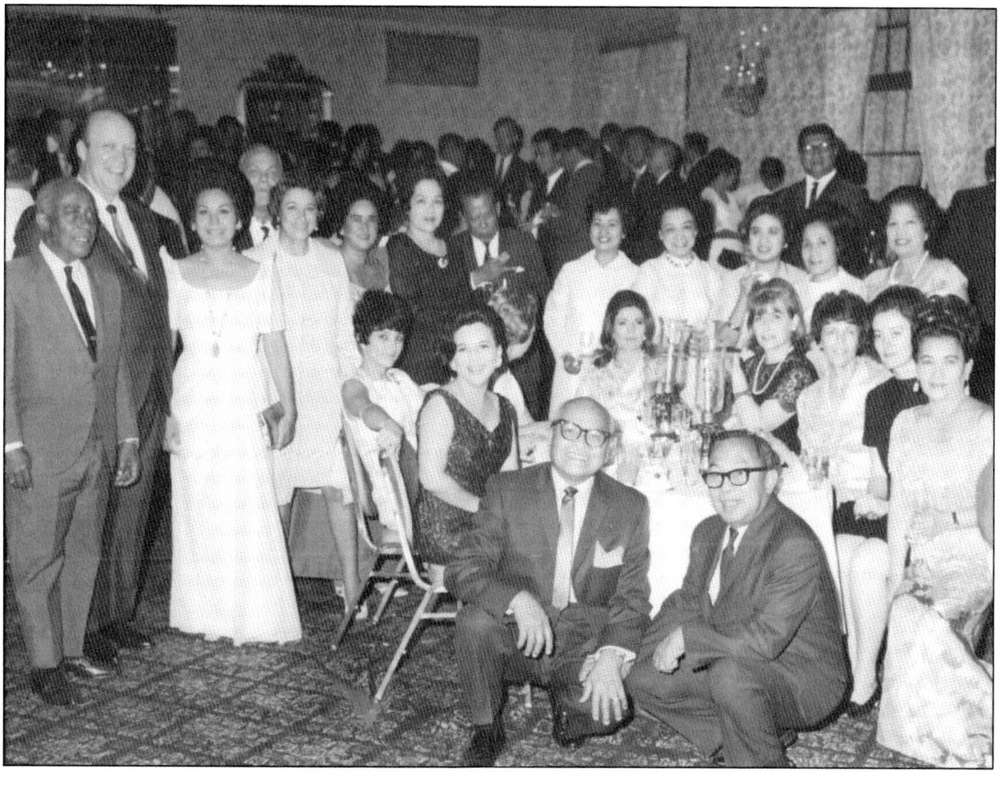

Filipino Community of L.A. Fetes Consul-General and Mrs. Holigores With Testimonial Dinner and Ball

The Philippines Star Press

The fabulous Biltmore Bowl, Biltmore Hotel in downtown Los Angeles burst in full glory when the Filipino Community of Los Angeles proudly honored one of the ablest Consul Generals the Philippine Government has ever sent abroad, The Honorable Alejandro F. Holigores. The testimonial dinner and ball was held Saturday, March 25, 1967.

Consul General Holigores, a career diplomat in the Philippine Foreign Service had remarkably served for five years [1962-1967] as Philippine Consul General in Los Angeles but recently he was given a definite order by the Philippine Government to go to New York to occupy the choice post vacated by Ambassador Bartolome Umayam, Philippine Consul General, New York, who was recently appointed Philippine Ambassador to Rome.

Prior to his consular assignment in Los Angeles, Minister Holigores was Philippine Consul General in Singapore, Malaysia. He left Los Angeles for New York, April 1, 1967. Carlos A. Faustino, Phillippine Consul General to Hongkong will succeed Consul General Holigores. He is due to take over by the middle of this month.

Among the distinguished City officials, guests and friends who attended the affair included The Honorable Hansrolf Kiderlen, Consul General of Germany.

(Continued on Page 4)

A COMMUNITY PAYS TRIBUTE

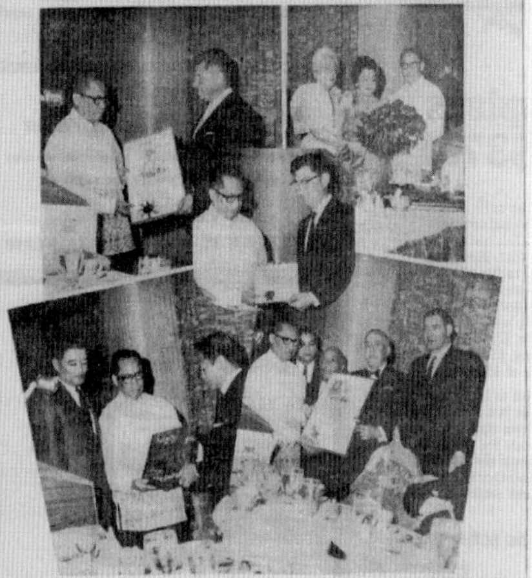

Civic leaders in the Southland present commendations, resolutions, plaque at the Los Angeles Filipino Community testimonial banquet and ball for departing minister and his wife. Lower photos, L. FCLA's plaque is shown being received by Minister Alejandro F. Holigores, center, for his unselfish cooperation with the Filipino Community of Los Angeles from Emile Eisma, right, chairman FCLA Board of Trustees. At left is FCLA's president, Benjamin Manibog. R., Los Angeles City Councils resolution of commendation was also read and presented to Minister Holigores at the testimonial dinner and ball tendered by the FCLA in honor of Minister and Mrs. Holigores at the Biltmore Bowl of the Biltmore Hotel in Los Angeles, March 25, 1967. Making the presentation is Councilman Paul Lamport, second from right. Others in the picture from left next to Minister Holigores are Monty Manibog, legal counsel of FCLA, Councilman Gilbert Lindsay and Councilman John Ferraro. Looking on admiringly at right foreground is Mrs. Holigores. (Top photos.) Minister Holigores, left, is shown receiving a resolution of commendation from the County Board of Supervisors from Robert Donahue, right, Field Deputy of Supervisor Ernest Debs. Mrs. Felipe Inocencio, third from right, past president of the Los Angeles Philippine Women's Club and prominent matron of the Caballeros de Dimas-Alang, presented a bouquet of red roses to Mrs. Holigores, second from right, while Minister Holigores looks on. (Center photo). Mayor Yorty's letter of commendation was read and presented to Minister Holigores, left, by George Saiki, right, Executive Assistant to Los Angeles Mayor Yorty.

Photos by N. D. Lagmey

A 1967 article covered a grand event in which the Filipino community highly honored the departing Filipino consul general Alejandro F. Holigores. In Consul General Holigores's parting message to the Filipino community in Los Angeles, he said "to let live and keep ever aflame the spirit of unity and cooperation among themselves." (Courtesy of Benita Q. Lagmay and Numeriano D. Lagmay.)

L.A. FILIPINO COMMUNITY FETES CONSUL GENERAL

(Continued from Page 1)

dean of the Los Angeles Consular Corps, Councilman and Mrs. Gilbert Lindsay, Councilman and Mrs. Paul Lamport, Councilman John Ferraro, George Saiki, Executive Assistant to Los Angeles City Mayor Samuel Wm. Yorty, Robert Donahue, Field Deputy to Los Angeles County Board of Supervisors Ernest E. Debs, Howard Chappel, Commissioner of Public Works, Los Angeles County, Philippine Consul Fe O. Palma, and The Rev. Felix Pasua of the Filipino Christian Church who gave the invocation.

Benjamin M. Manibog, President of The Filipino Community of Los Angeles, Incorporated gave the Welcome Address.

One of the featured highlights of the affair was the presentation of commendations to Minister Holigores by the following:

a. A letter of commendation from Los Angeles City Mayor Samuel Wm. Yorty, read by Executive Assistant George Saiki.

b. A Board of Supervisors' resolution, read and presented by Field Deputy Robert Donahue who represented Supervisor Ernest E. Debs.

c. Los Angeles City Council resolutions, read and presented by Councilman Paul Lamport. The resolution was signed by all the councilmen of Los Angeles City Council.

d. A plaque from The Filipino Community of Los Angeles, presented by Emile Eisma, Chairman of the Board of Trustees.

e. A plaque from Manila Post 464, American Legion, presented by Commander Numeriano D. Lagmay.

f. Caballeros de Dimasalang's plaque, presented by Felipe Inocencio, Commander of the Su-

g. A plaque from Filipino Alumni Association, presented by Mrs. Ruben Guerrero, "Mrs. Philippines of 1966", who represented Roque De La Ysla, President of the Filipino Alumni Association, Inc.

Sharing with all the laurels and honors was of course the charming and amiable wife of the Consul General, Mrs. Sofia Holigores, who was also presented a bouquet of red roses by Mrs. Felipe Inocencio, "in admiration to her being the moving spirit and the living inspiration behind the enviable successes of her beloved husband."

In his stirring parting message, Minister Holigores exhorted the officers and members of The Filipino Community to let live and keep ever aflame the spirit of unity and cooperation among themselves; to keep the link of friendship between the Filipino Community and the City Government eternally firm, striving to let this unique friendship continue and expand through the years.

Attorney G. Monty M. Manibog, FCLA Legal Counsel, was the master of ceremonies. Mrs. Salud Albarico, third Vice President, FCLA, was General Chairman. The affair wound up at two o'clock in the morning with Johnny Aquino, and his orchestra providing the music. The affair was a tremendous success, an affair to remember.

Pictured here in 1961 are Ray Buhen (left, owner of Tiki Ti) and his son Mike Buhen. After almost three decades of making drinks for customers, Ray Buhen decided to open his own tiki bar in Hollywood in 1961. Loyal patrons from his bartending days at the many popular Hollywood bars and restaurants would visit him at Tiki Ti for a drink. The Tiki Ti is still open for business after 46 years. (Courtesy of Mike Buhen.)

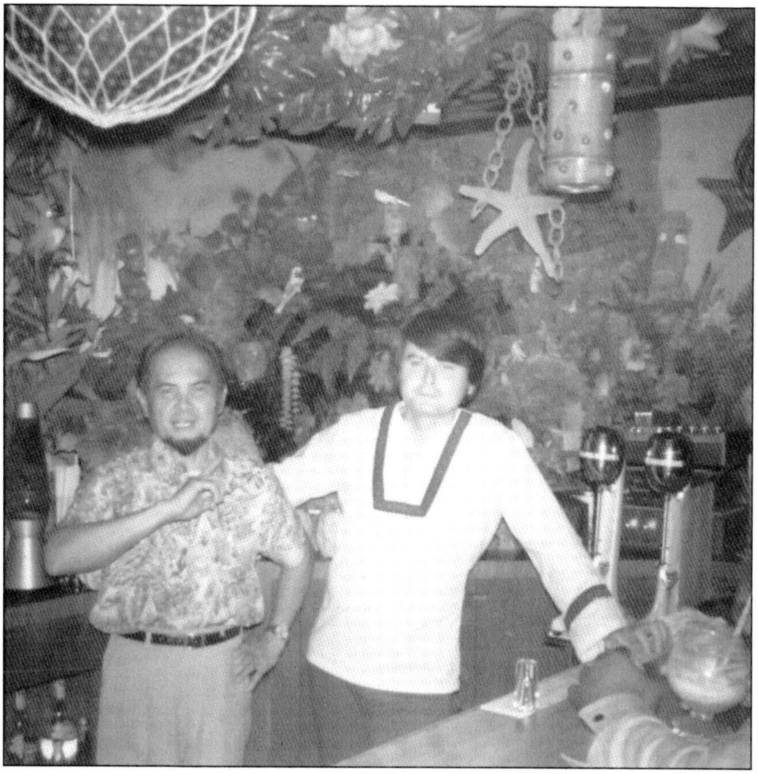

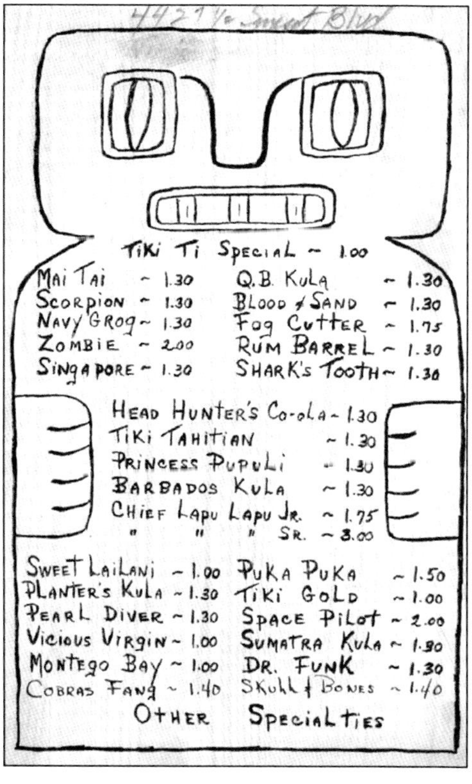

This original Tiki Ti of Hollywood bar menu dates to 1961. (Courtesy of Mike Buhen.)

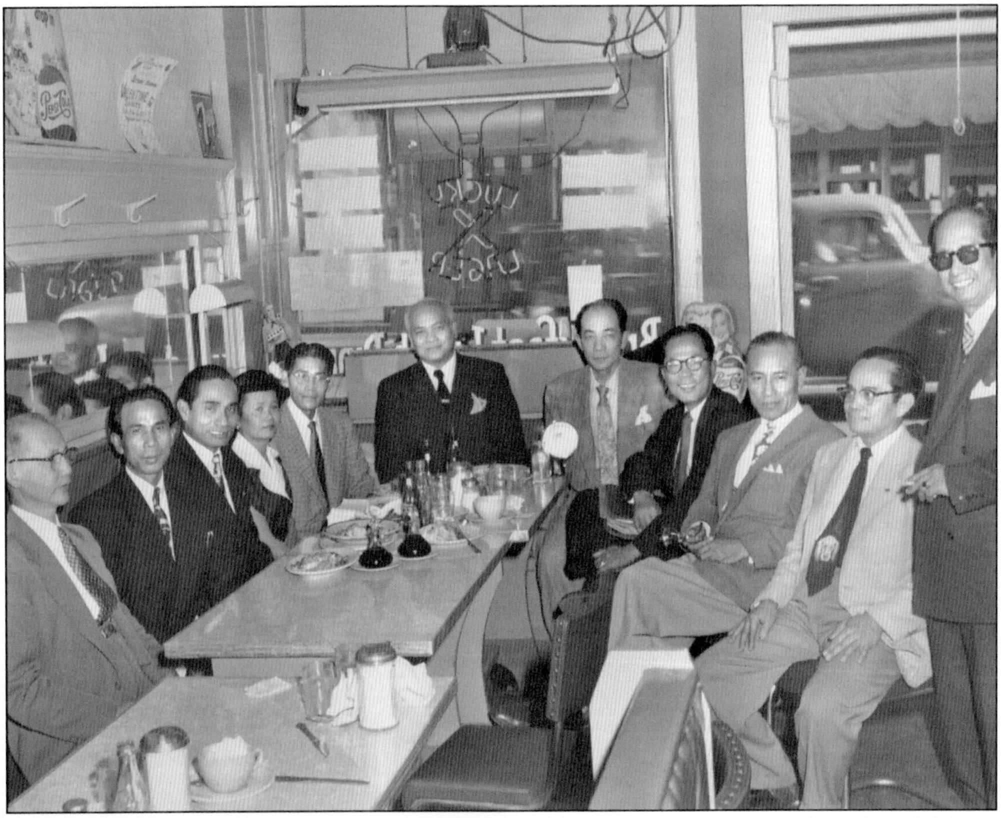

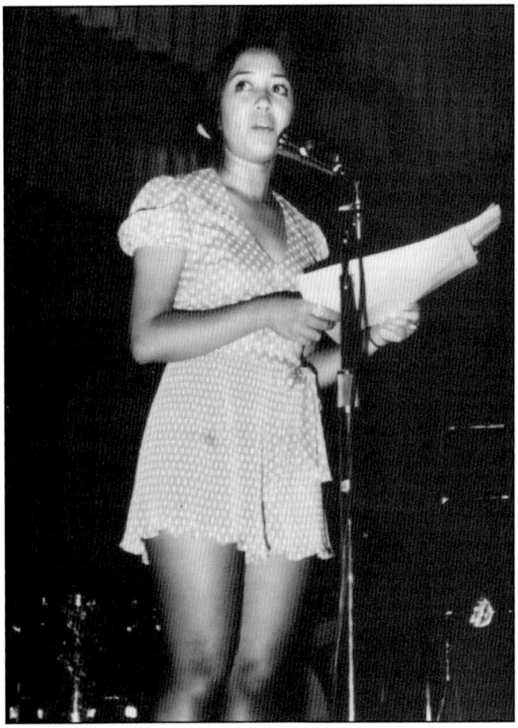

Numeriano D. Lagmay (third from left) is shown at a diner with friends in the 1960s. Bonds of friendship were lifelong and getting together frequently was common. (Courtesy of Benita Q. Lagmay and Numeriano D. Lagmay.)

Daughter of longtime Angeleno and Filipino American activist Remedios Geaga, Joselyn Geaga-Rosenthal presents an introduction at the Fourth of July event held at the Hollywood Palladium in the 1960s. (Courtesy of Joselyn Geaga-Rosenthal.)

Numeriano D. Lagmay was photographed in the 1960s atop Mount Wilson. Mount Wilson is known as a metro-media center for its broadcasting of radio and television frequencies for the Greater Los Angeles area. (Courtesy of Benita Q. Lagmay and Numeriano D. Lagmay.)

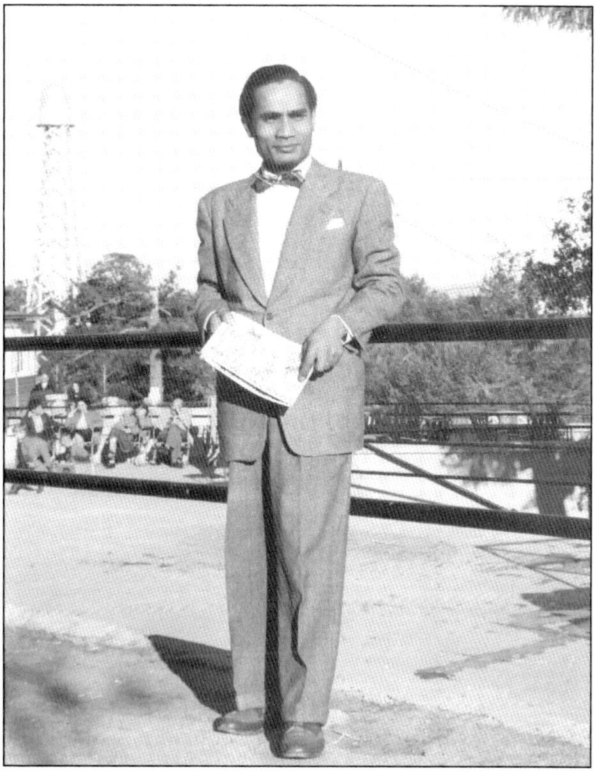

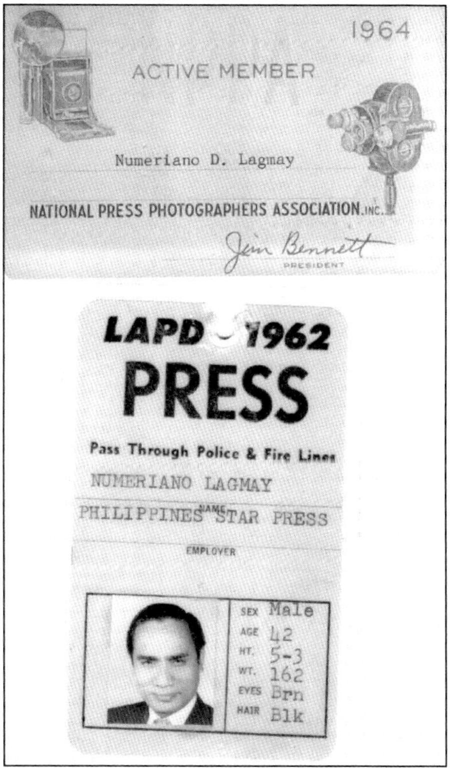

This is a 1964 photograph of Numeriano D. Lagmay's press badge, which allowed him entry into all events in the city. He was the primary photographer for the Filipino community for almost four decades, covering and preserving the history of Filipino families and events that otherwise would have been left undocumented in the early years. (Courtesy of Benita Q. Lagmay and Numeriano D. Lagmay.)

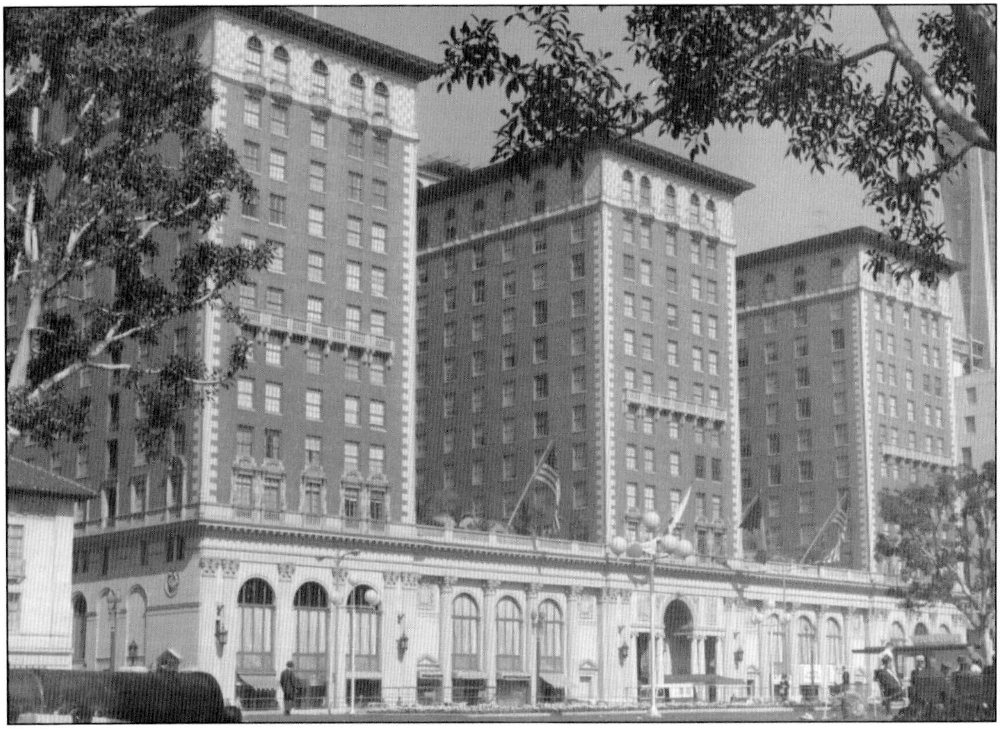

Beauty pageants, debutant balls, and weddings are huge milestone events in the Filipino community. Outwardly, it would sometimes appear that no expense in celebrating such an event was sparred. Above is the grand Biltmore Hotel in Los Angeles where such events were held. (Courtesy of Juliet Lagmay-Akiaten.)

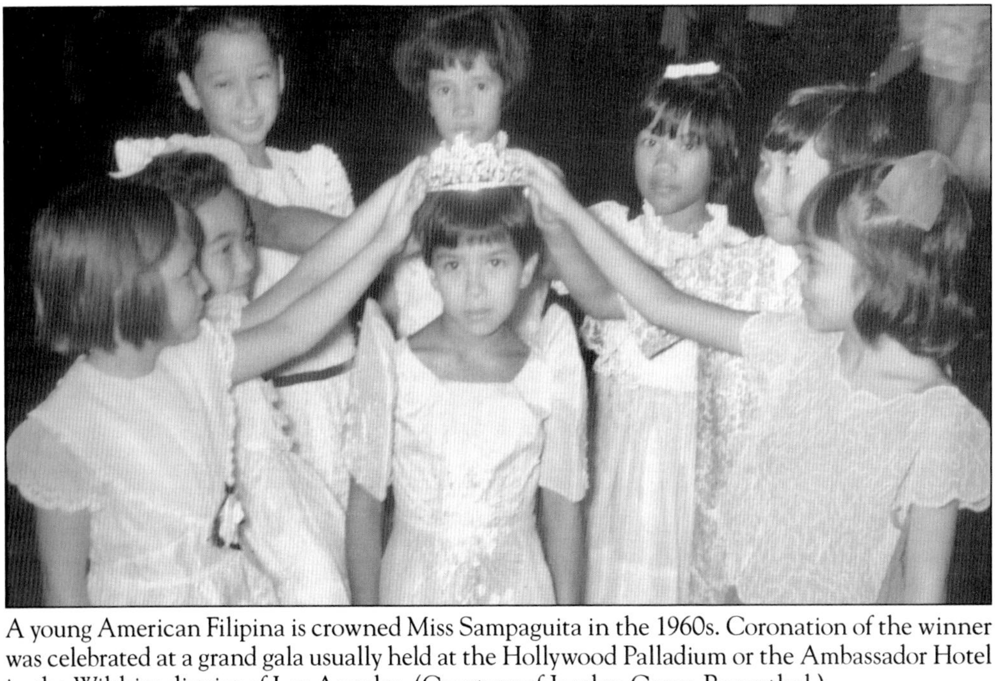

A young American Filipina is crowned Miss Sampaguita in the 1960s. Coronation of the winner was celebrated at a grand gala usually held at the Hollywood Palladium or the Ambassador Hotel in the Wilshire district of Los Angeles. (Courtesy of Joselyn Geaga-Rosenthal.)

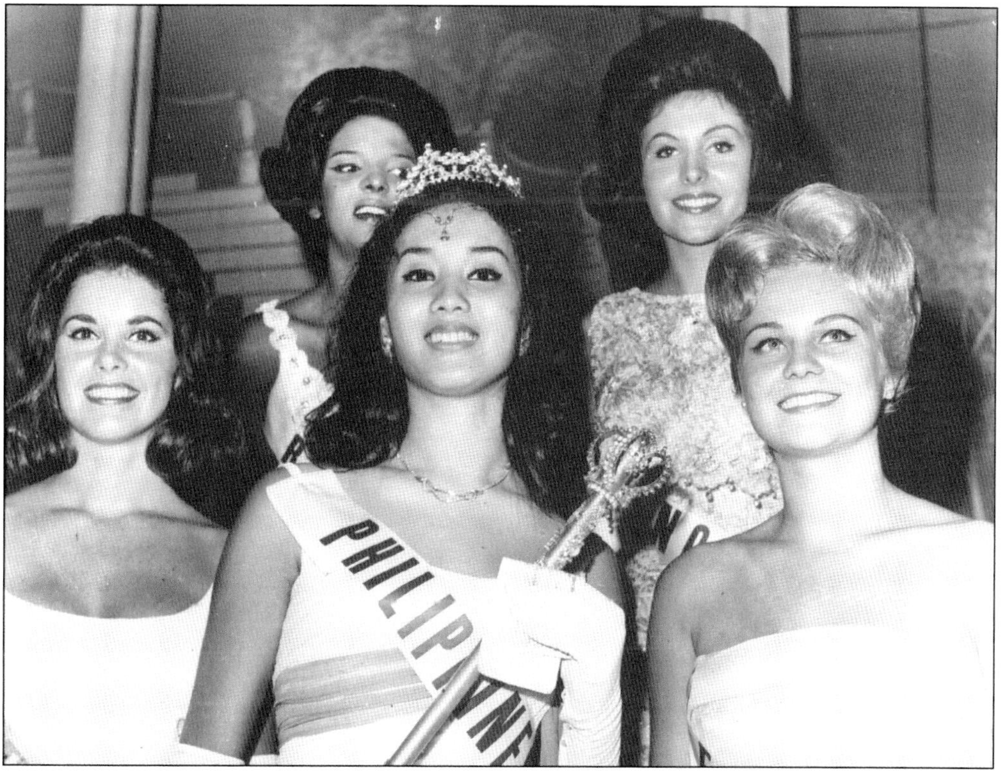

Gemma G. Cruz (above, front center) won the title of Miss Philippines in the 1960s and later won the crown of Miss International in 1965 (right). She was the first Filipina to win two beauty pageant titles, and her success garnered national recognition. (Both, courtesy of Benita Q. Lagmay and Numeriano D. Lagmay.)

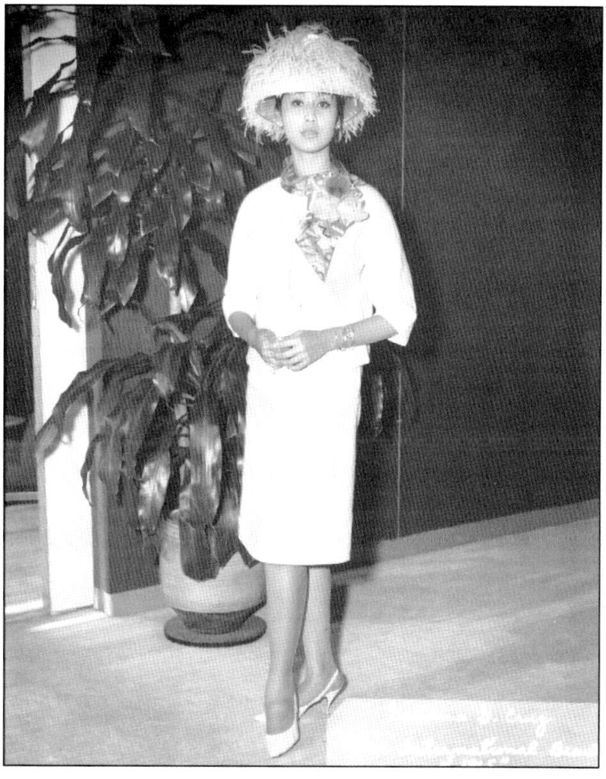

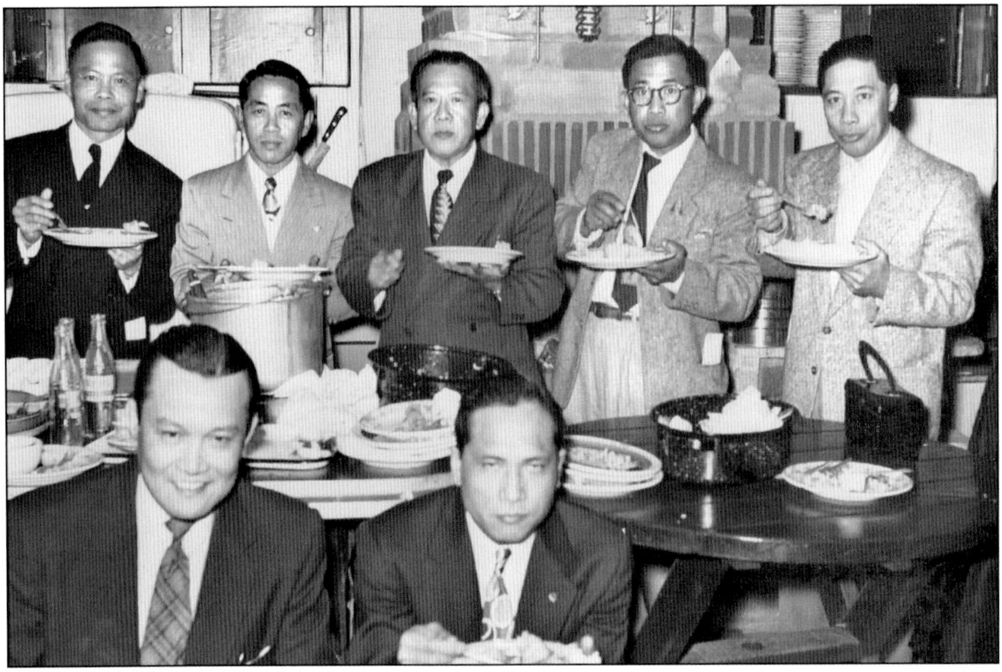

Filipino men gather in the kitchen at a Santa Maria Ilocos Sur Association event in the 1960s. The club, formed in the 1940s and named after a *barangay*, or province, on the south China coast of Luzon, consisted of mainly families. The club organized many family-oriented events and focused on issues to better the organization and community. The Santa Maria Association was one of several Filipino organizations that began to take a political interest in furthering the Filipino community. (Courtesy of Benita Q. Lagmay and Numeriano D. Lagmay.)

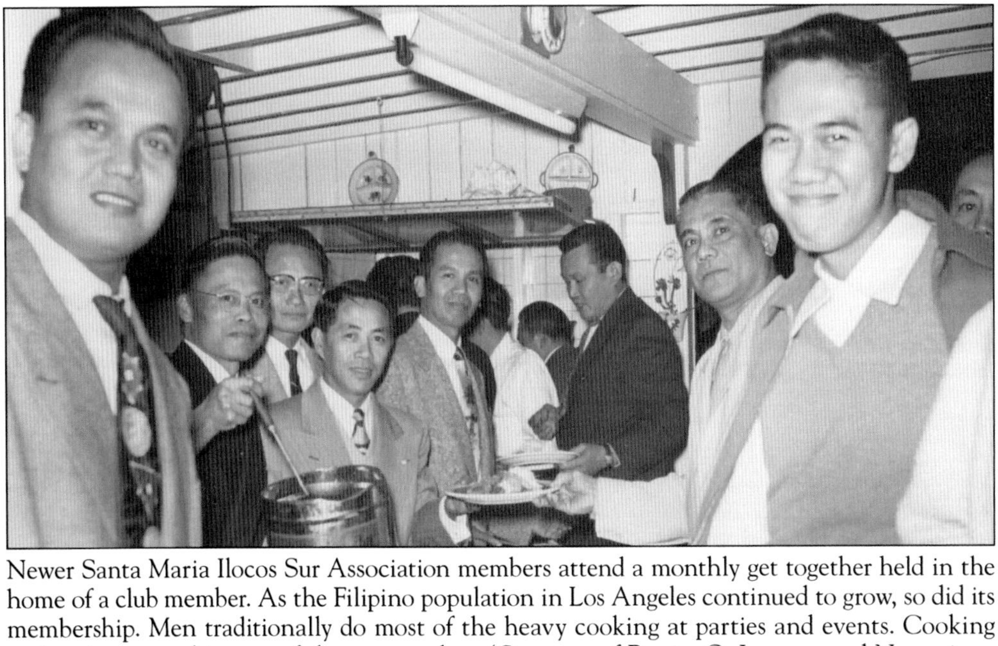

Newer Santa Maria Ilocos Sur Association members attend a monthly get together held in the home of a club member. As the Filipino population in Los Angeles continued to grow, so did its membership. Men traditionally do most of the heavy cooking at parties and events. Cooking and eating was a big part of the get-together. (Courtesy of Benita Q. Lagmay and Numeriano D. Lagmay.)

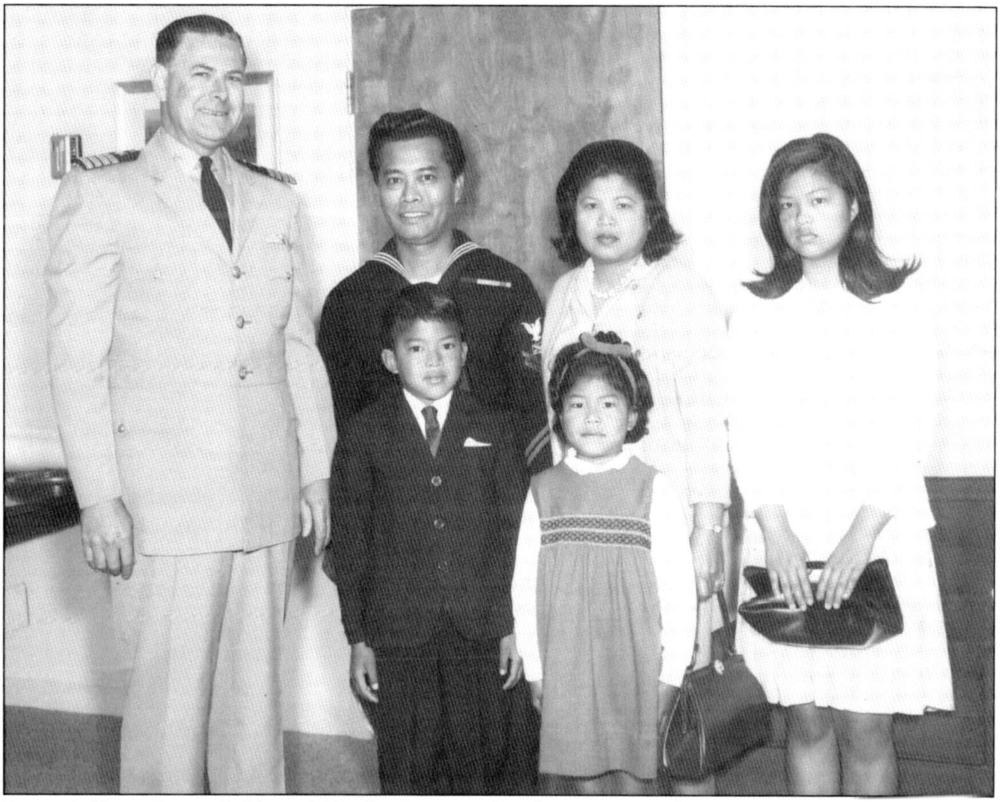

Petty Officer Second Class Alfredo Taganas (back row, second from left) and his family are pictured here in the 1960s. He was the personal chef of an admiral (back row, far left) in the U.S. Navy. (Courtesy of Celina Taganas-Duffy.)

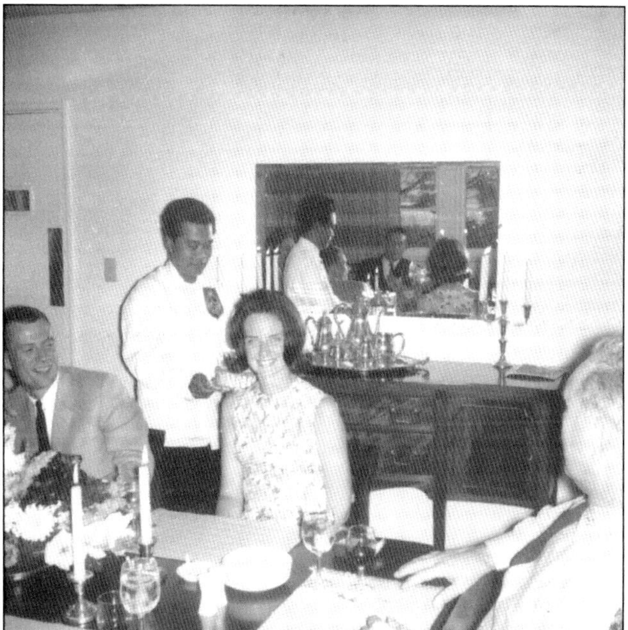

Alfredo Taganas serves a birthday cake to Anne Dolan at the admiral's home on July 3, 1965. Taganas also served the admiral's family while off duty during his enlistment in the U.S. Navy. (Courtesy of Celina Taganas-Duffy.)

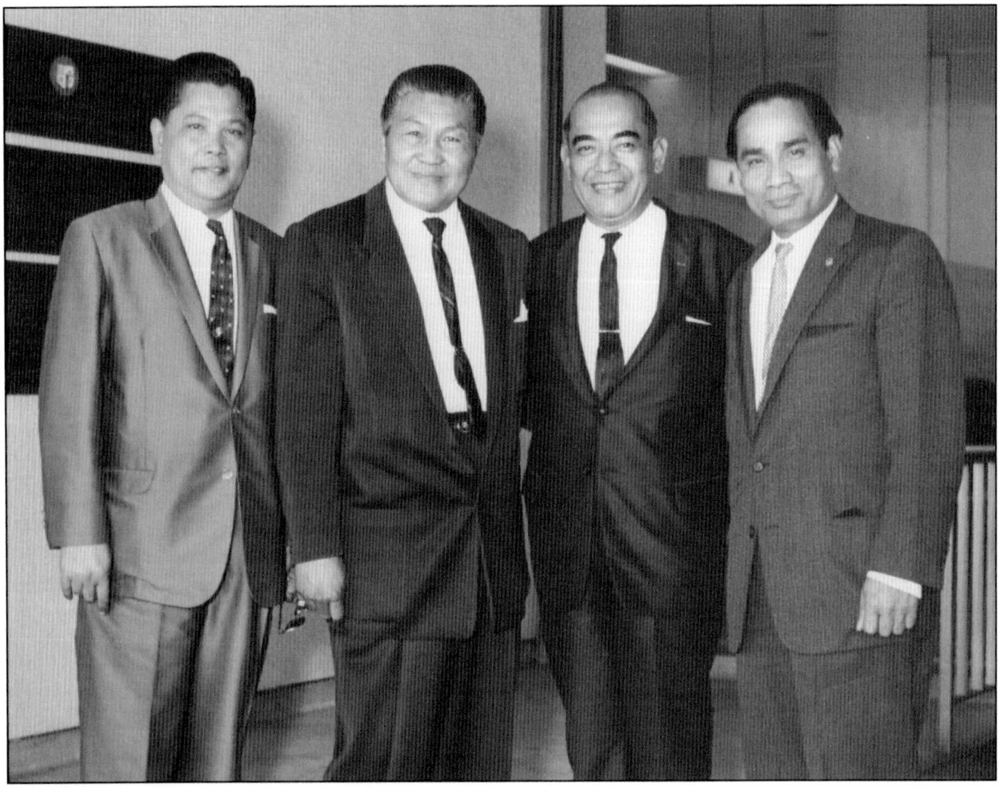

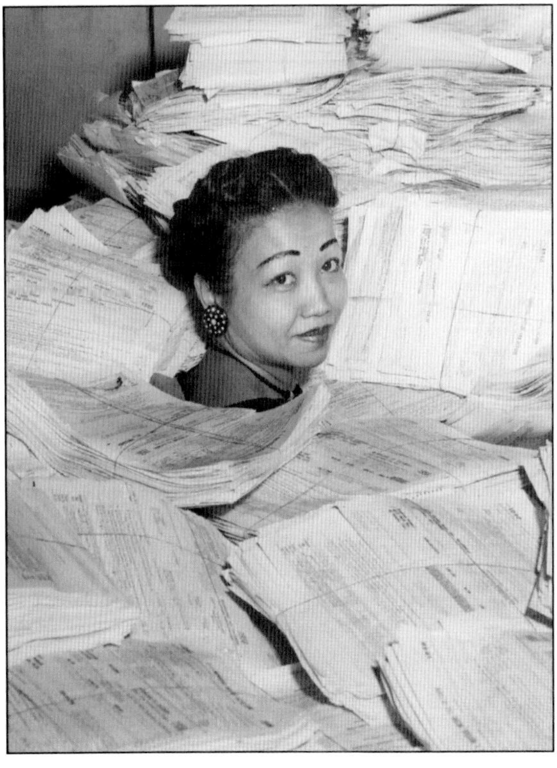

Filipino community activist and leader Numeriano D. Lagmay (far right) poses with fellow community leaders in the 1960s. Filipino activism and leadership greatly helped the Filipino community expand within the city and opened doors for the new generation. (Courtesy of Benita Q. Lagmay and Numeriano D. Lagmay.)

A 1960s photograph of Amparo Domingo, president of the Filipino Community Association of Los Angeles, shows her buried in stacks of mortgage loan documents from the purchase and refinance of the Filipino community center. The mortgages of the center were paid off during Domingo's presidency. (Courtesy of Benita Q. Lagmay and Numeriano D. Lagmay.)

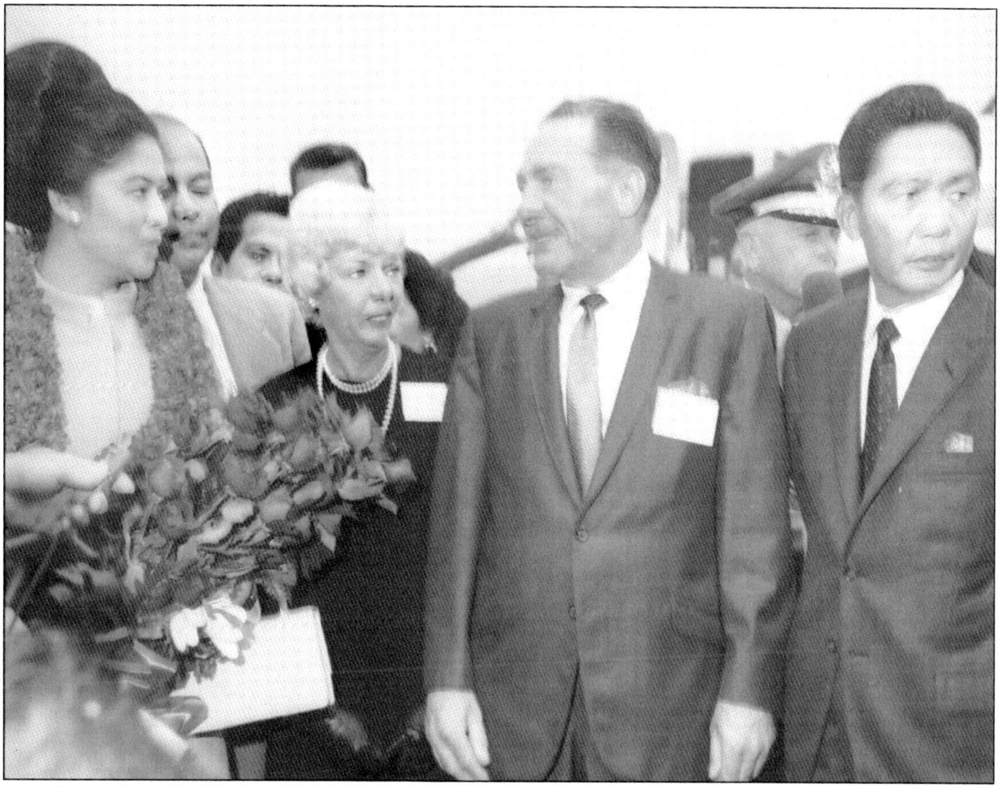

Imelda Marcos (far left) and her husband, Pres. Ferdinand Marcos (far right), are pictured with Mrs. Sam Yorty (second from left) and Los Angeles mayor Sam Yorty during a visit to the city in the 1960s (above). Mayor Yorty acknowledged the Filipino American community and often attended its many events and celebrations, including this welcoming reception for President Marcos (right). (Both, courtesy of Benita Q. Lagmay and Numeriano D. Lagmay.)

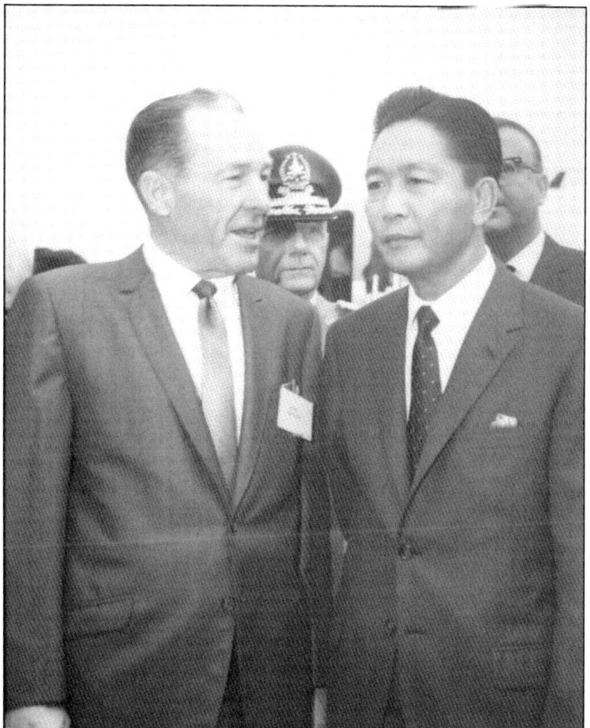

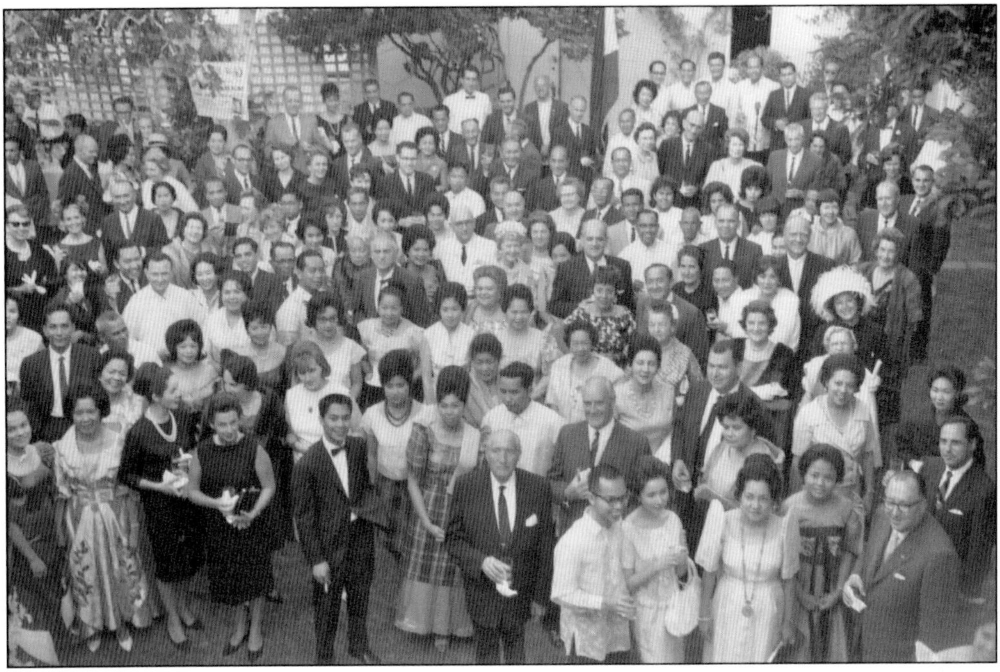

The Filipino consul general of Los Angeles in the 1960s, Alejandro F. Holigores opened his home to many Filipino events, usually receptions honoring visiting Filipino dignitaries, religious leaders, celebrities, Miss Philippines and Miss Universe winners, and American Filipino community leaders in the city. The mayor of Los Angeles was often a guest at these events. These 1960s photographs, above and below, were receptions for Filipino dignitaries. (Both, courtesy of Benita Q. Lagmay and Numeriano D. Lagmay.)

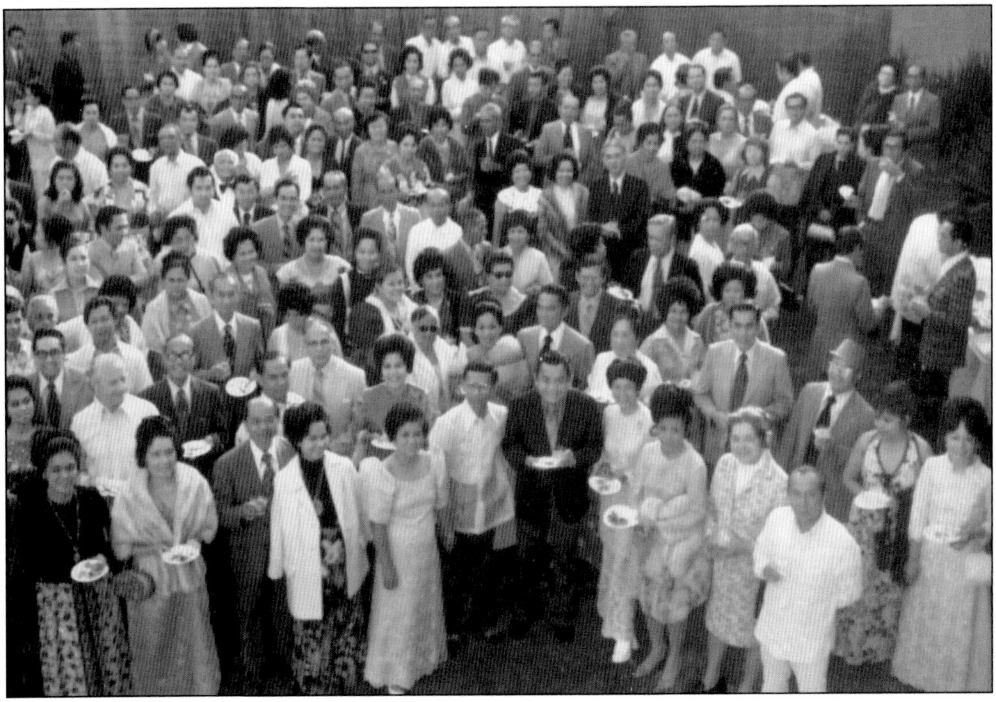

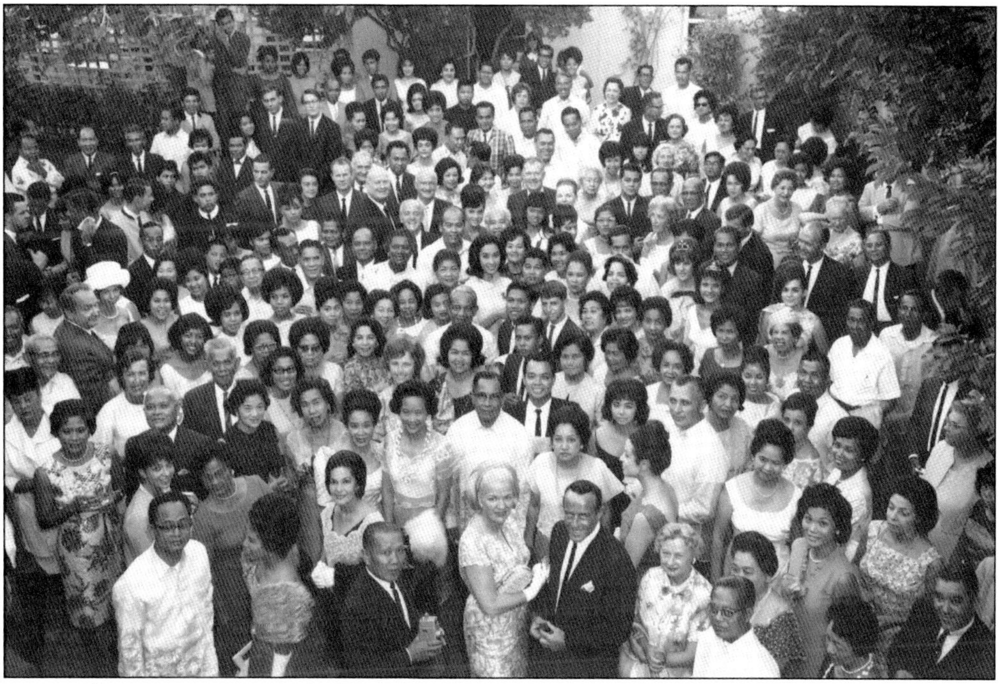

A typical 1960s reception at the home of the Philippine consul general of Los Angeles is depicted with leaders of the Filipino community center. (Courtesy of Benita Q. Lagmay and Numeriano D. Lagmay.)

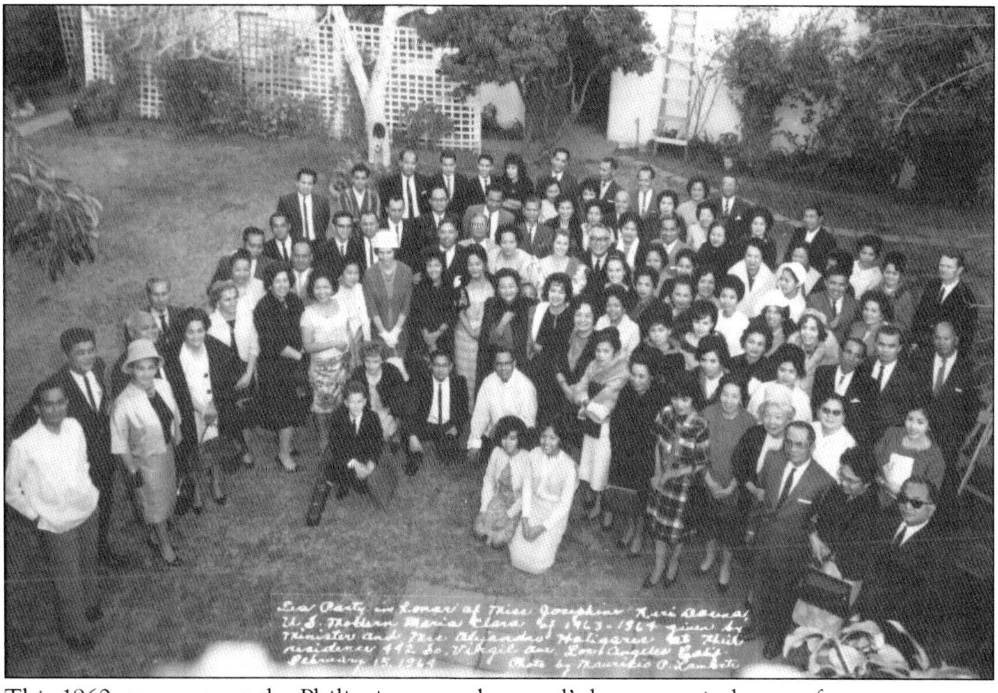

This 1960s tea party at the Philippine consul general's home was in honor of a young woman who was a member of the organization called Maria Clara in Los Angeles. (Courtesy of Benita Q. Lagmay and Numeriano D. Lagmay.)

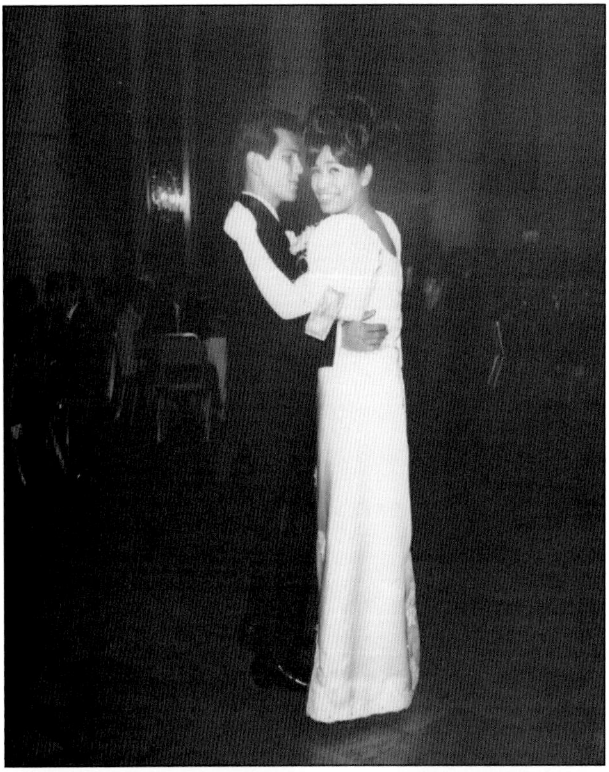

Juliet Lagmay and her future husband, Eugene Akiaten, dance at a grand debutante ball given by her parents, Numeriano D. and Benita Q. Lagmay, in 1966. It is a cultural Filipino tradition to hold a debut—the ceremonial presentation of a young Filipina—as a popular rite of passage. Because of a debutante ball's grandness, debuts are a measure of the upward mobility of Filipinos. (Courtesy of Juliet Lagmay-Akiaten.)

Juliet Lagmay and her escort, Eugene Akiaten, greet guests after her formal presentation ceremony. (Courtesy of Juliet Lagmay-Akiaten.)

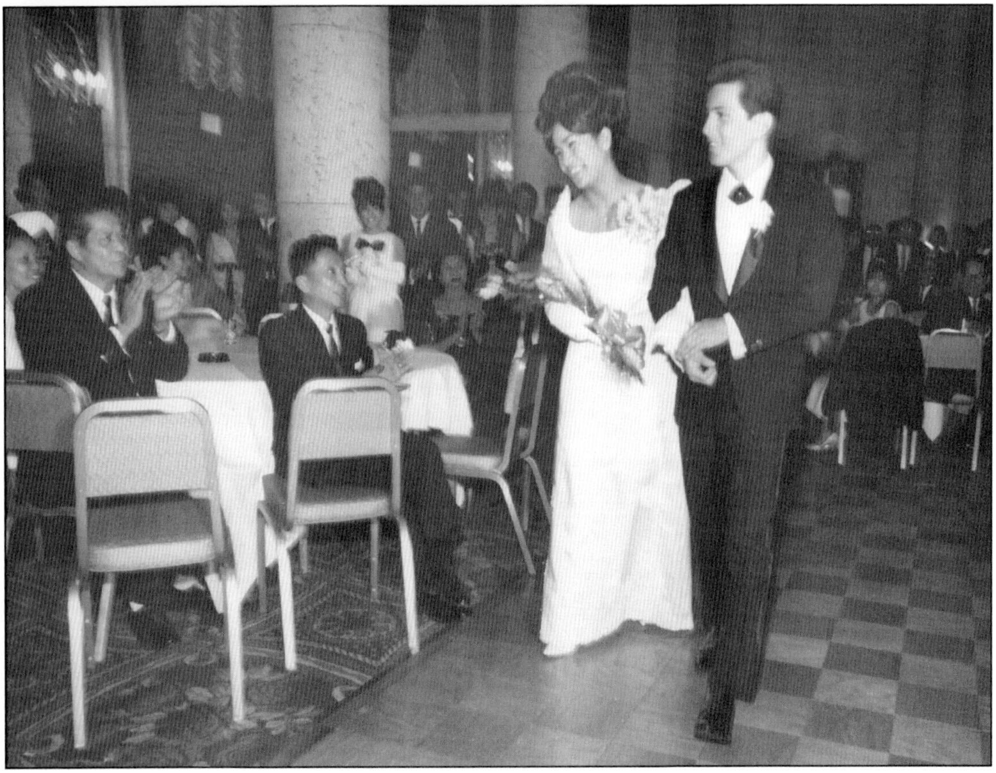

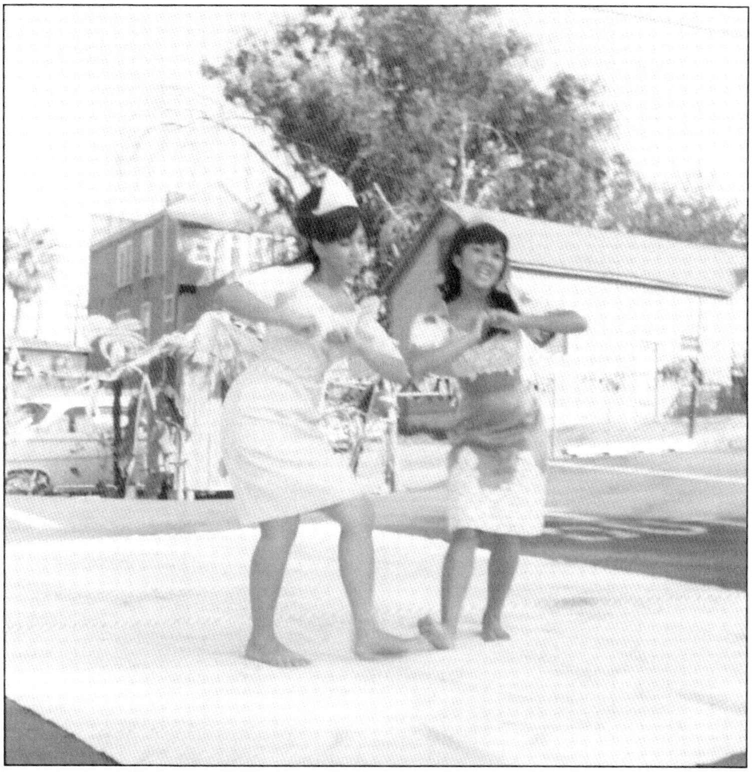

Joselyn Geaga-Rosenthal (right) performs a traditional Filipino dance for members of the Los Angeles Filipino community in the 1960s. (Courtesy of Joselyn Geaga-Rosenthal.)

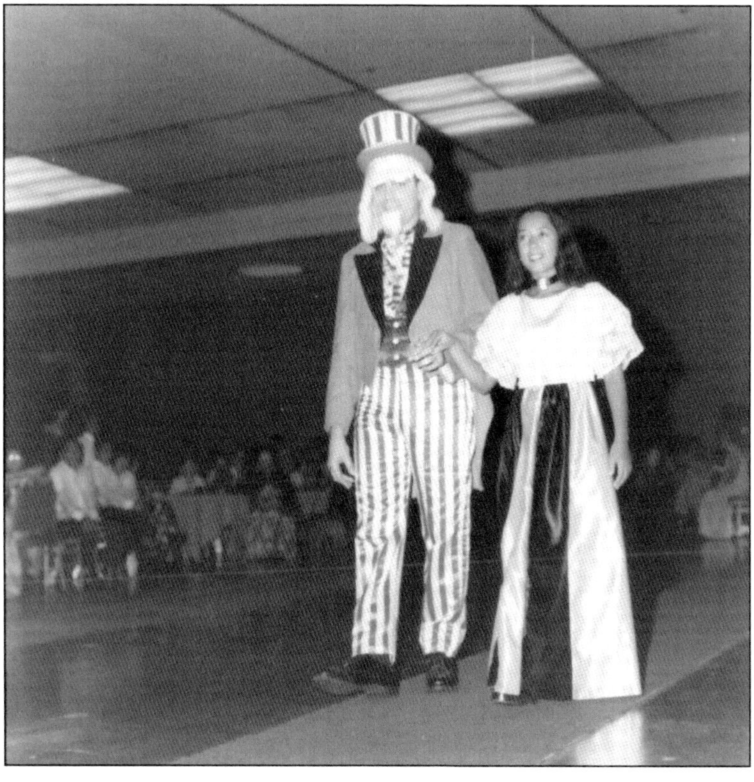

Joselyn Geaga-Rosenthal (right) performs at the Hollywood Palladium with a co-performer in a Fourth of July celebration in the 1960s. (Courtesy of Joselyn Geaga-Rosenthal.)

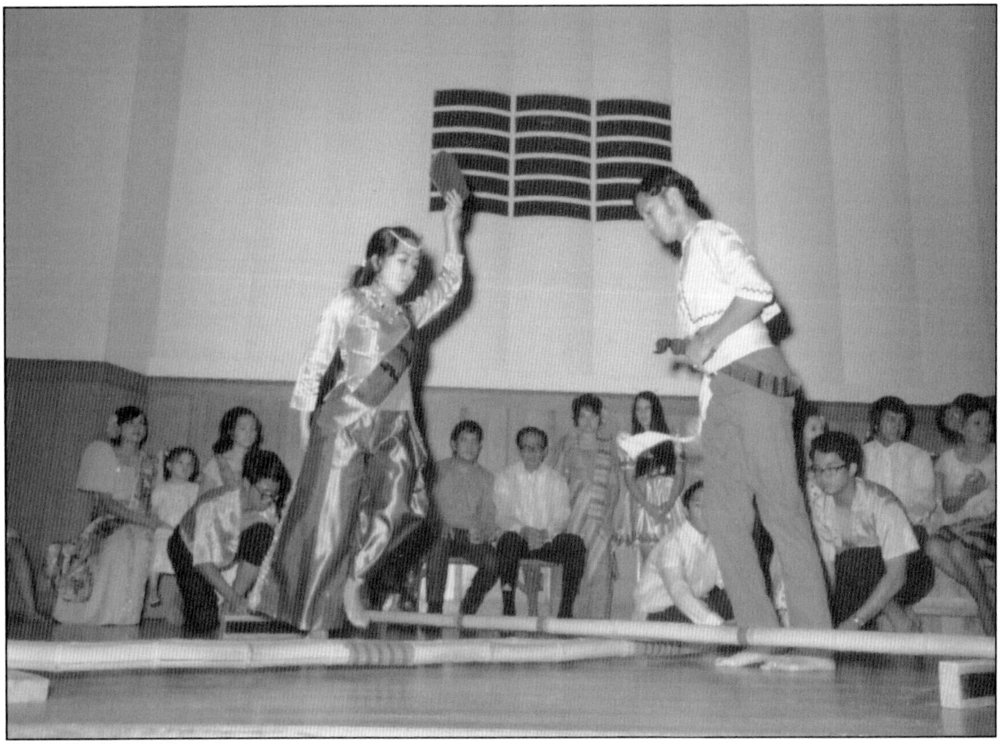

Joselyn Geaga-Rosenthal (left) was a popular traditional Filipino folk dancer who performed in many Filipino American events held in Hollywood and in grand hotels in Los Angeles. Here she is performing at the Ambassador Hotel in the 1970s. (Courtesy of Joselyn Geaga-Rosenthal.)

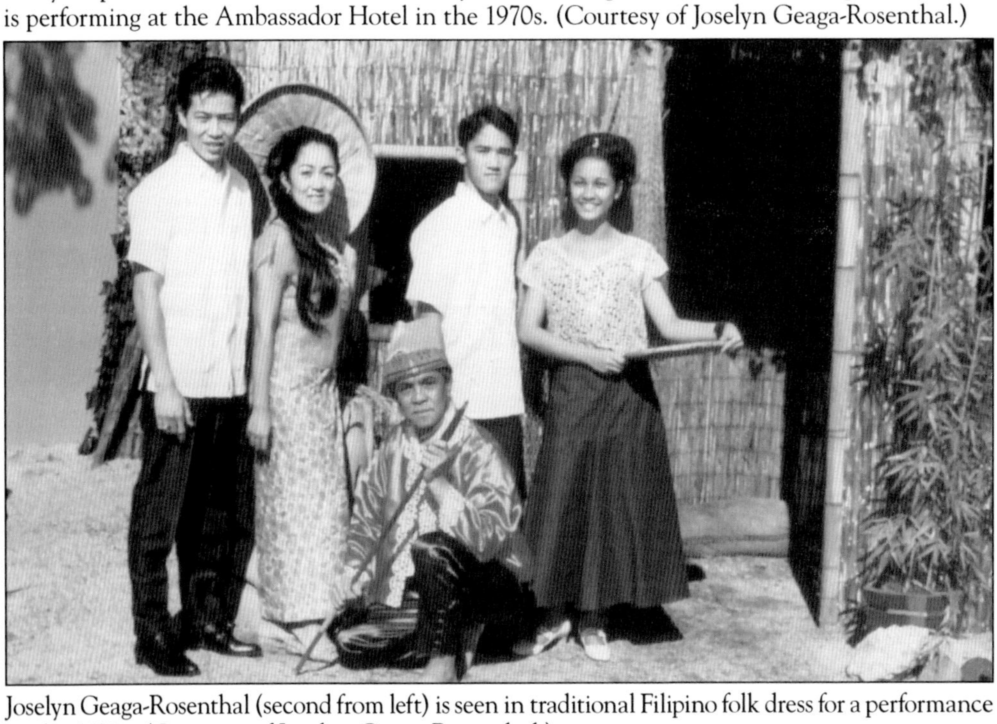

Joselyn Geaga-Rosenthal (second from left) is seen in traditional Filipino folk dress for a performance in the 1970s. (Courtesy of Joselyn Geaga-Rosenthal.)

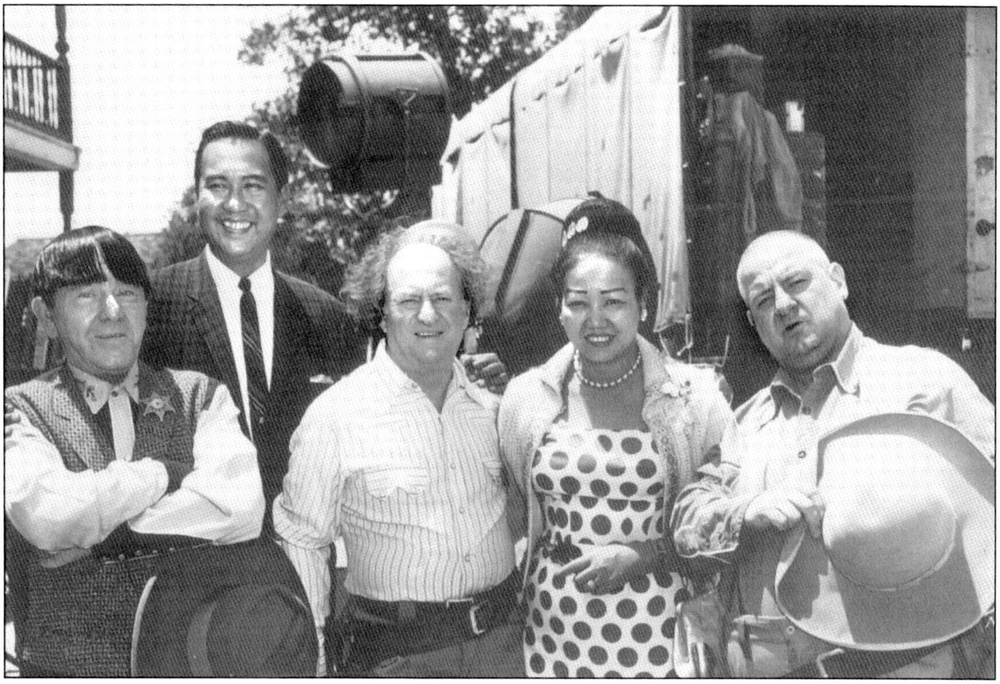

President of the Filipino American Community Center, Amparo Domingo (second from right), a former stand-in for actress Dorothy Lamour, poses with the three stooges, from left to right, Moe Howard, Larry Fine, and Curly Howard in the 1970s. An unidentified Filipino dignitary is seen in back. Domingo utilized her connection with Hollywood's industry to give visiting Filipino dignitaries Hollywood studio tours. (Courtesy of Toni Thomas.)

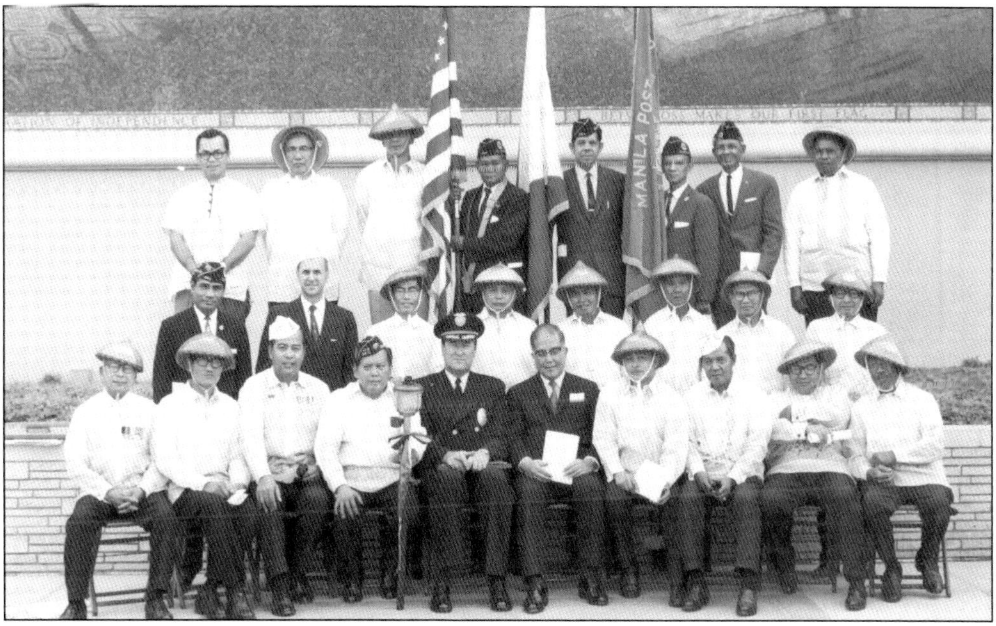

Filipino American veterans attend an event honoring the American Legion/Filipino American Veterans, Manila Post No. 464, held at the Hollywood Forest Lawn historical memorial building in the 1970s. (Courtesy of Benita Q. Lagmay and Numeriano D. Lagmay.)

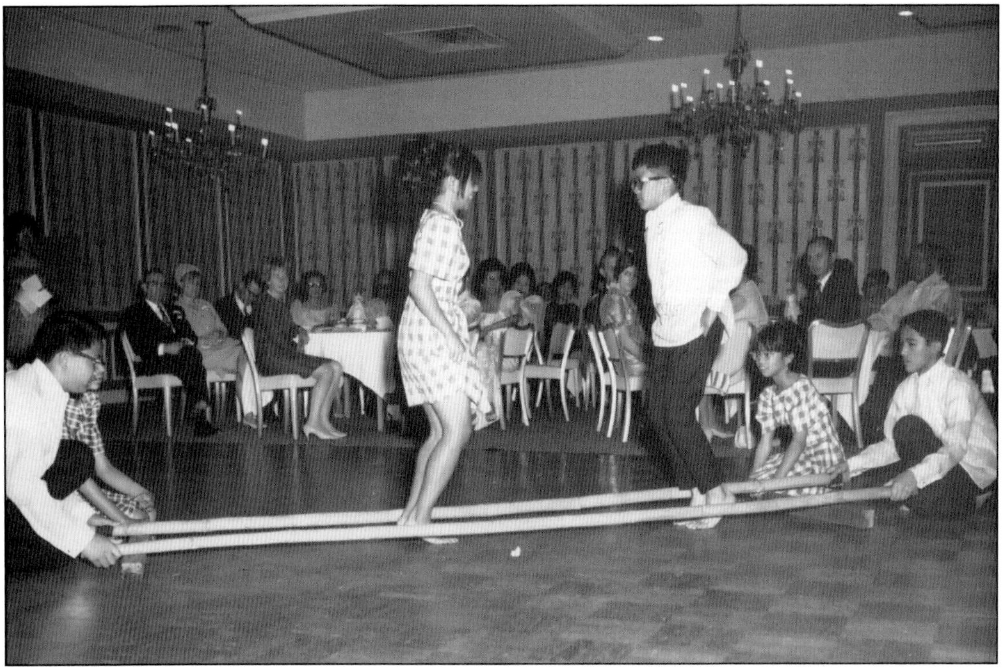

At an event held at the famed Ambassador Hotel in the 1970s by the Sampaguita Women's Circle, Filipino youths perform the traditional *tinikling* dance for entertainment. (Courtesy of Joselyn Geaga-Rosenthal.)

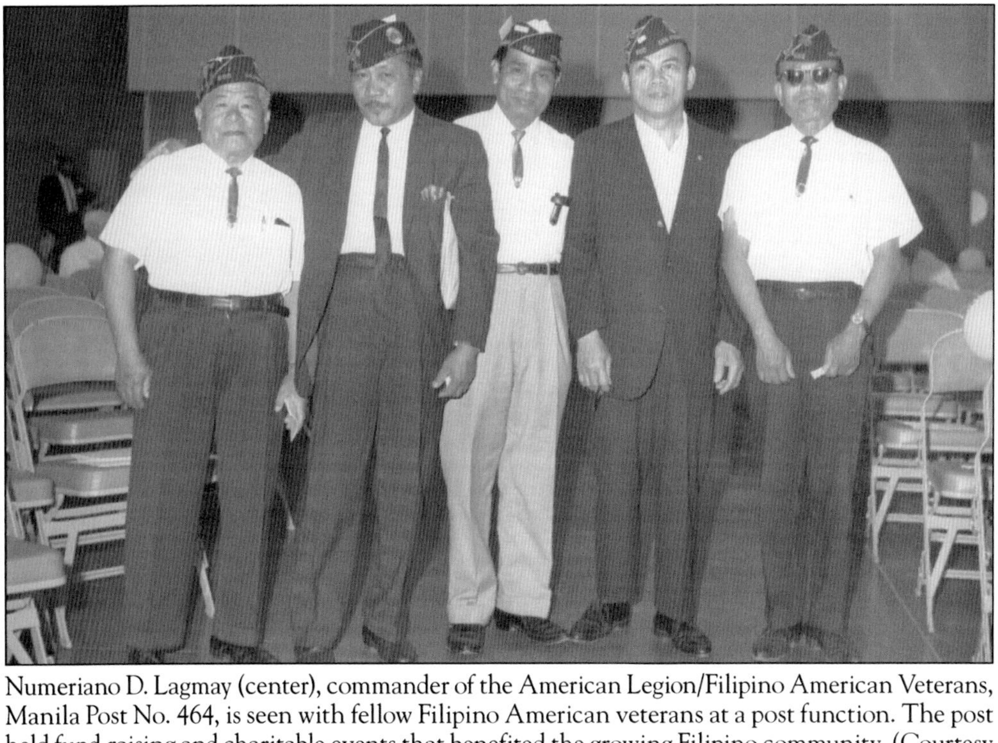

Numeriano D. Lagmay (center), commander of the American Legion/Filipino American Veterans, Manila Post No. 464, is seen with fellow Filipino American veterans at a post function. The post held fund-raising and charitable events that benefited the growing Filipino community. (Courtesy of Benita Q. Lagmay and Numeriano D. Lagmay.)

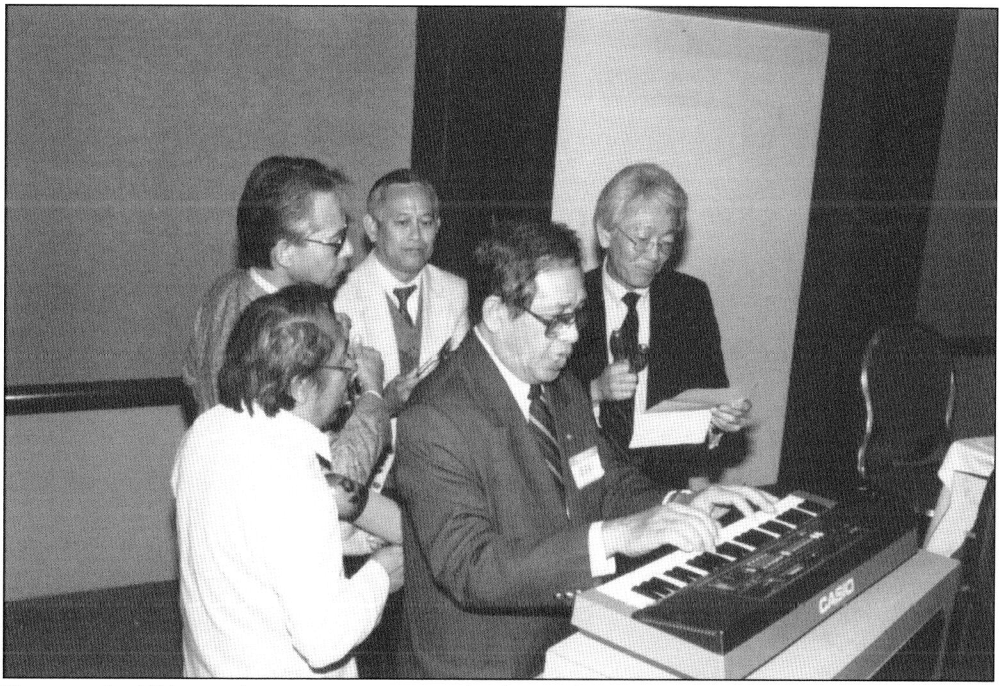

Distinguished Filipino American community leaders and activists play the keyboard at a gathering in Los Angeles in the 1960s. The exact order of the men is uncertain, but their names are Royal Morales, Dr. Ben Marte, Al Mendoza, Jimmy Avo, and one unidentified. (Courtesy of Joselyn Geaga-Rosenthal.)

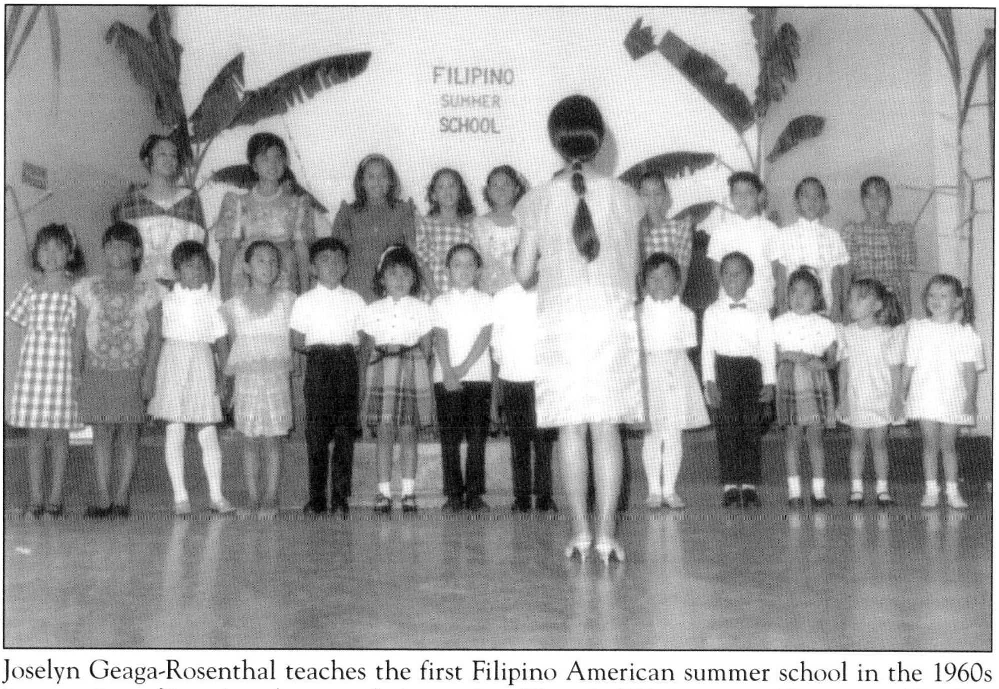

Joselyn Geaga-Rosenthal teaches the first Filipino American summer school in the 1960s in a section of Los Angeles now designated as Historic Filipinotown. (Courtesy of Joselyn Geaga-Rosenthal.)

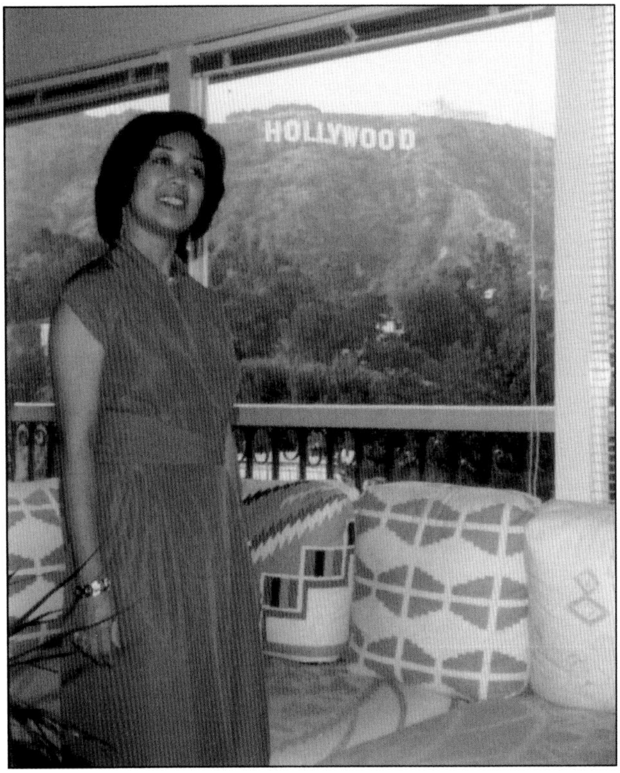

Joselyn Geaga-Rosenthal poses in front of her living room window, which overlooks the Hollywood sign in the Hollywood Hills. It is a fittingly symbolic photograph of the Filipinos' general progress, advancement, and assimilation in a city that once discriminated against them. From the 1920s to 1950s, Filipinos were forced to live in the impoverished section of downtown Los Angeles, but many worked in the homes located in the Hollywood Hills. Today many Filipino families own homes in the Hollywood Hills. (Courtesy of Joselyn Geaga-Rosenthal.)

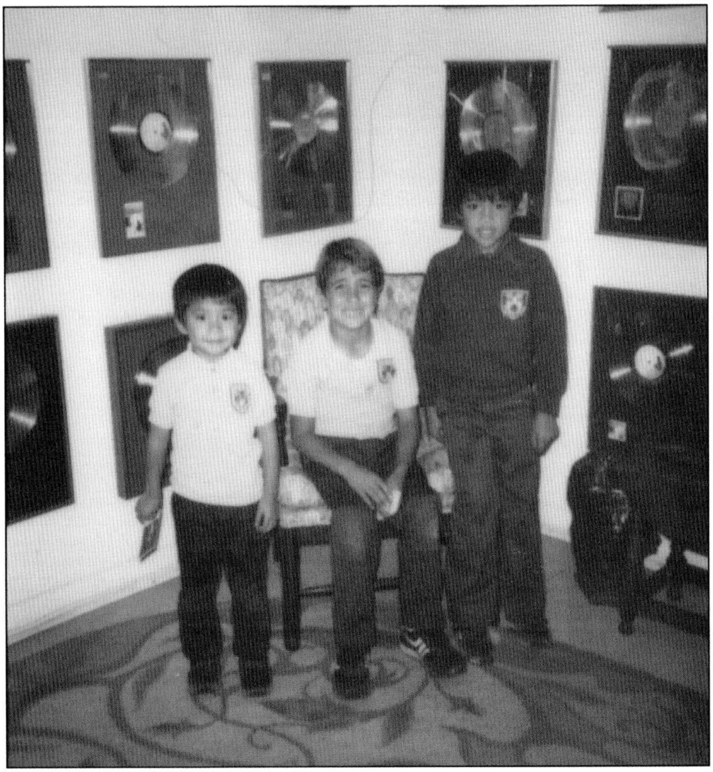

These young Filipino American music hopefuls, Jason Yap (left) and Jonathan Yap (right), are pictured with a friend in legendary singer Neil Diamond's studio. (Courtesy of Joselyn Geaga-Rosenthal.)

Four

Moving Forward

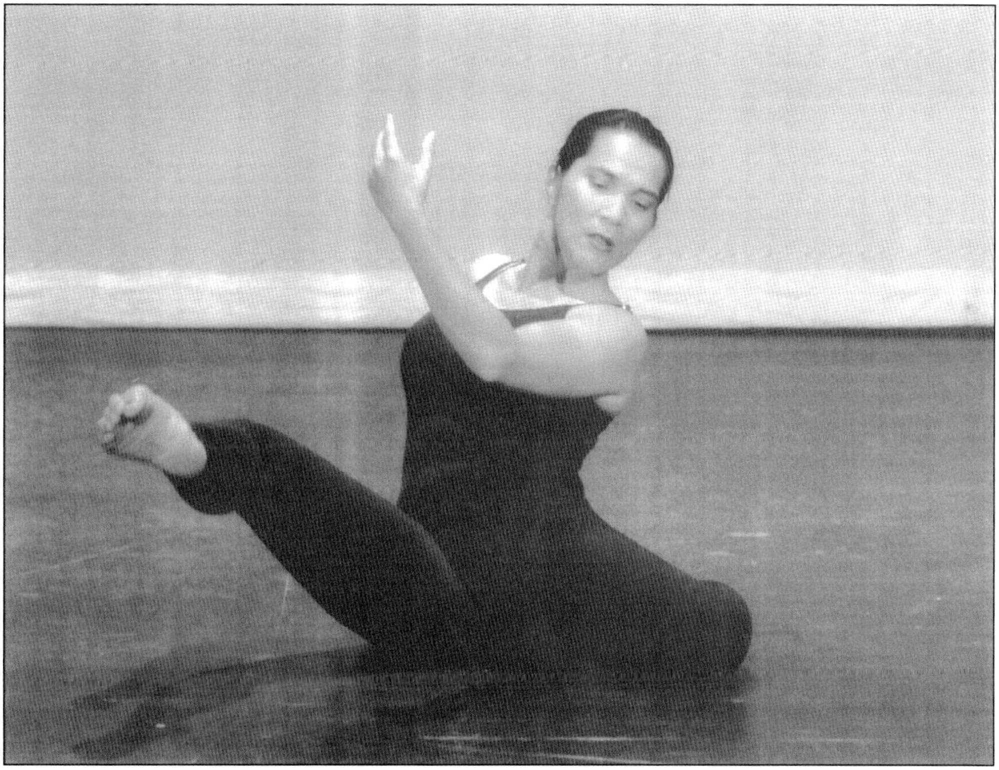

Born and raised in the Philippines, Joanne Mallillin came to the United States after winning the International Dance Fever Competition in Manila in 1984. Merv Griffin Productions brought her and her co-performing sister Marie to Hollywood to perform on the syndicated television program *Dance Fever*. After Joanne and Marie were the runner-up act of the year on *Dance Fever*, the sisters remained in the United States. Joanne became a U.S. citizen in 1996. She continues to pursue her passion for modern dance, choreography, directing, producing, and performing on college and community stages, including for the Hermosa (Beach) Arts Foundation. (Courtesy of Jerry Roberts.)

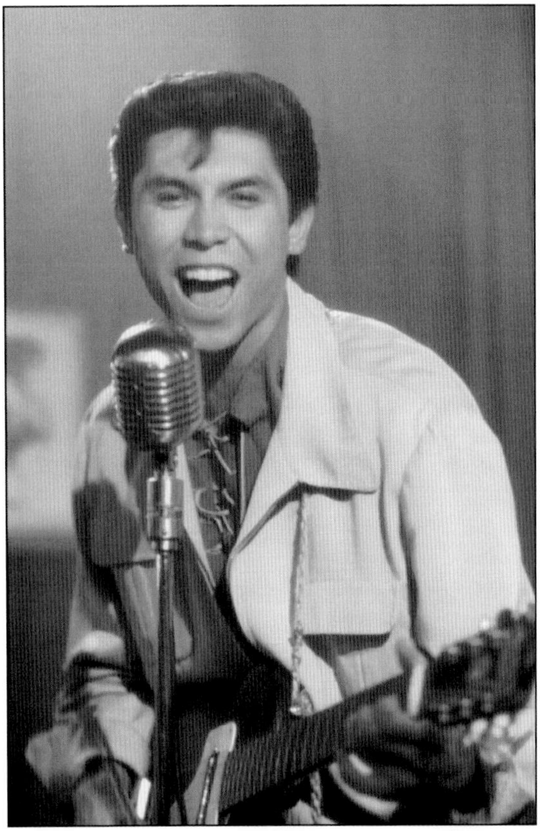

Born at Subic Bay Naval Station in the Philippines, Lou Diamond Phillips has been an acclaimed actor, director, writer, and producer in Hollywood since the 1980s. He portrayed popular singer Ritchie Valens in the film *La Bamba* in 1987. The film was nominated for a Golden Globe Award for best motion picture–drama in 1988. (Courtesy of Everett Collection.)

Lou Diamond Phillips is pictured in character as Hank Storm with Kiefer Sutherland (left) in the 1989 film *Renegades*. Phillips has starred in dozens of movies and television shows. (Photograph by NBC; courtesy of Sthanlee B. Mirador.)

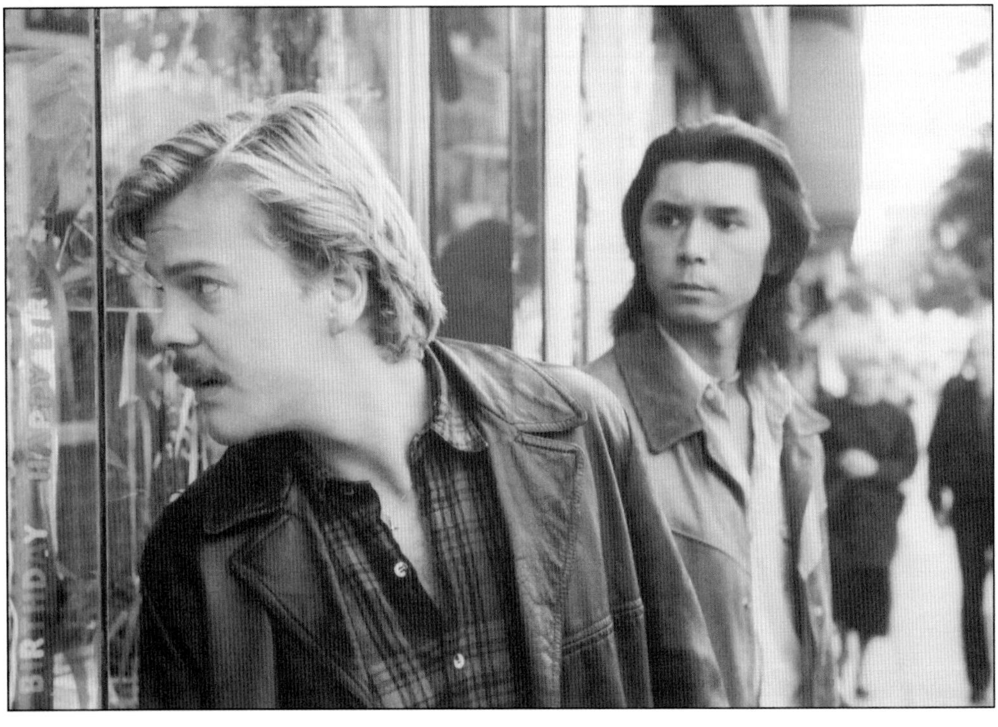

Tia Carrera is depicted in the 1997 film *Kull the Conqueror*, in which she played the character of Akivasha. Born in Hawaii, Carerra has modeled; recorded the album *Dream*; performed all the songs in the movie *Wayne's World*; was featured in *Playboy* magazine in 2003; was named one of 50 most beautiful people in the world by *People* magazine in 1992; and was ranked No. 69 in *FHM-USA*'s 100 sexiest women in 2001. She was nominated for an ALMA award for outstanding lead actress in a syndicated drama series, *Relic Hunter*, 1999; nominated in 1995 for a Saturn award for best supporting actress for *True Lies*; nominated in 1995 for an MTV award for best dance sequence for *True Lies*; and was nominated in 1992 for an MTV award for most desirable female for *Wayne's World*. (Courtesy of Everett Collection.)

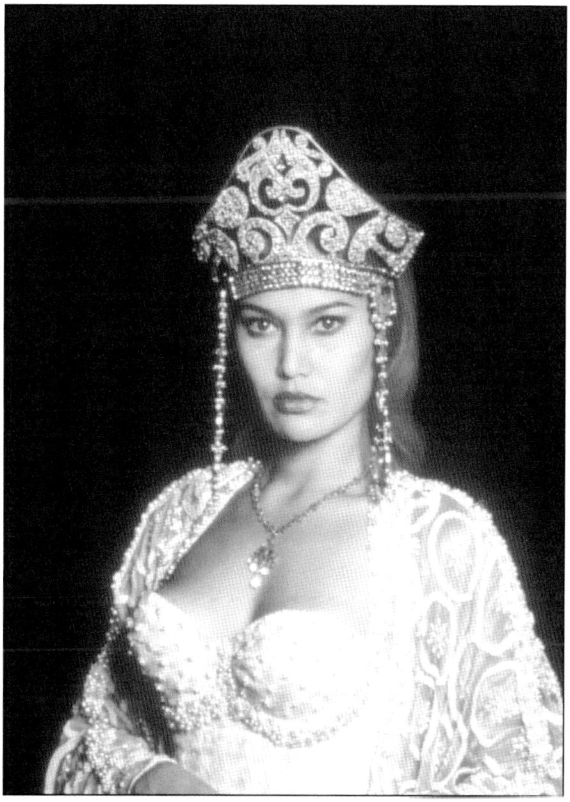

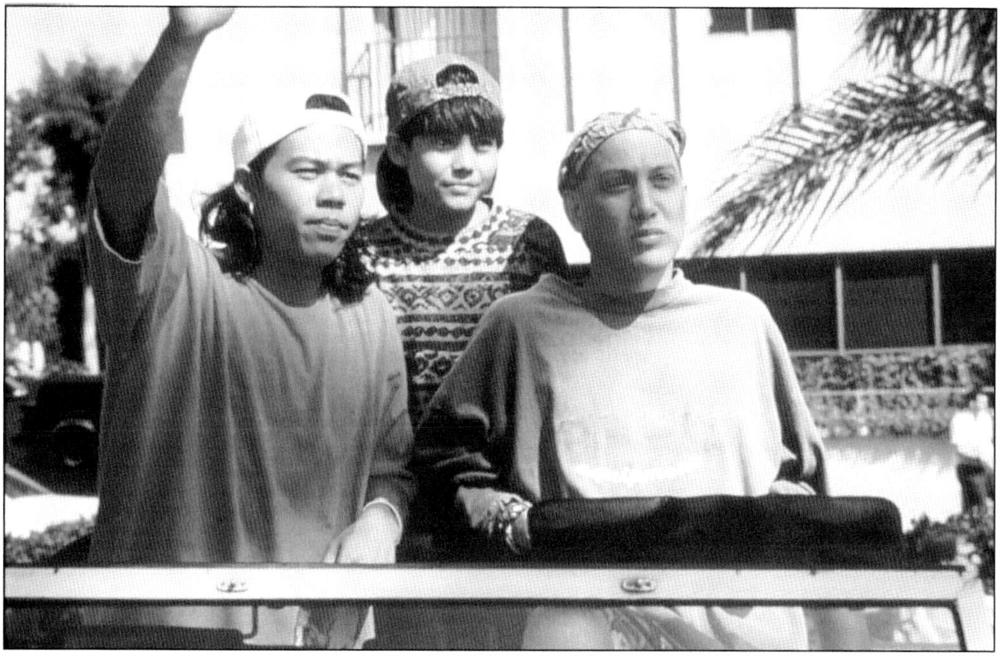

Rob Schneider (right) and Ernie Reyes Jr. (left) starred in the 1993 movie *Surf Ninjas*. Reyes was nominated in 1994 for the Young Artist Award for best youth actor in a leading role in a motion picture drama. (Courtesy of Everett Collection.)

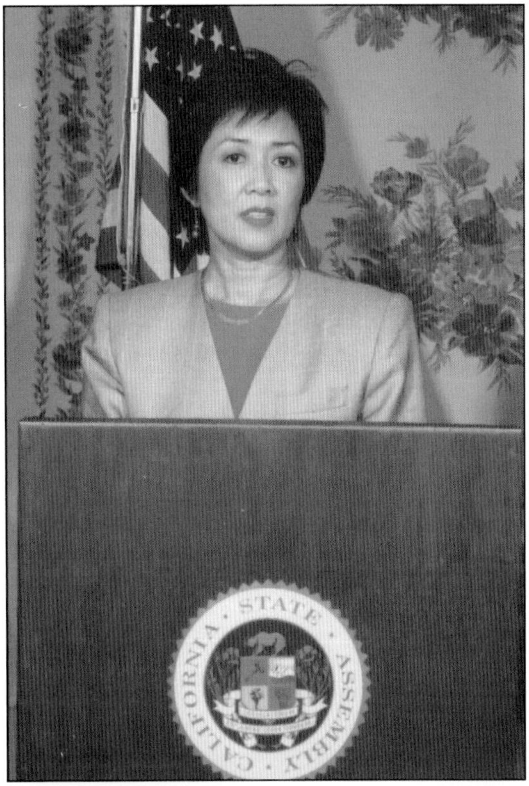

Joselyn Geaga-Rosenthal is seen in 1991 during her candidacy in a special election for a seat in the California State Assembly in the 46th District. A longtime Angeleno and Filipino community activist, Joselyn continues the efforts begun by her mother, Remedios Geaga, in furthering the interests of the Filipino community. She is the founder and owner of Remy's on Temple. (Courtesy of Joselyn Geaga-Rosenthal.)

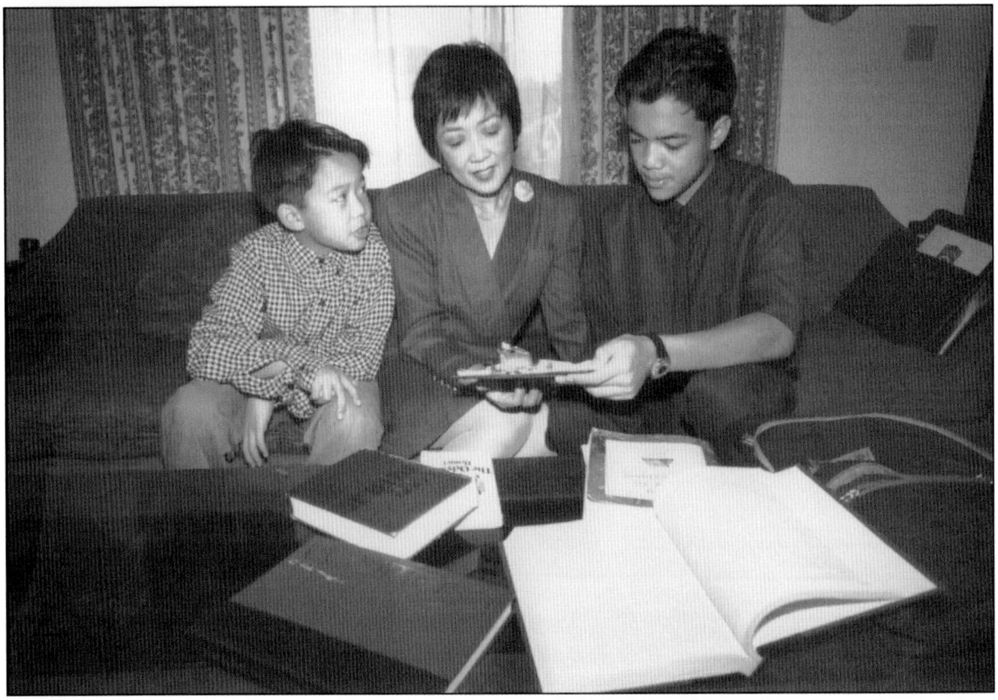

Joselyn Geaga-Rosenthal poses with her children, Jason (left) and Jonathan Yap. (Courtesy of Joselyn Geaga-Rosenthal.)

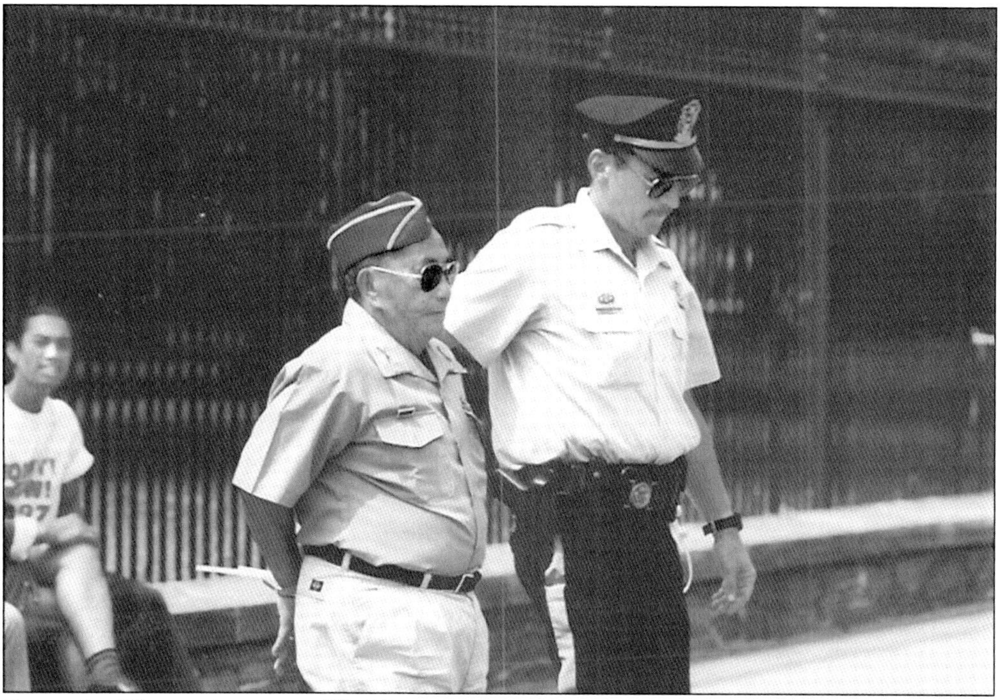

Pictured is Filipino American, World War II veteran Faustino "Peping" Baclig, who was handcuffed and arrested in 1997 during a protest in front of the White House in Washington, D.C. Baclig and fellow veterans chained themselves to the White House fence in a staged protest in their long fight for America's recognition that Filipino American soldiers should be granted benefits equal to those received by their fellow American soldiers. (Courtesy of Faustino "Peping" Baclig.)

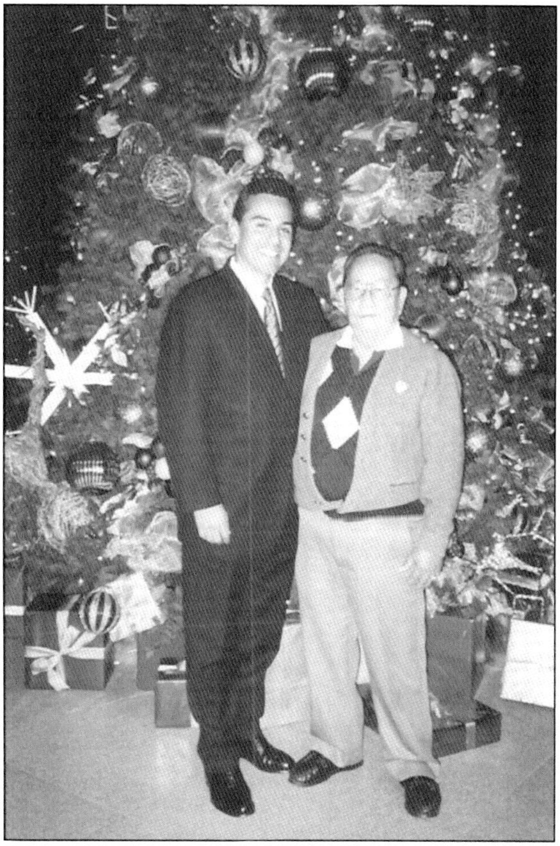

When Antonio Villaraigosa was California state assemblyman for the 45th District, he posed for this photograph with Filipino American Service Group, Inc., member and World War II veteran Faustino "Peping" Baclig in support and recognition of the Filipino American Library. Villaraigosa was later elected mayor of Los Angeles in 2005. (Courtesy of Faustino "Peping" Baclig.)

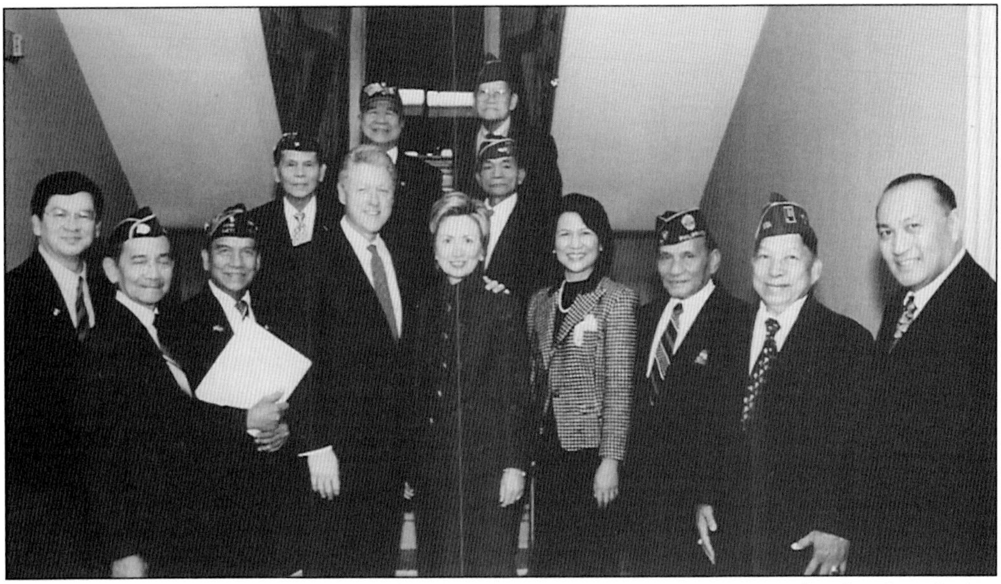

In the continued quest for equal rights for Filipino American veterans who fought side-by-side with American soldiers during World War II, the veterans persistently fight for America's recognition of its soldiers to be granted benefits equal to those enjoyed by American soldiers. Pictured are former president Bill Clinton and Hillary Clinton (center) in the 1990s. (Courtesy of Faustino "Peping" Baclig.)

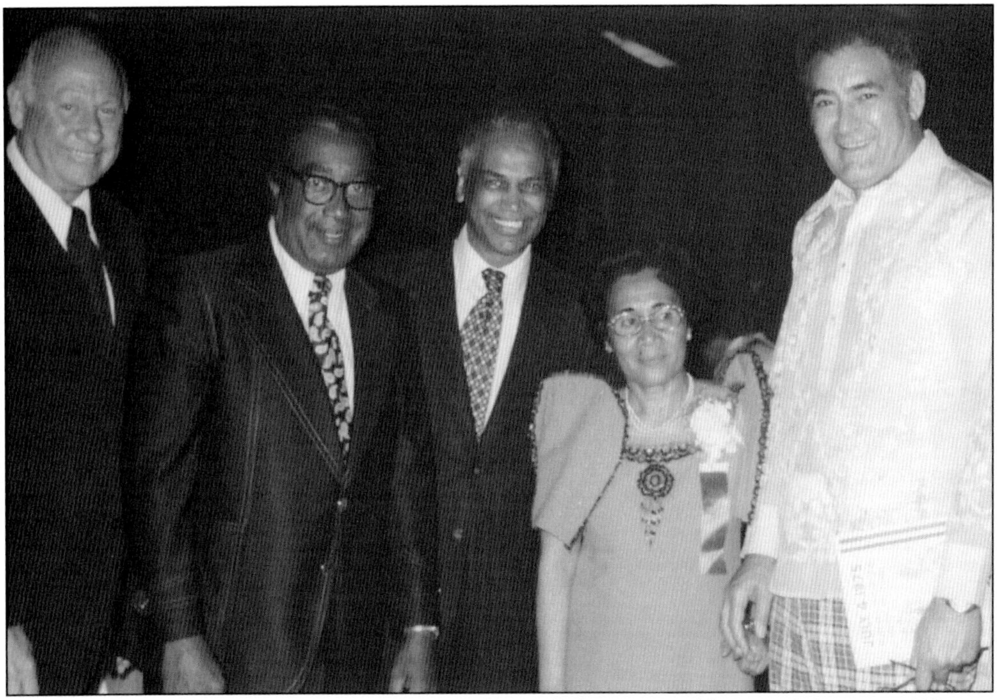

City of Los Angeles councilman John Ferraro (far right) is pictured here with longtime Filipino American activist and president of FACLA in the 1970s, Remedios Geaga (second from right), and three unidentified Los Angeles leaders. Geaga helped voice the Filipino community's interests in Los Angeles. (Courtesy of Joselyn Geaga-Rosenthal.)

Five

The New Generation

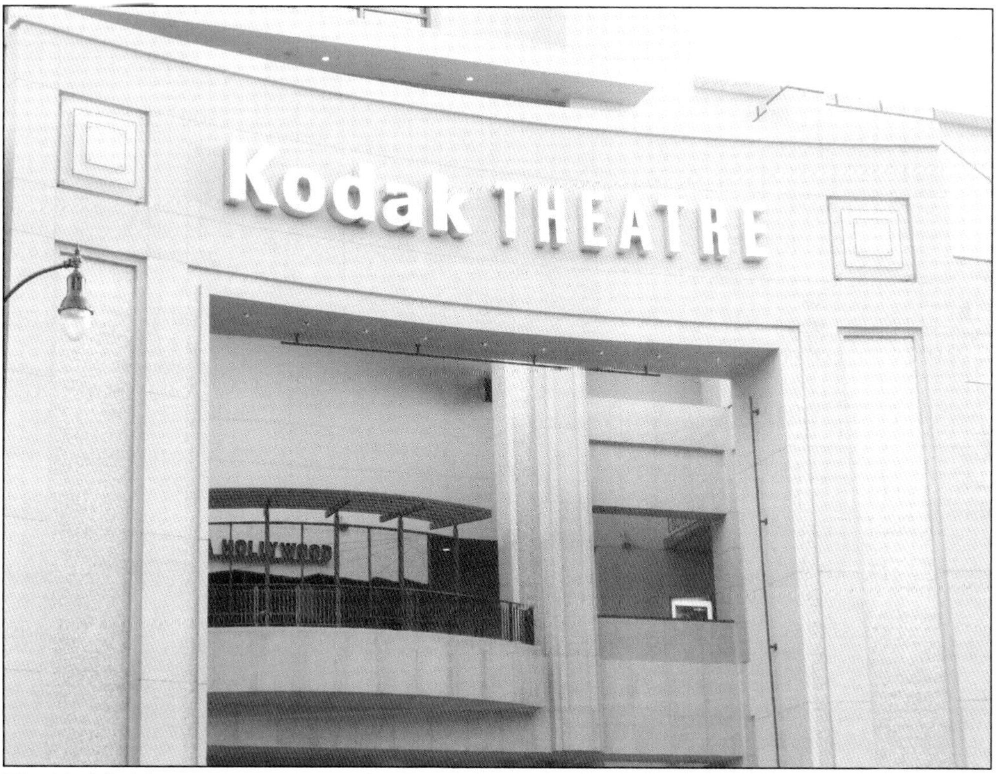

The Kodak Theatre, seen in 2007, has become a 21st-century Hollywood landmark. Opened in 2001, the theater is the first permanent home of the annual Academy Awards. Since its opening, it has hosted a range of prestigious artists and events. Some notable events include the *American Idol* finals, the American Film Institute's Lifetime Achievement Awards, the Daytime Emmy Awards, and others. (Courtesy of Steven De La Vega.)

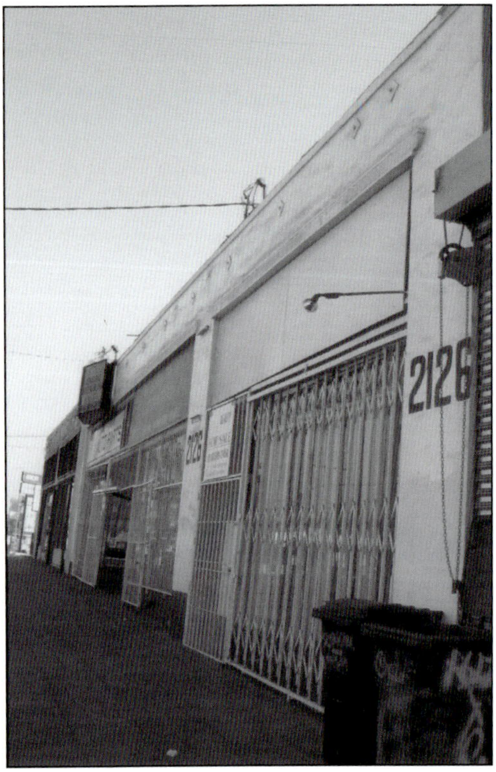

Remy's on Temple, seen before its renovation, was founded in 2005 by Joselyn Geaga-Rosenthal and named after her mother, Remedios Geaga, a longtime Angeleno and Filipino American activist. Remy's on Temple is an art gallery that serves as host to Philippine American artists and writers, and is located in the heart of Historic Filipinotown. (Courtesy of Joselyn Geaga-Rosenthal.)

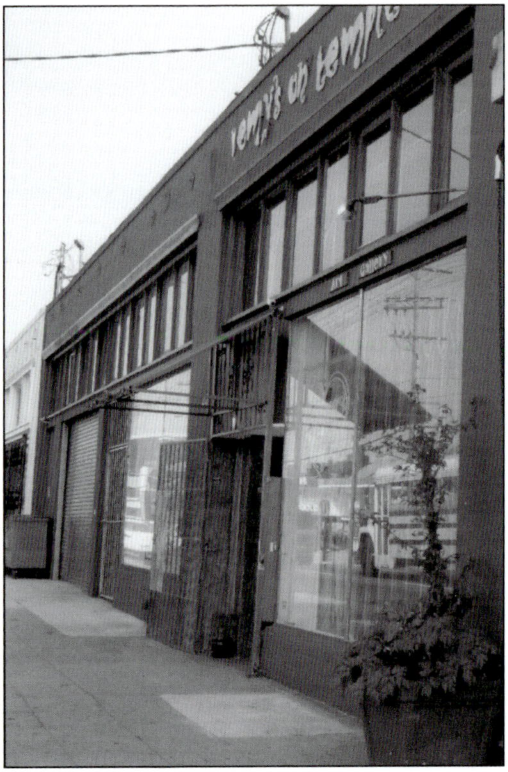

Another shot of Remy's on Temple depicts the gallery after its renovation. (Courtesy of Joselyn Geaga-Rosenthal.)

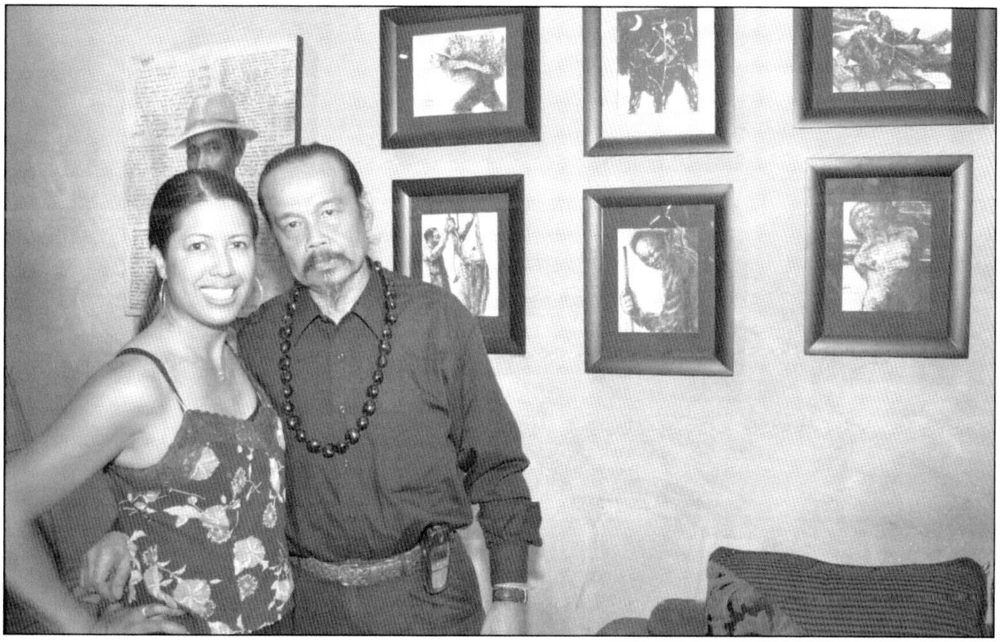

Celina Taganas-Duffy (left), the cochair of the Los Angeles Centennial Committee, is depicted with artist Faustino Caigoy in front of his artwork. (Photograph by Vics Magsaysay; courtesy of Celina Taganas-Duffy.)

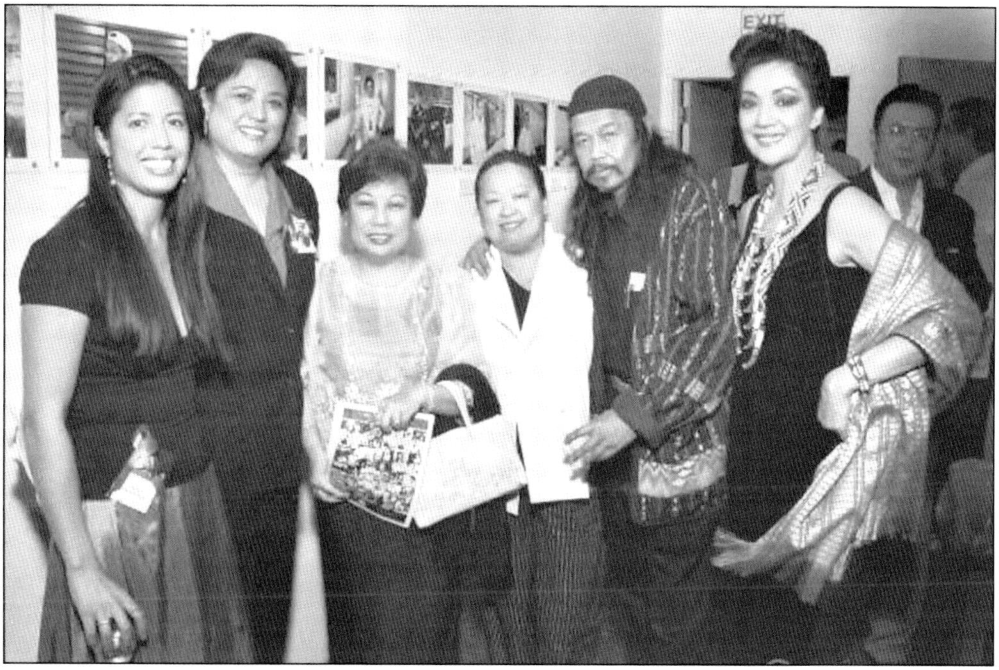

Pictured from left to right are Celina Taganas-Duffy, Yey Coronel, Consulate General Mary Jo Bernardo-Aragon, chef Cecilia De Castro, artist Faustino Caigoy, and City of Glendale arts commissioner Zen Lopez at the *I Am Today's Filipino* VIP reception, an exhibit depicting exceptional Filipino individuals in the Los Angeles and Hollywood communities. (Photograph by Vics Magsaysay; courtesy of Celina Taganas-Duffy.)

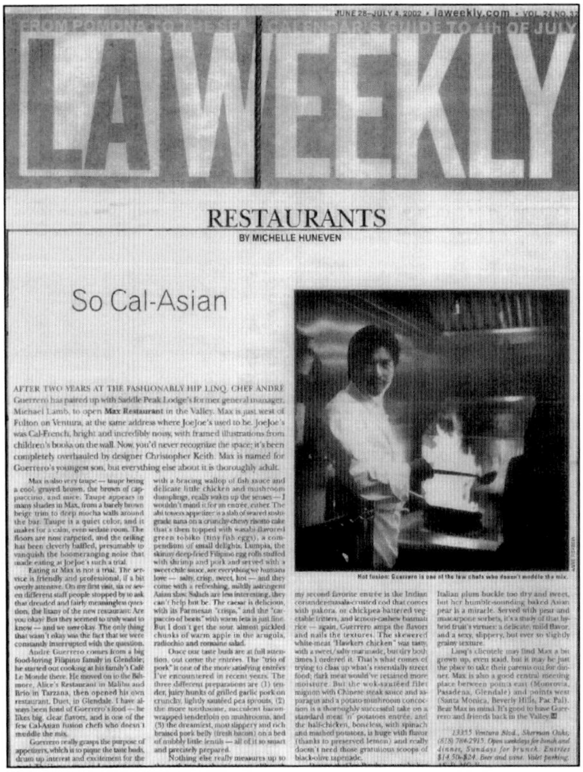

JUNE 28–JULY 4, 2002 • laweekly.com • VOL. 24 NO. 32

FROM POMONA TO THE SEA: CALENDAR'S GUIDE TO 4th OF JULY

LA WEEKLY

RESTAURANTS

BY MICHELLE HUNEVEN

So Cal-Asian

AFTER TWO YEARS AT THE FASHIONABLY HIP LINQ, CHEF ANDRE Guerrero has paired up with Saddle Peak Lodge's former general manager, Michael Lamb, to open **Max Restaurant** in the Valley. Max is just west of Fulton on Ventura, at the same address where JoeJoe's used to be. JoeJoe's was Cal-French, bright and incredibly noisy, with framed illustrations from children's books on the wall. Now, you'd never recognize the space; it's been completely overhauled by designer Christopher Keith. Max is named for Guerrero's youngest son, but everything else about it is thoroughly adult.

Max is also very taupe — taupe being a cool, grayed brown, the brown of cappuccino, and mice. Taupe appears in many shades in Max, from a barely brown beige trim to deep mocha walls around the bar. Taupe is a quiet color, and it makes for a calm, even sedate room. The floors are now carpeted, and the ceiling has been cleverly baffled, presumably to vanquish the boomeranging noise that

with a bracing wallop of fish sauce and delicate little chicken and mushroom dumplings, really wakes up the senses — I wouldn't mind it for an entrée, either. The ahi towers appetizer is a slab of seared sushi-grade tuna on a crunchy-chewy risotto cake that's then topped with wasabi-flavored green tobiko (tiny fish eggs), a compendium of small delights. Lumpia, the skinny deep-fried Filipino egg rolls stuffed

Hot fusion: Guerrero is one of the few chefs who doesn't muddle the mix.

Born in the Philippines, Andre Guerrero immigrated to the United States with his family as a child in 1961. The family moved to Los Angeles from San Francisco and have remained in the Los Angeles area for 35 years. Guerrero is a graduate of the University of California, Los Angeles, with a degree in Fine Arts, but later studied restaurant management and became a chef in his family's restaurant, Café le Monde, in 1979. (Courtesy of MAX Restaurant.)

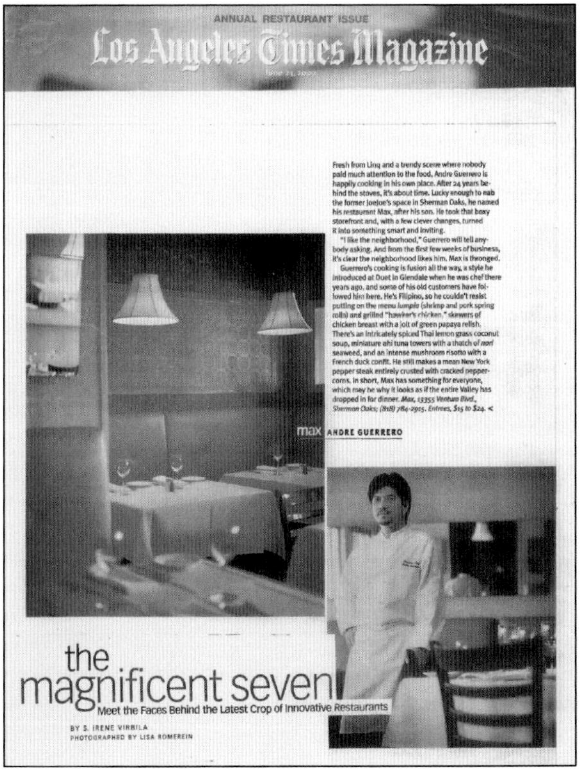

ANNUAL RESTAURANT ISSUE

Los Angeles Times Magazine

Fresh from Linq and a trendy scene where nobody paid much attention to the food, Andre Guerrero is happily cooking in his own place. After 24 years behind the stoves, it's about time. Lucky enough to nab the former JoeJoe's space in Sherman Oaks, he named his restaurant Max, after his son. He took that boxy storefront and, with a few clever changes, turned it into something smart and inviting.

"I like the neighborhood," Guerrero will tell anybody asking. And from the first few weeks of business, it's clear the neighborhood likes him. Max is thronged.

Guerrero's cooking is fusion all the way, a style he introduced at Duet in Glendale when he was chef there years ago, and some of his old customers have followed him here. He's Filipino, so he couldn't resist putting on the menu *lumpia* (shrimp and pork spring rolls) and grilled "hawker's chicken," skewers of chicken breast with a jolt of green papaya relish. There's an intricately spiced Thai lemon grass coconut soup, miniature ahi tuna towers with a thatch of *nori* seaweed, and an intense mushroom risotto with a French duck confit. He still makes a mean New York pepper steak entirely crusted with cracked peppercorns. In short, Max has something for everyone, which may be why it looks as if the entire Valley has dropped in for dinner. *Max, 13355 Ventura Blvd., Sherman Oaks; (818) 784-2915. Entrees, $15 to $24.* <

max ANDRE GUERRERO

the magnificent seven

Meet the Faces Behind the Latest Crop of Innovative Restaurants

BY S. IRENE VIRBILA

PHOTOGRAPHED BY LISA ROMEREIN

In 2002, the *Los Angeles Times Magazine* featured chef Andre Guerrero's MAX Restaurant as one of the magnificent seven new restaurants in Los Angeles. (Courtesy of MAX Restaurant.)

In 2002, chef Andre Guerrero's MAX Restaurant was featured in *Angeleno* as a San Fernando Valley hot spot. (Courtesy of MAX Restaurant.)

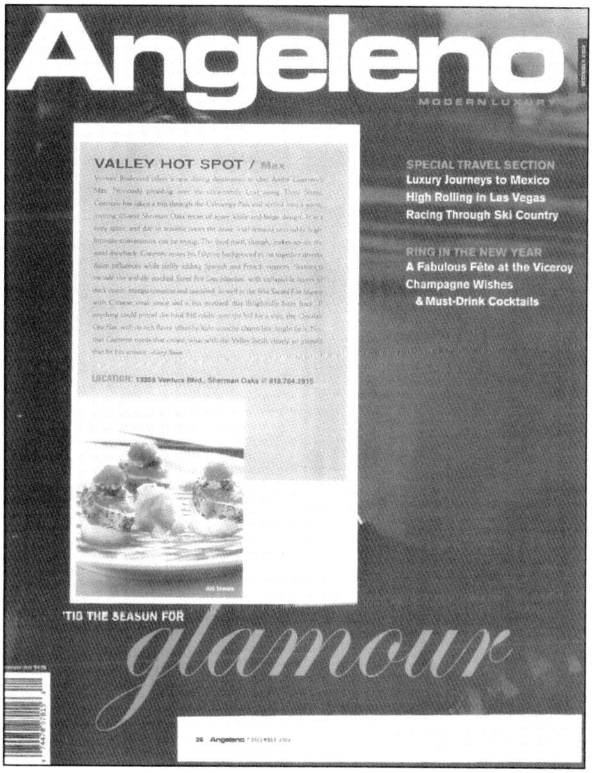

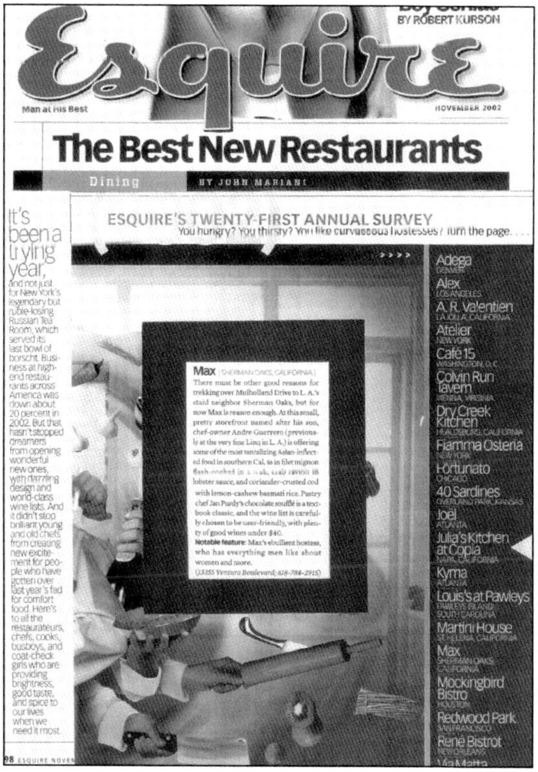

In November 2002, MAX restaurant was bestowed the *Esquire* magazine award for "best new restaurants in America." (Courtesy of MAX Restaurant.)

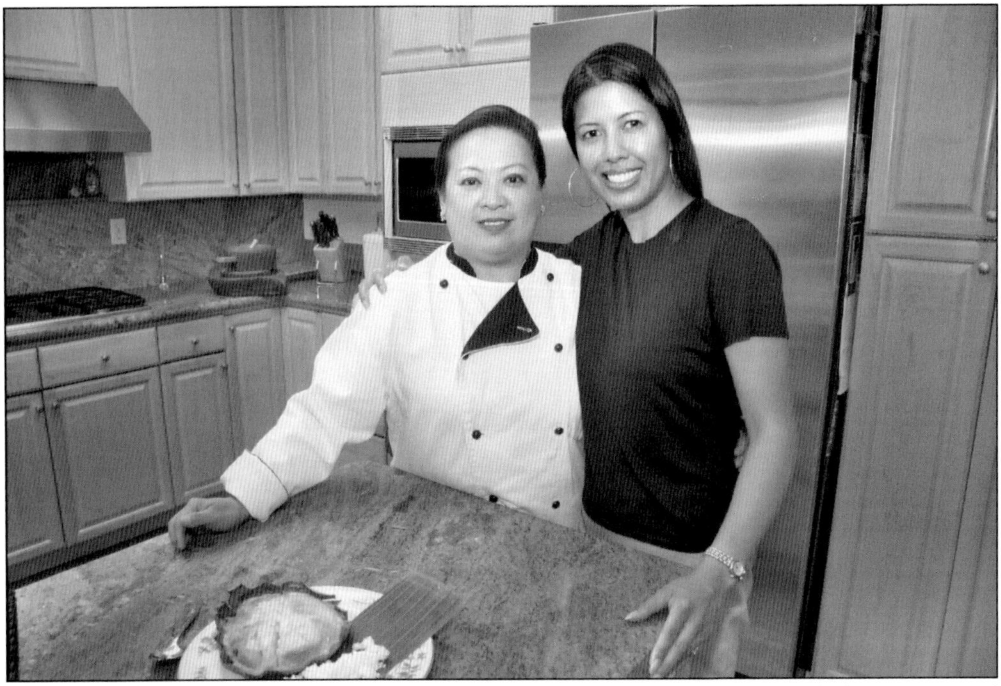

Chef Cecilia de Castro (left), executive chef for the Food Channel's *Wolfgang Puck Show*, is pictured with Celina Taganas-Duffy. De Castro has been referred to as Puck's right hand. (Courtesy of Celina Taganas-Duffy and Ray Carbullido.)

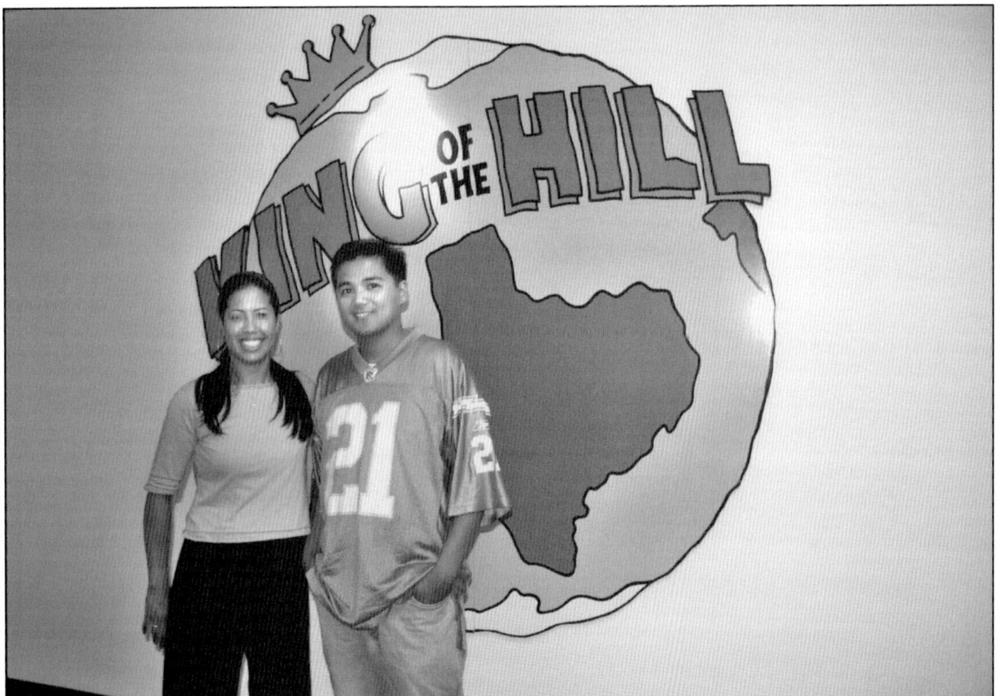

Ronald Rubio (right), the director of *King of the Hill*, the animated television series created for Fox broadcasting, is shown with Celina Taganas-Duffy. (Courtesy of Celina Taganas-Duffy.)

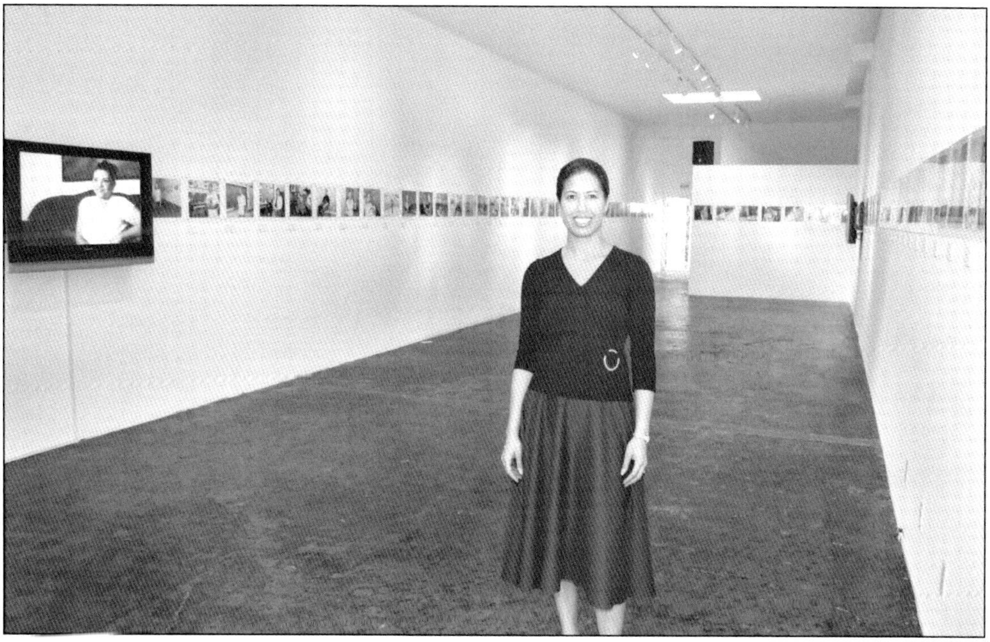

Artist Celina Taganas-Duffy is pictured at the installation of *I Am Today's Filipino* (IATF), a photography and video exhibit on the many special individuals of the Filipino community. (Courtesy of Celina Taganas-Duffy and Ray Carbullido.)

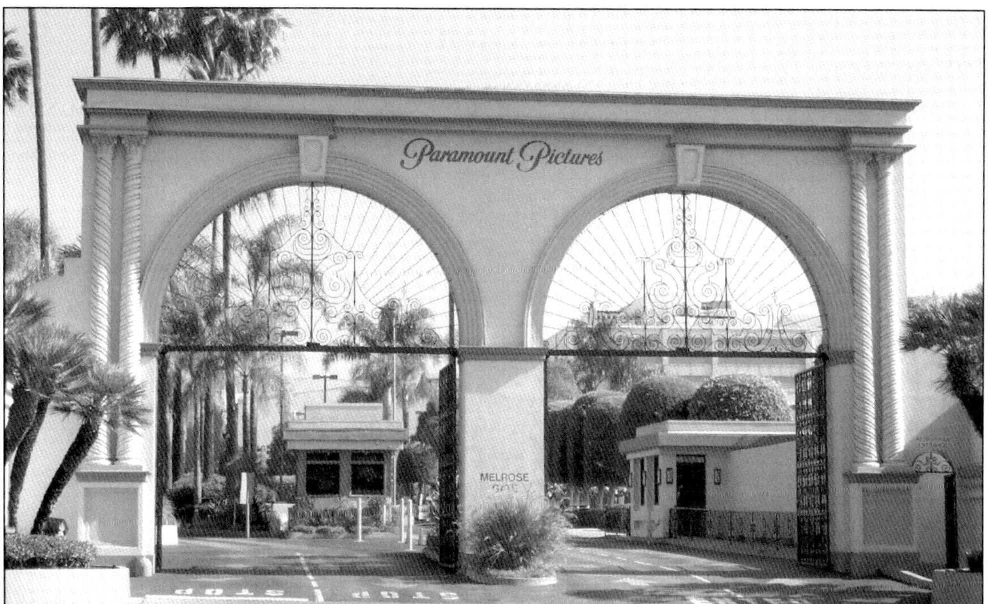

In 2007, the Paramount Pictures lot is quite a different place than it and the other Hollywood studios were for Filipinos in the early and mid-20th century. Filipino Americans such as Vincent P. Ching, executive director of contract accounts for Paramount Pictures, occupy high positions within Hollywood's movie industry. Ron Sato is vice president of corporate publicity for Sony Pictures Television International. Dean Devlin is chief executive officer of Electric Entertainment. (Courtesy of Steven De La Vega.)

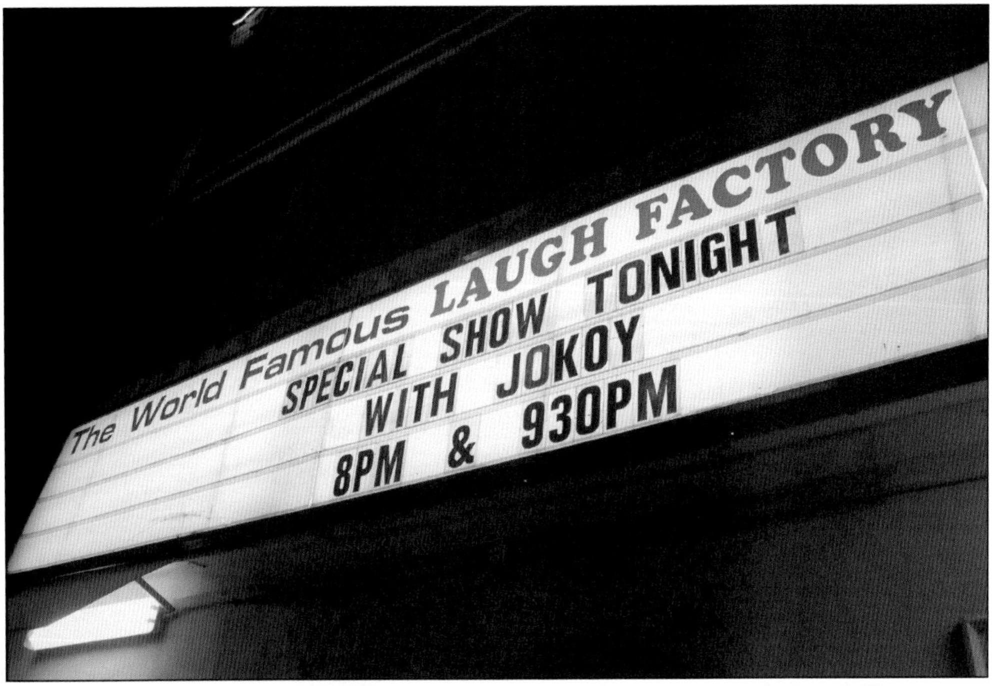

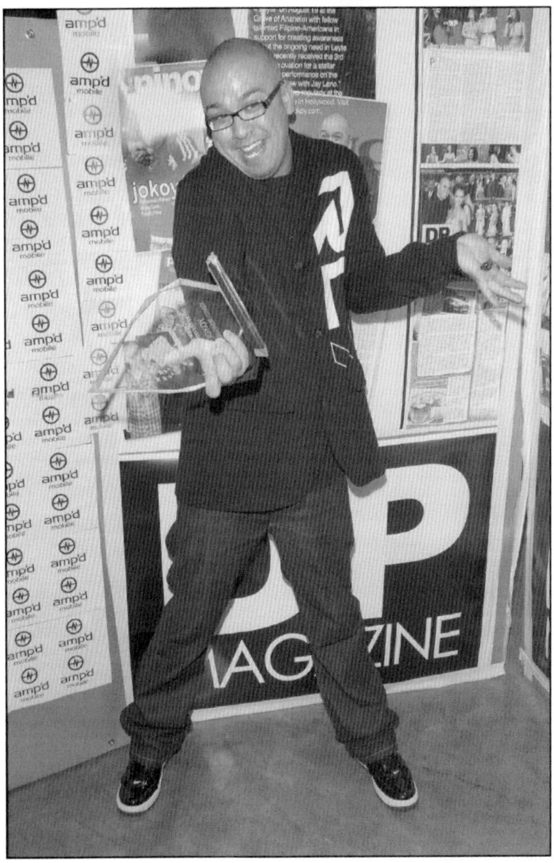

The marquee at the Laugh Factory in West Hollywood features Jokoy, a comedian. The Laugh Factory, a comedy club that opened in 1979, features stand-up comics. (Courtesy of Sthanlee B. Mirador.)

Jokoy, also known as Jo Koy, was named one of the 10 comics to watch in 2007 by *Daily Variety*. He began his comedy career in 1996 in Las Vegas coffee houses. Having starred in several television, stand-up comedy specials, he has also appeared in several television shows. He is a regular featured comedian at the Laugh Factory. (Courtesy of Sthanlee B. Mirador.)

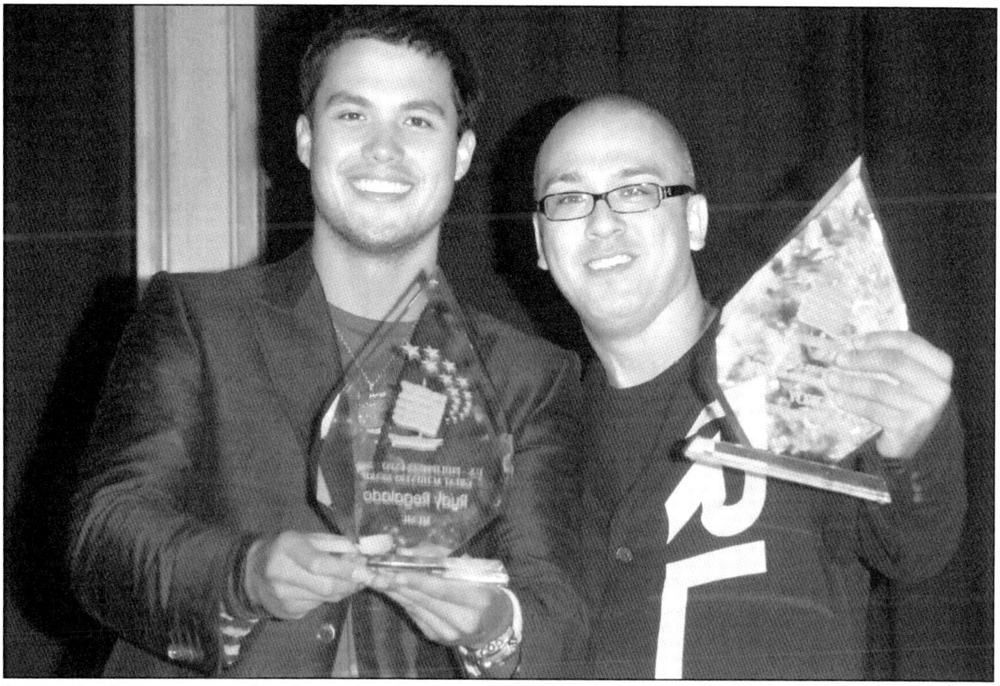

Jo Koy (right) is pictured with Michael Copon in 2006. Copon was awarded the Philippine Expo 2006 Great Achievers Award in television/film. (Courtesy of Sthanlee B. Mirador.)

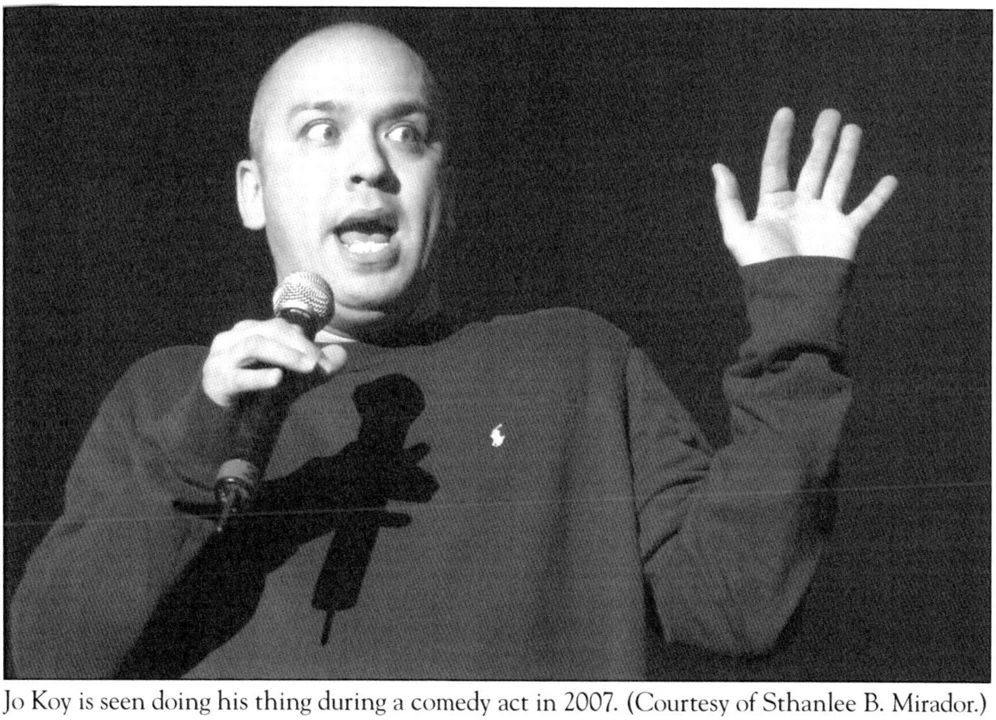

Jo Koy is seen doing his thing during a comedy act in 2007. (Courtesy of Sthanlee B. Mirador.)

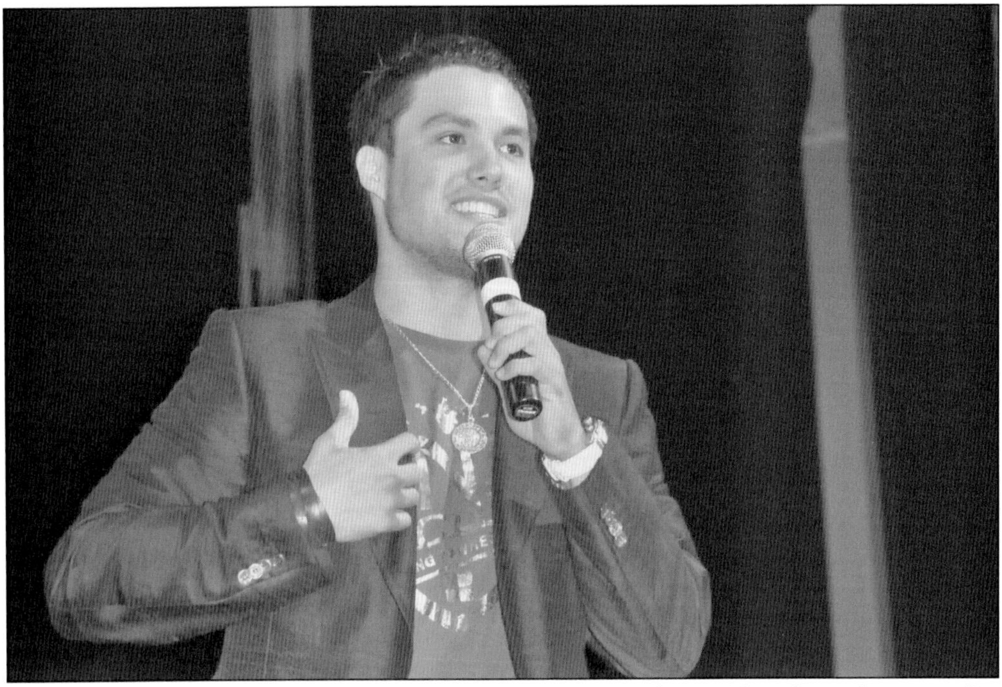

Actor, model, and singer Michael Copon won the VH1 Award in 2005 in the reality series *But Can They Sing?* He was named as one of *People* magazine's 50 hottest bachelors in 2005. (Courtesy of Sthanlee B. Mirador.)

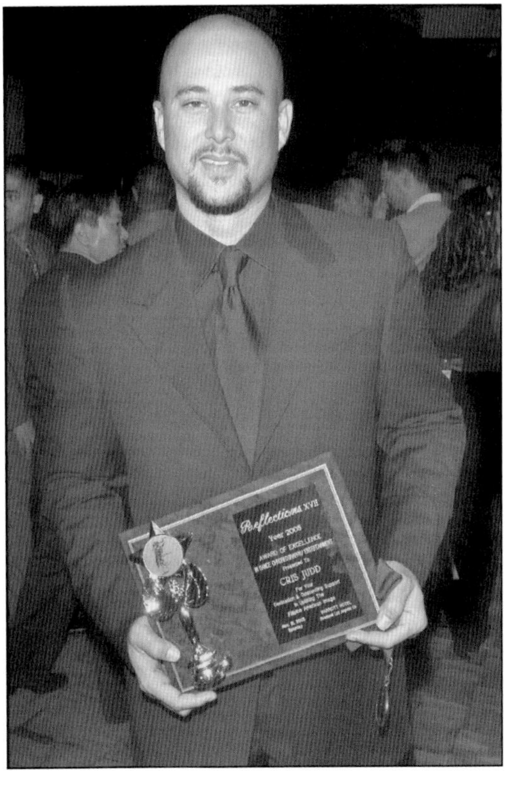

Dancer, choreographer, and actor Cris Judd was awarded the Reflections XVII award of excellence for dance/choreography entertainment in 2005. He was selected as one of *People* magazine's 25 hottest bachelors and *In Touch* magazine's 20 "hottest hunks." (Courtesy of Sthanlee B. Mirador.)

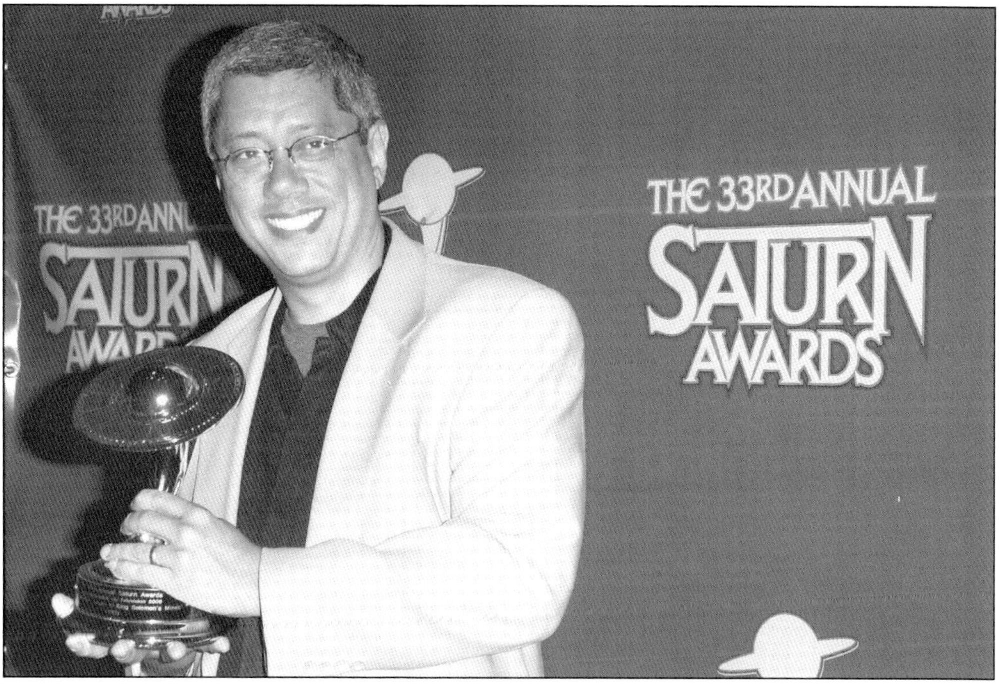

Dean Devlin, a producer and writer, attended the 33rd Annual Saturn Awards held at Universal City in May 2007. He was the winner of best presentation on television for *The Librarian: Return to King Solomon's Mines*. Earlier in his career he was an actor, but Devlin went on to write and produce films with director Roland Emmerich, particularly *Stargate*, *Independence Day*, *Godzilla*, and *The Patriot*. (Courtesy of Sthanlee B. Mirador.)

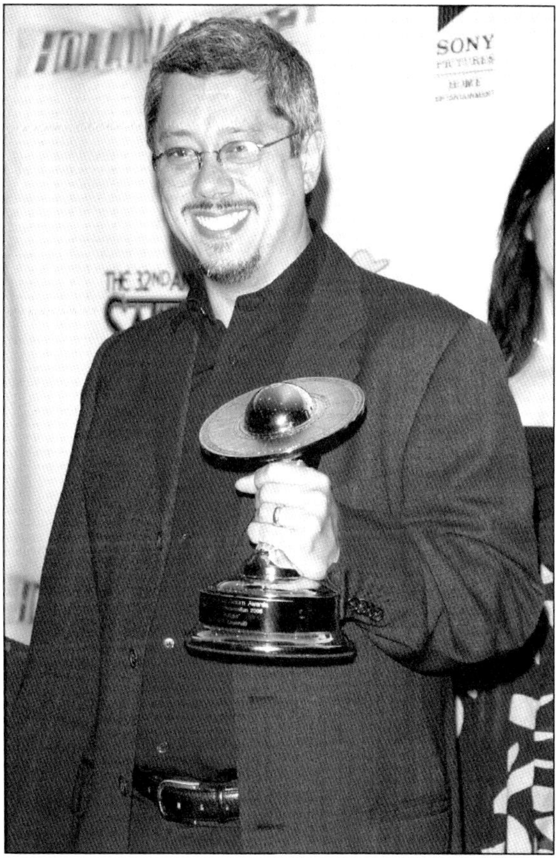

Dean Devlin is seen at the 32nd Annual Saturn Awards in 2005 for his work on *The Triangle*. It won the best television presentation. (Courtesy of Sthanlee B. Mirador.)

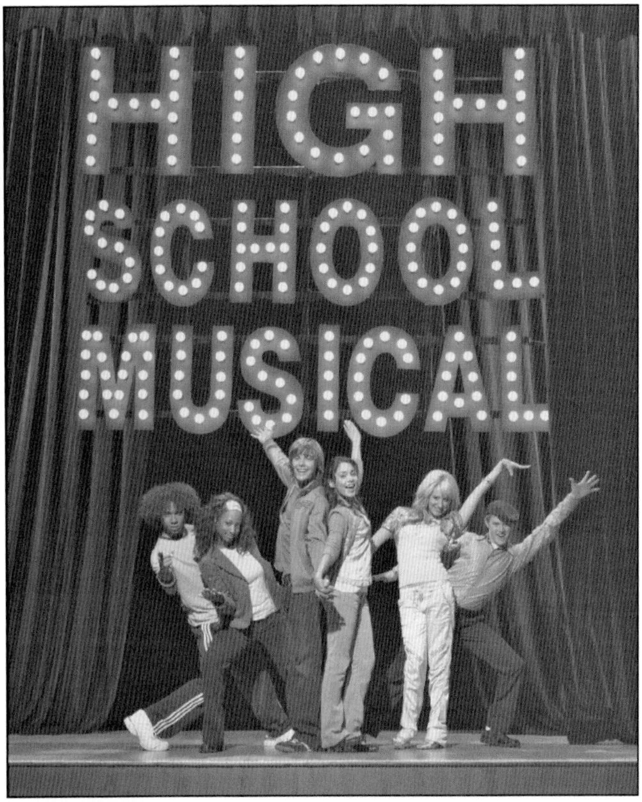

Vanessa Hudgens performs here in the *High School Musical* (third from right) as character Gabriella Montez. The musical was nominated for several awards, and it won two Emmys. (Photograph by Fred Hayes/Disney; courtesy of Sthanlee B. Mirador.)

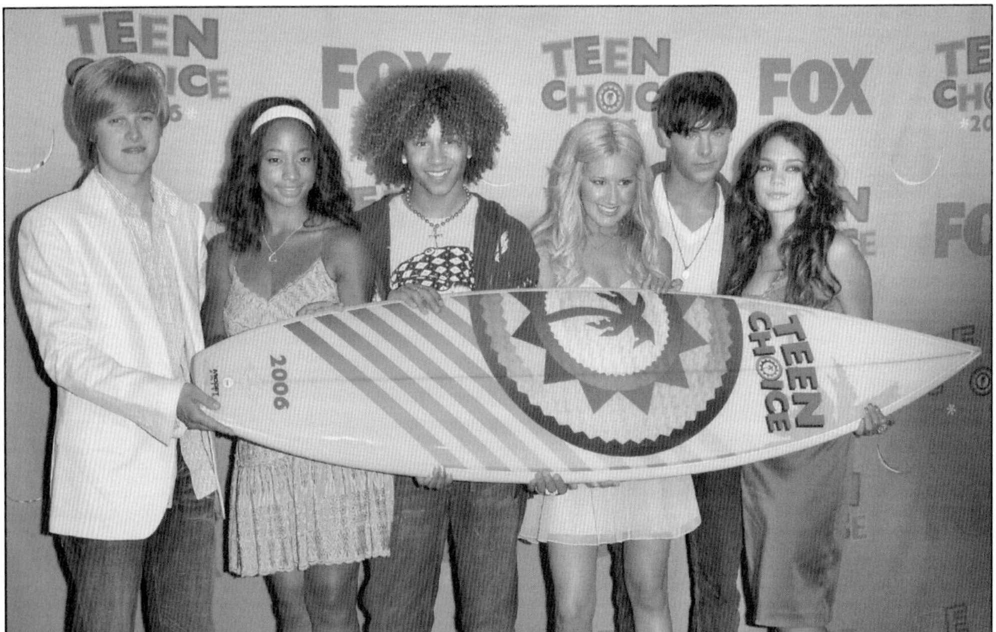

Vanessa Hudgens (far right) is shown with the *High School Musical* cast at the Teen Choice Awards in 2006. (Photograph by Fred Hayes/Disney; courtesy of Sthanlee B. Mirador.)

Brad Viratal was one of 20 castaways in CBS's reality series *Survivor.* The contestants, who boarded an ancient ship in the middle of the South Pacific, were divided into four tribes: Asian American, Caucasian, Latino, and African American. They were challenged to survive the next 39 days, provided they were not voted out before the game ended. (Photograph by Bill Inoshita/ CBS; courtesy of Sthanlee B. Mirador.)

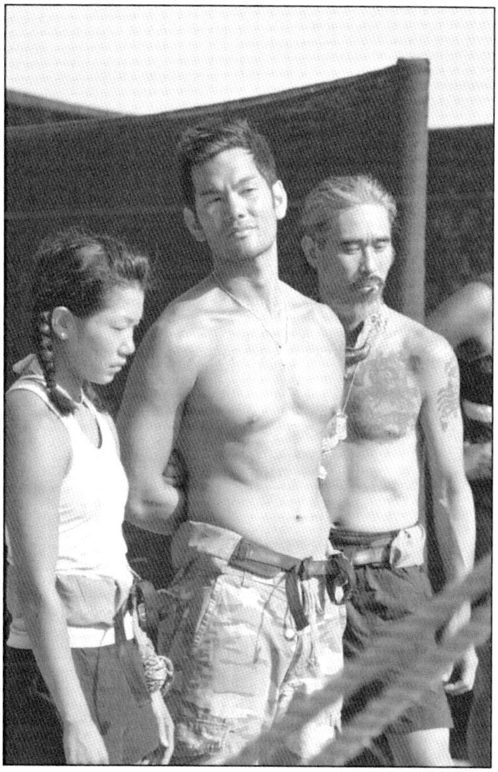

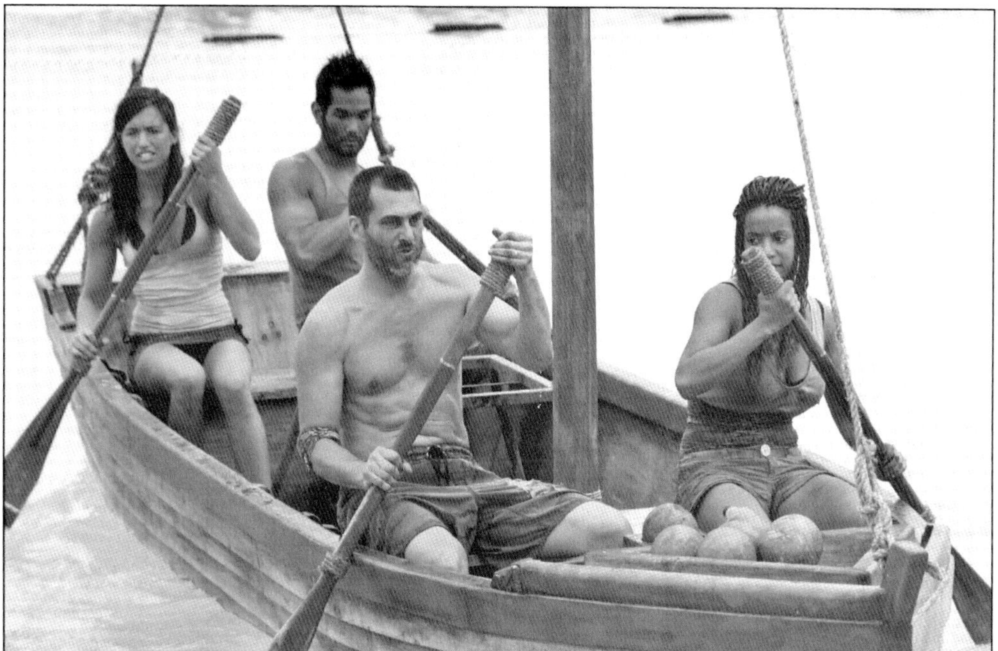

Brad Viratal helps paddle a boat in CBS's reality series *Survivor: Cook Islands* in 2006. The reunion of the Cook Islands castaways was watched by 13.5 million viewers. (Photograph by Bill Inoshita/CBS; courtesy of Sthanlee B. Mirador.)

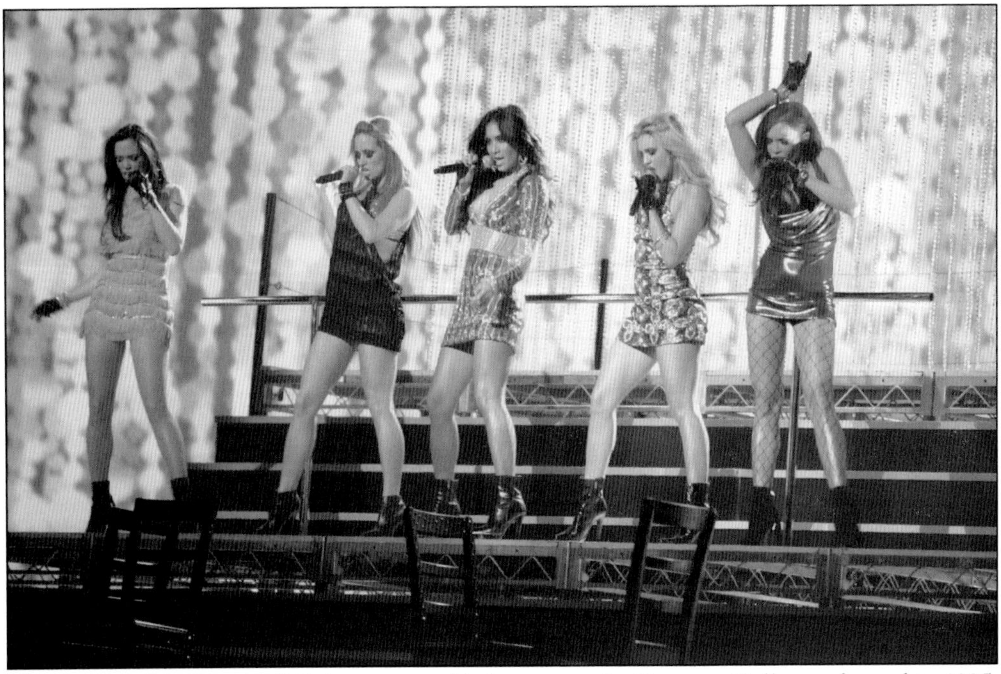

The American pop and R&B dance ensemble known as the Pussycat Dolls was formed in 1995. In 2003, Nicole Scherzinger (center) became the group's lead singer. The Pussycat Dolls released their first single in 2004, and in 2005, they received their first hit single "Don't Cha." The song went to No. 1 in several countries and reached No. 2 on the Billboard Hot 100. The group won a Billboard Music Award for the song and was also nominated for the top-selling single of the year and the top-selling dance single of the year. (Photograph by Craig Sjodin/ABC; courtesy of Sthanlee B. Mirador.)

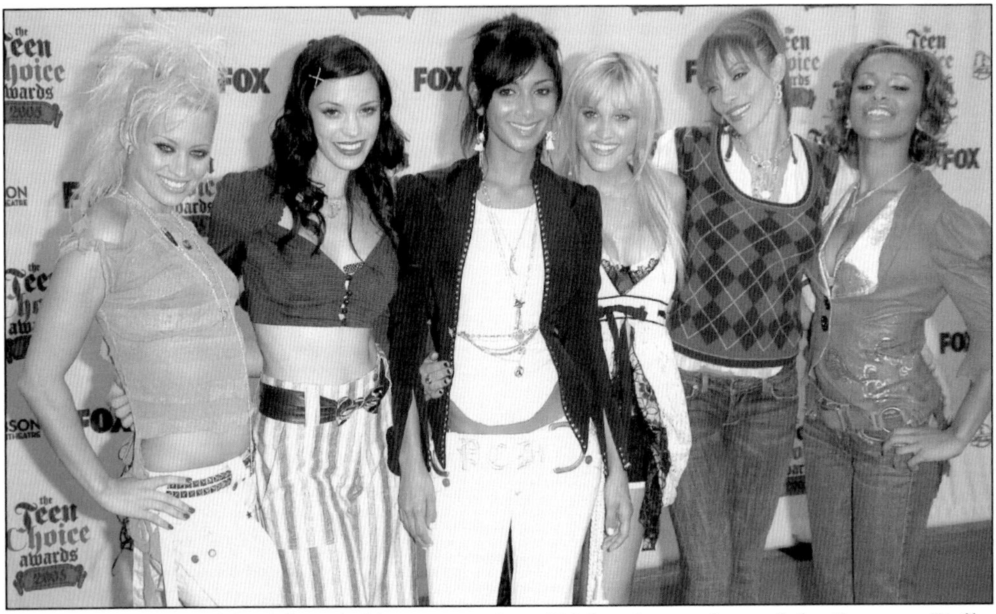

Nicole Scherzinger (third from left) is pictured in 2006 with members of the Pussycat Dolls. (Courtesy of Sthanlee B. Mirador.)

Vanessa Minnillo, seen here at the Golden Globe Awards in 2007, was Miss South Carolina Teen USA in 1998 and went on to be crowned Miss Teen USA that year. She cohosted the Miss Teen USA Pageant in 2004 and the Miss Universe Pageant in 2007. (Courtesy of Sthanlee B. Mirador.)

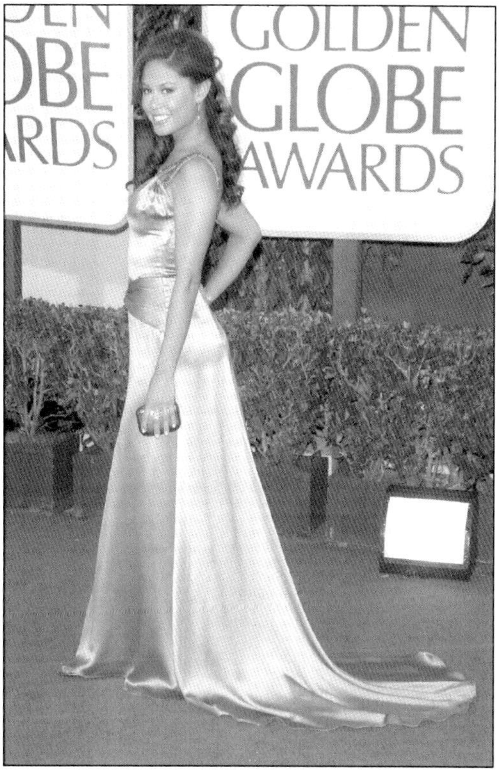

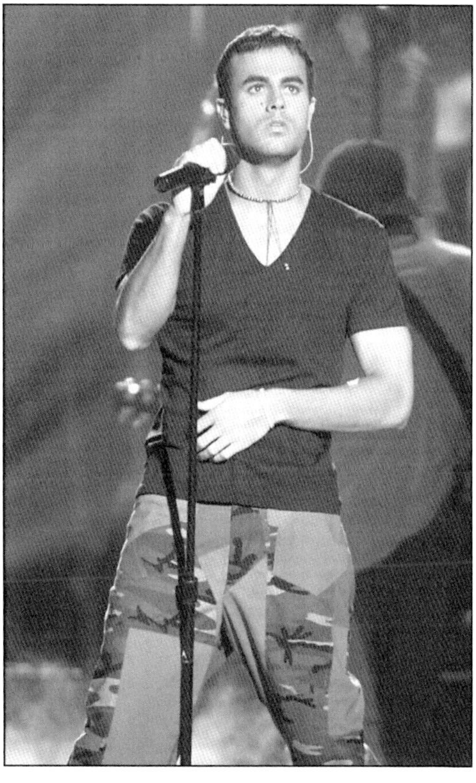

Enrique Iglesias appeared at the Teen Choice Awards in 2002. Born in Madrid, Spain, Iglesias is the son of Julio Iglesias and Filipina Isabel Preysler. He has 16 No. 1 hit songs and has acted in both film and television. In 1999, he was nominated for an ALMA award for "outstanding performance by an individual in a series" at the 26th American Music Awards of 1998. In 2000, he was nominated for a Blockbuster Entertainment Award for favorite song (Internet) for the movie *Wild Wild West*, 1999. (Courtesy of Everett Collection.)

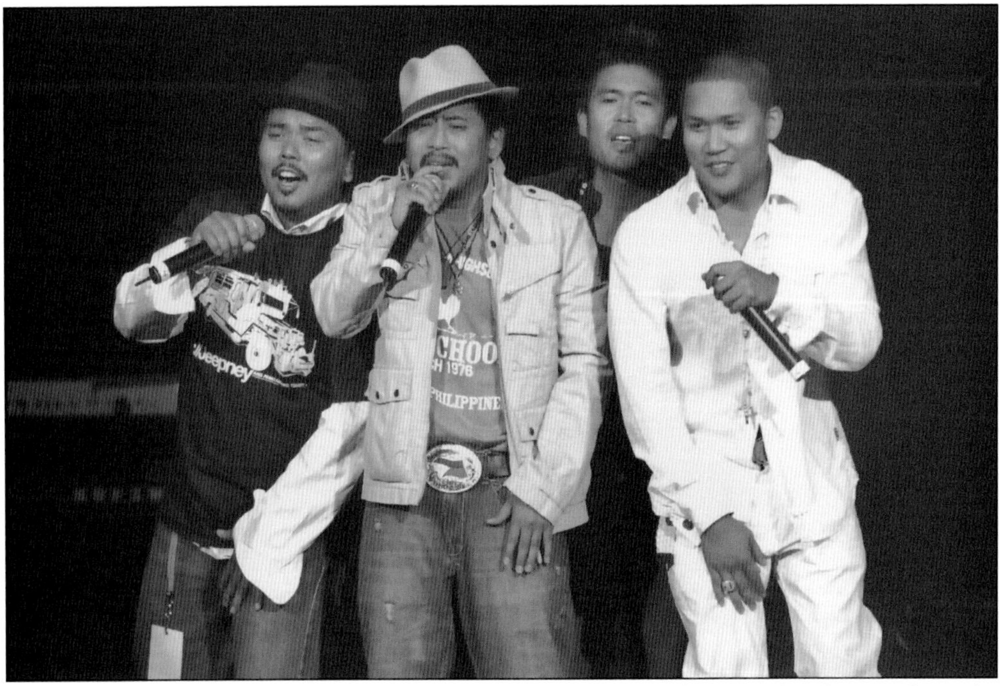

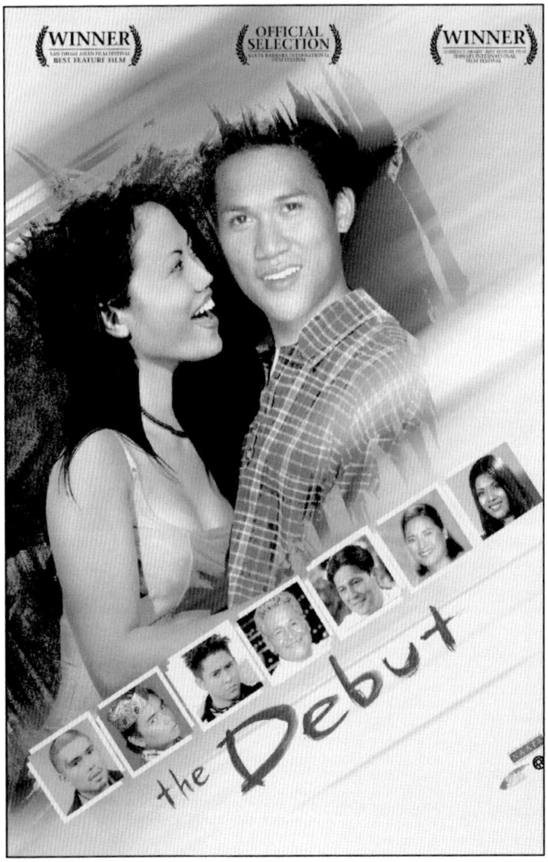

In 2006, the Basco brothers performed at a benefit concert called Love for Leyte at the Grove in Anaheim, California, to benefit the landslide victims on the island of Leyte in the Philippine archipelago. The Basco brothers—Dante, Dion, Darion, and Derek—are seen here in 2007. A talented family, the brothers act, sing, and dance. Dante (far right) is most noted for his performance in the movie *The Debut* and as the costar of the film *Take the Lead*. (Courtesy of Sthanlee B. Mirador.)

Written by Gene Cajayon and John Manal Castro, and directed by Gene Cajayon, *The Debut* is the first Filipino American theatrical movie. It won the Audience Award for best feature in the Hawaii International Film Festival in 2000, as well as the Jury Award for best dramatic narrative feature in the San Diego Asian Film Festival that same year. (Courtesy of Gene Cajayon.)

Ernie Reyes Jr., pictured here in 2002, counts among his identities actor, martial artist, director, and producer. He was nominated in 1987 for the exceptional performance by a young actor in a new television comedy or drama series for *Sidekicks*; nominated in 1992 for best young actor co-starring in a motion picture for *Teenage Mutant Ninja Turtles II: The Secret of the Ooze*; and nominated in 1994 for best youth actor in a leading role in a motion picture drama for *Surf Ninjas*. (Courtesy of Sthanlee B. Mirador.)

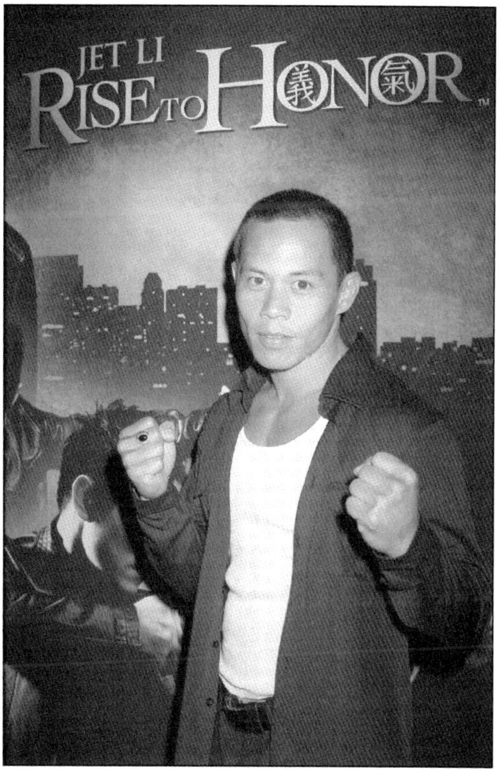

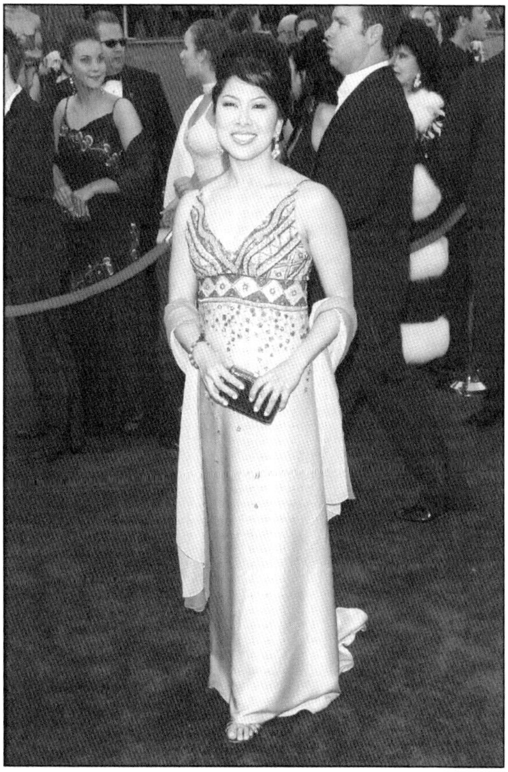

Actress and producer Pia Clemente, seen here in 2006, is the first Filipina to be nominated for a competitive Academy Award. Her Oscar nomination was for the short film *Our Time is Up* (2004). (Courtesy of Sthanlee B. Mirador.)

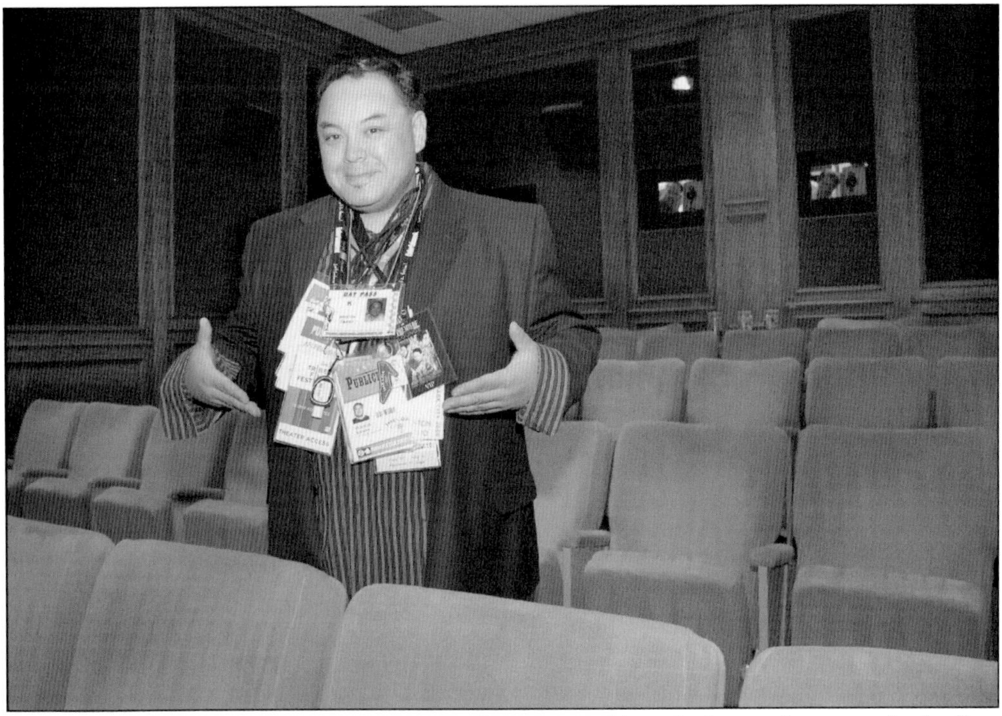

Pictured is publicist Winston Emano wearing his many publicist badges and passes, which allow him theater access to shows and events. (Courtesy of Celina Taganas-Duffy.)

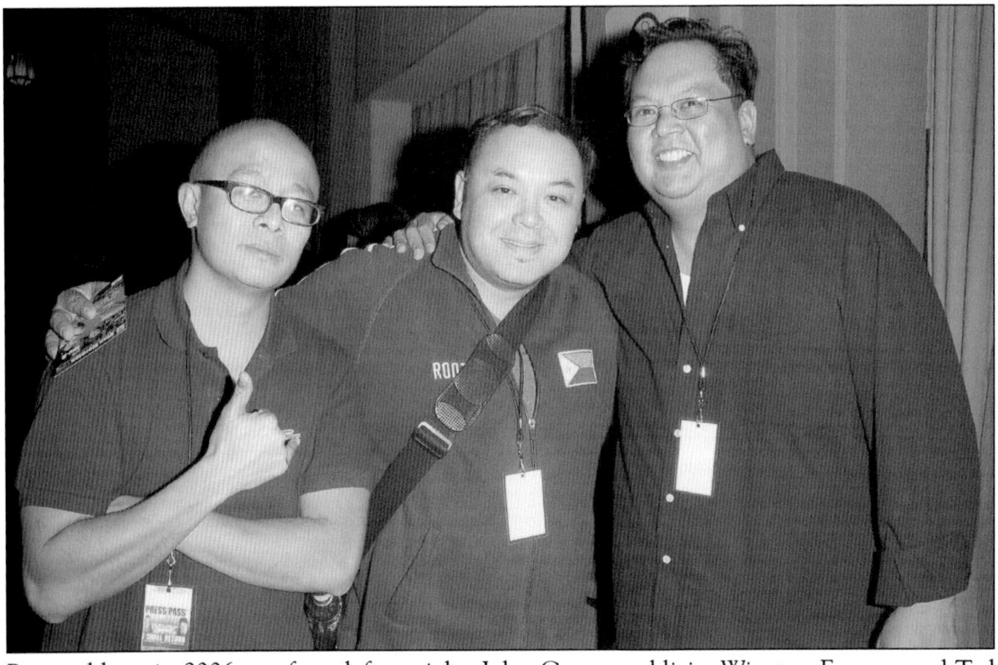

Pictured here in 2006 are, from left to right, John Castro, publicist Winston Emano, and Ted Benito. Castro, an independent filmmaker, wrote and directed the short film *Diary of a Gangsta Sucka* and was co-writer on the Filipino American movie *The Debut*. (Courtesy of Sthanlee B. Mirador.)

Cheryl Burke (left) is shown in 2007 competing with her partner Emmitt Smith on the ABC show *Dancing with the Stars*. She is the only two-time winner on *Dancing with the Stars*. Smith, a three-time Super Bowl champion as a running back with the Dallas Cowboys, is the National Football League's all-time rusher. (Photograph by Adam Lafkey/ABC; courtesy of Sthanlee B. Mirador.)

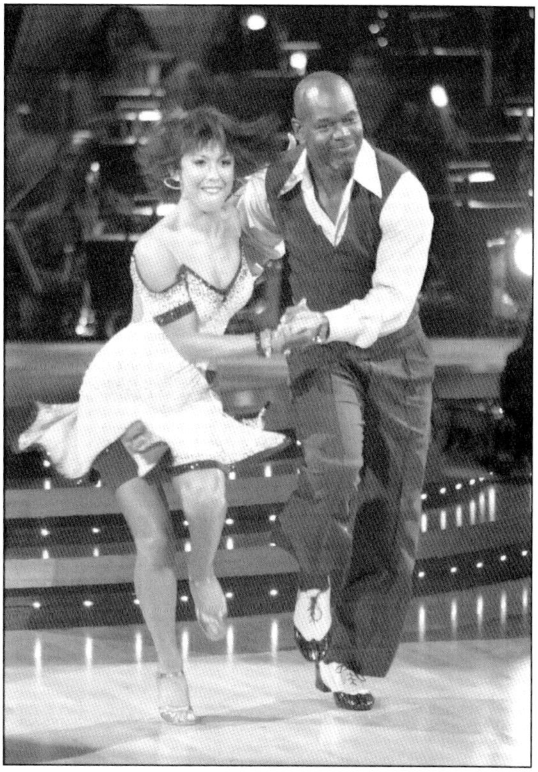

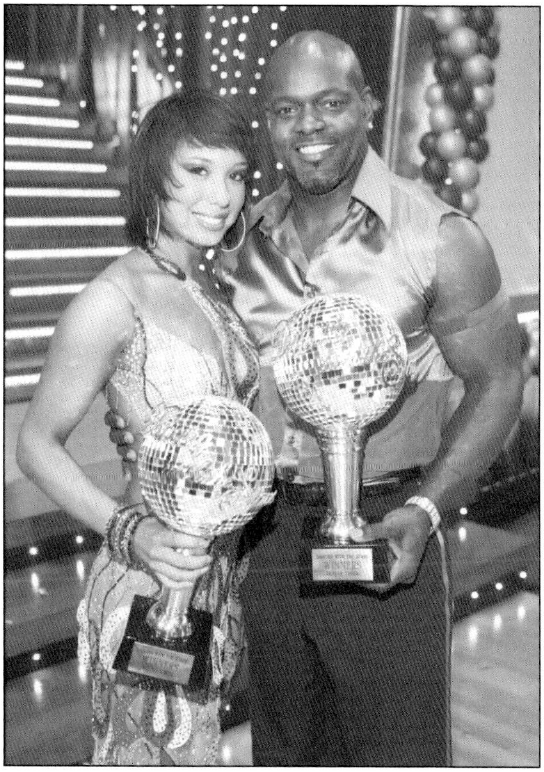

Together, Cheryl Burke and Emmitt Smith won ABC's *Dancing with the Stars* competition. (Photograph by Adam Lafkey/ABC; courtesy of Sthanlee B. Mirador.)

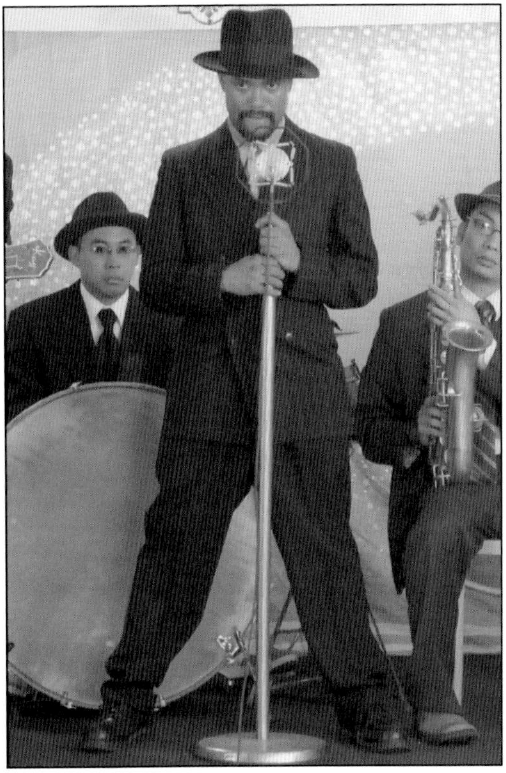

Apl.de.ap, a member of the Grammy Award–winning group Black Eyed Peas, is pictured here in a scene from the video *Bebot (Generation One)*, directed by filmmaker Patricio Ginelsa. (Courtesy of Sthanlee B. Mirador.)

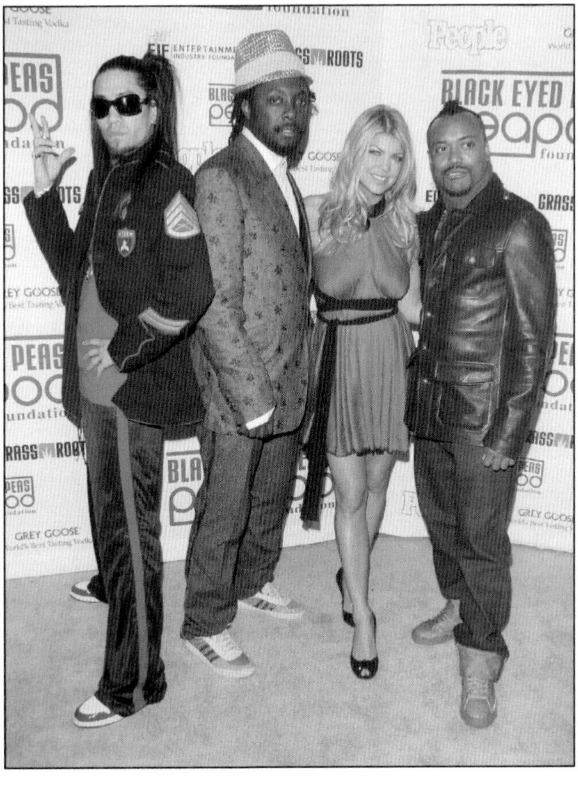

Allen Pineda Lindo, also known as apl.de.ap (far right), is seen with Black Eyed Peas members Taboo (far left), Will.i.am (second from left), and Fergie in 2007. (Courtesy of Sthanlee B. Mirador.)

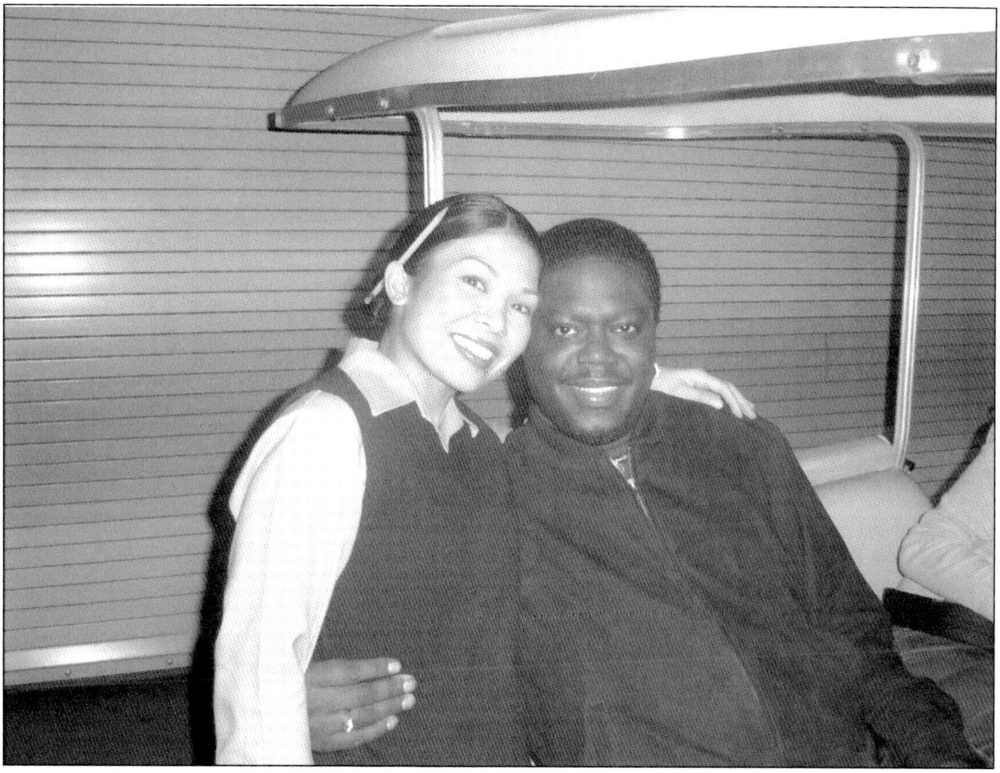

Actress Liza Del Mundo is seen here with actor Bernie Mac on the set of *The Bernie Mac Show* in 2005. She has appeared in several television episodes, commercials, and as the titular character in *Imelda*, a musical that premiered at East West Players in 2005. (Courtesy of Liza Del Mundo.)

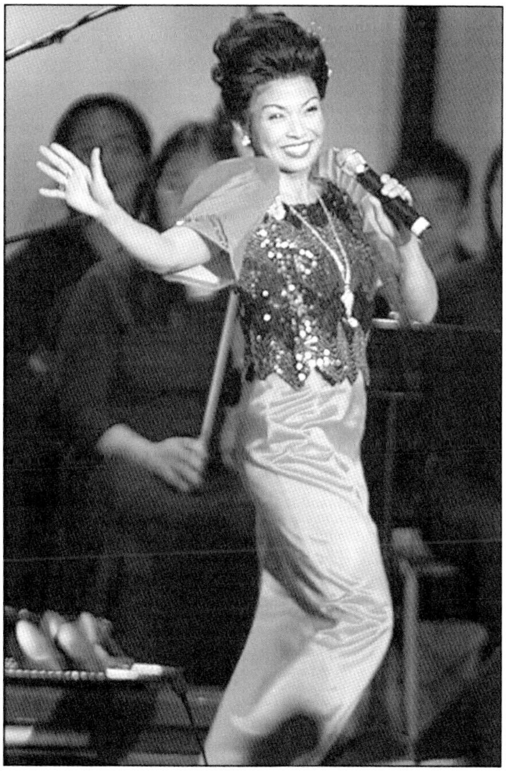

Liza Del Mundo performs at the East West Players 39th anniversary Visionary Awards gala at the Hilton Universal City. The cast of the East West Players' musical *Imelda* sang two songs from the show. (Courtesy of East West Players.)

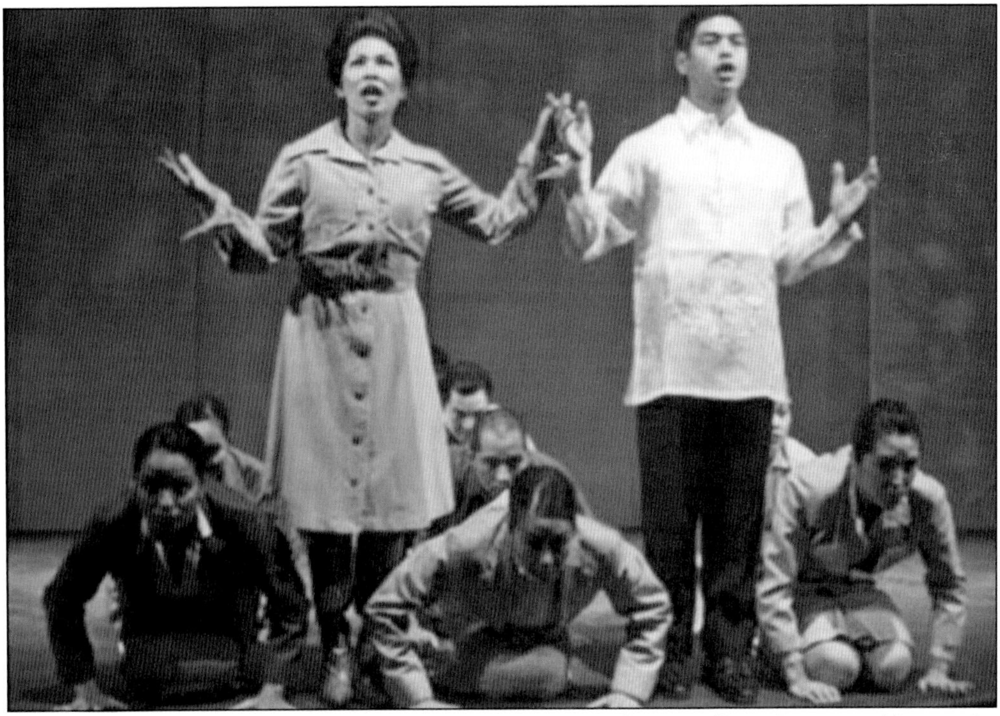

Liza Del Mundo portrays Imelda in the scene known as "Like a God" in the musical biography *Imelda*. (Courtesy of East West Players.)

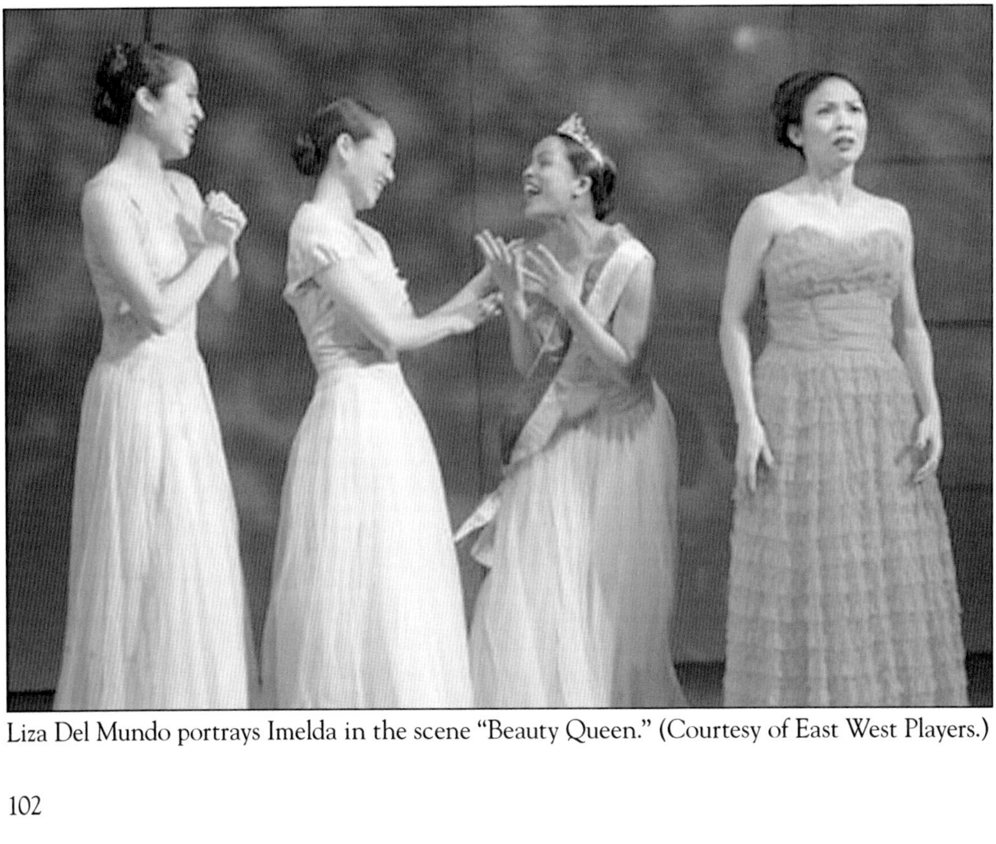

Liza Del Mundo portrays Imelda in the scene "Beauty Queen." (Courtesy of East West Players.)

Actress and writer Camille Mana is pictured here in 2007. She played the character role of Lisa on UPN's hit sitcom *One on One*, which ran for five years. In 2007, she produced her first film, *Equal Opportunity*, a satire on racial prejudices. It won the Best Film award in NBC/Universal's First Annual Comedy Shortcuts Film Festival. (Courtesy of Sthanlee B. Mirador.)

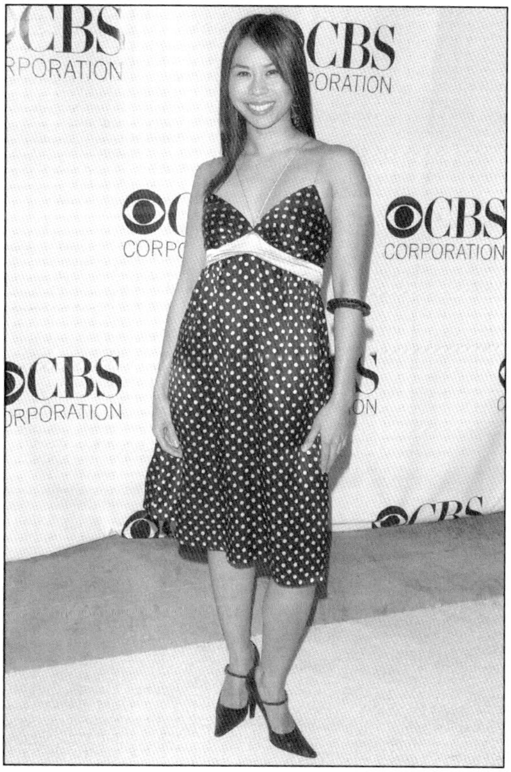

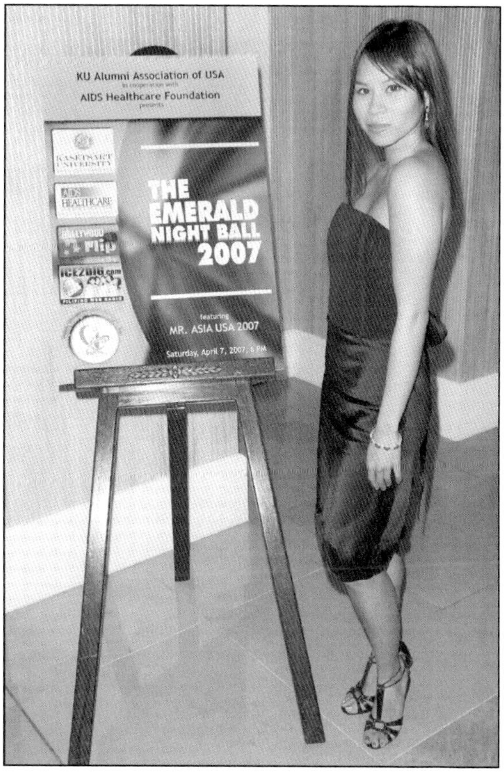

Camille Mana is shown attending the 2007 Emerald Night Ball benefit for the AIDS Healthcare Foundation. (Courtesy of Sthanlee B. Mirador.)

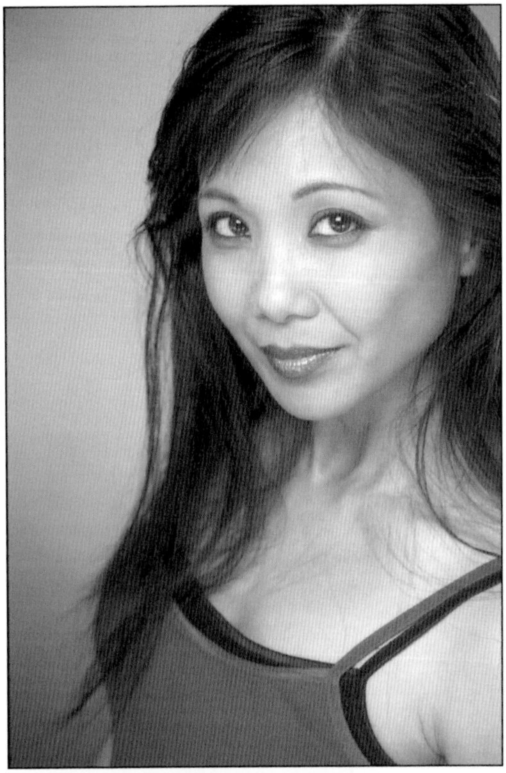

A graduate of the University of California, Los Angeles, with a degree in Economics, Jennifer Aquino is an accomplished martial artist who has appeared in many television shows, including JAG, *Caroline in the City*, and *City of Angels*. (Photograph by Phil Nee; courtesy of Jennifer Aquino.)

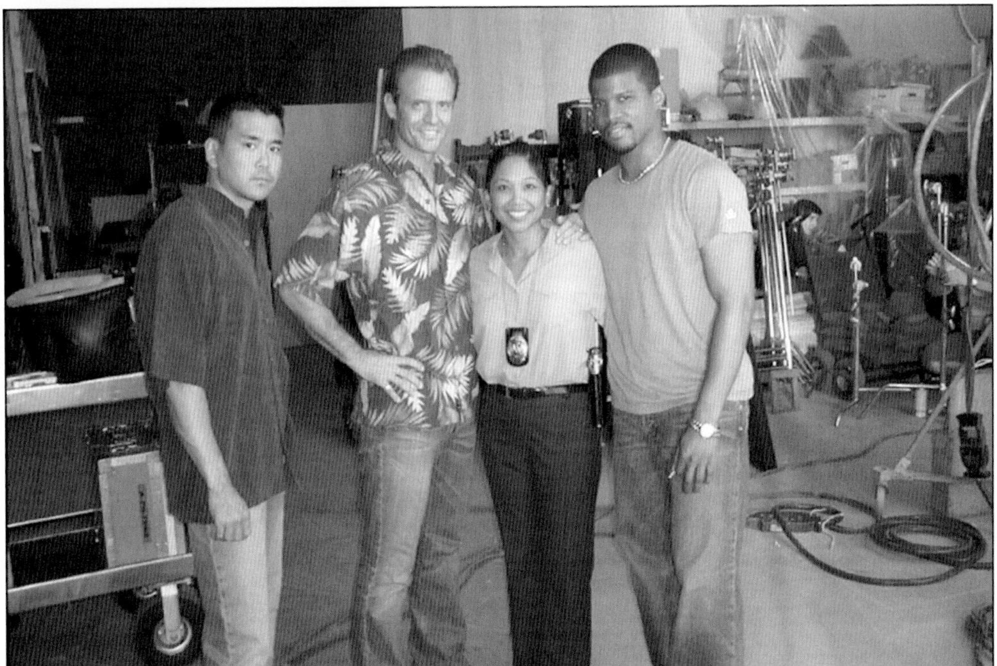

Jennifer Aquino (second from right) played the role of detective Laura Hannigan with Michael Sun Lee (far left), Michael Biehn (second left), and Sharif Atkins on the set of *Hawaii*, a 2004 CBS television series. (Courtesy of Jennifer Aquino.)

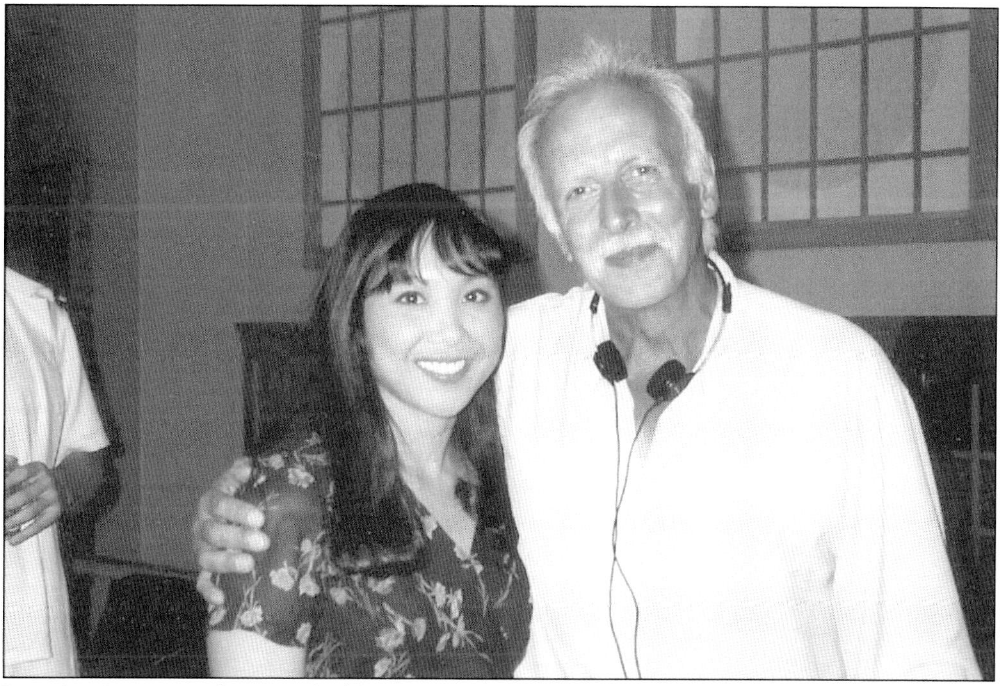

Jennifer Aquino is photographed here in 1998 with director Tony Wharmby on the set of the CBS television show *JAG*. (Courtesy of Jennifer Aquino.)

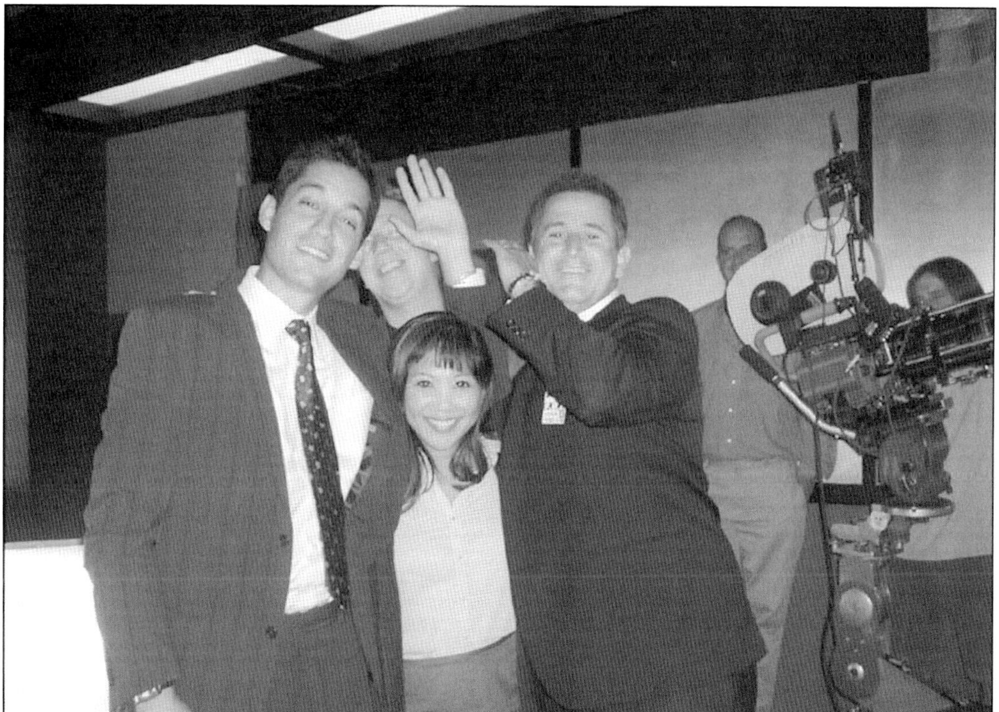

Actress Jennifer Aquino is pictured here between takes on the television show *Without a Trace* in 2004. (Courtesy of Jennifer Aquino.)

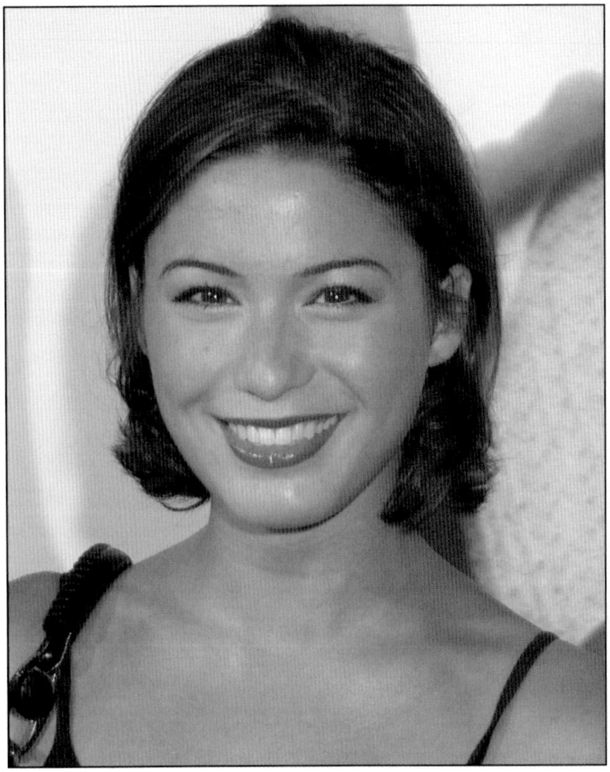

Actress Lori Trespicio is pictured here in 2001. She has appeared in several television shows, most notably *The Real World*. She also was ranked No. 72 in *Stuff* magazine's "102 Sexiest Women in the World" in 2002. (Courtesy of Sthanlee B. Mirador.)

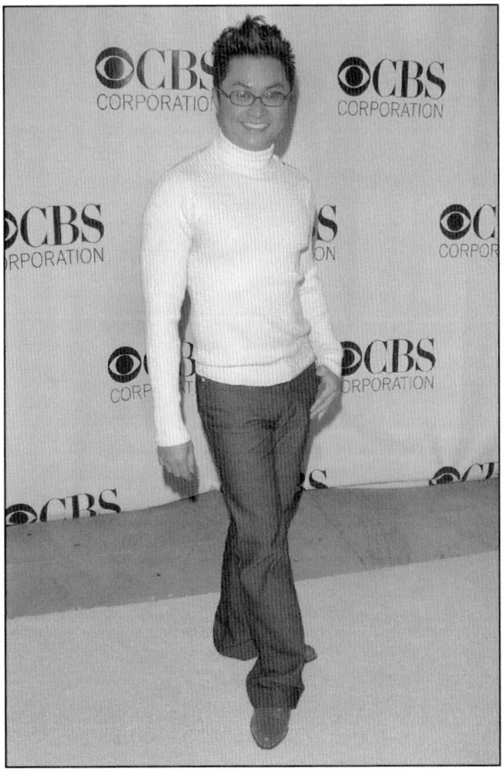

Award-winning actor, comedian, and writer Alec Mapa is shown in 2006. He has appeared in several television programs and films, including *Dharma & Greg*, *Desperate Housewives*, and *Ugly Betty*. (Courtesy of Sthanlee B. Mirador.)

In 2001, actress Joy Bisco holds a poster for the film *Lumpia* by Patricio Ginelsa, which she narrated. Lumpia is a traditional Filipino food much like egg rolls. Bisco also co-starred in the Filipino American film *The Debut*. (Courtesy of Sthanlee B. Mirador.)

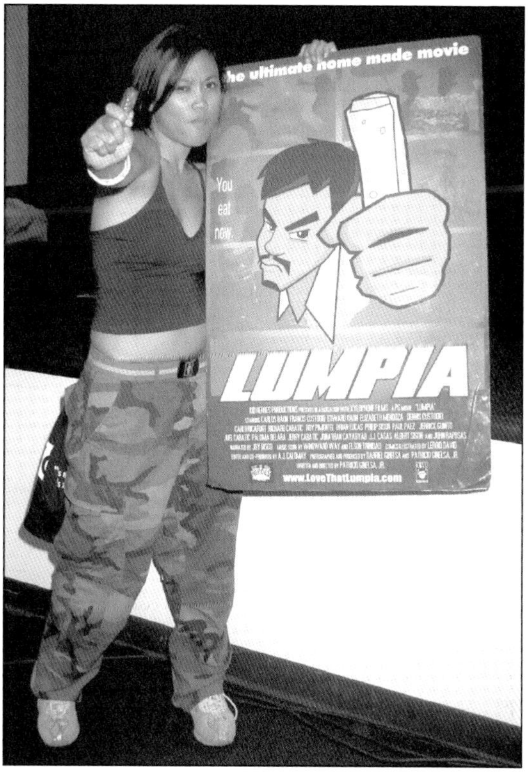

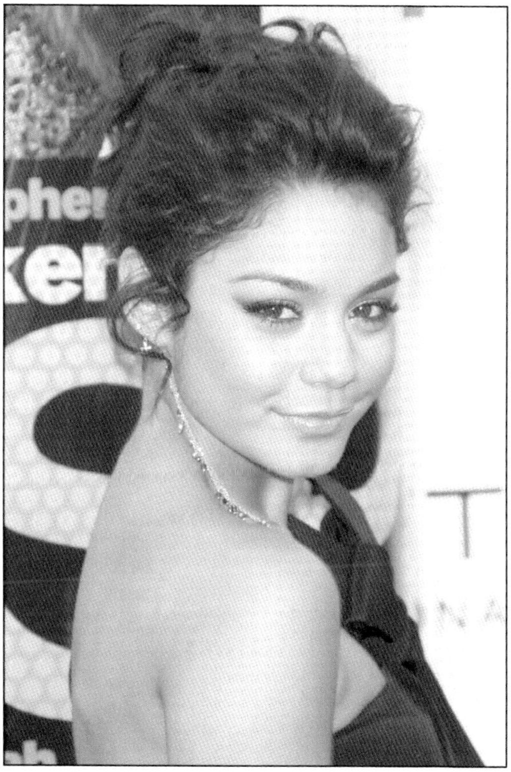

Pictured here is actress Vanessa Hudgens in 2007. She has appeared in the films *Thirteen* and *Thunderbirds*. Her musical theater roles include ones in *Evita*, *Carousel*, *The Wizard of Oz*, *The King & I*, *The Music Man*, *Cinderella*, *Damn Yankees*, *The Hunchback of Notre Dame*, and *The Little Mermaid*. She is best known for her role in the *High School Musical*. (Photograph by Fred Hayes/Disney; courtesy of Sthanlee B. Mirador.)

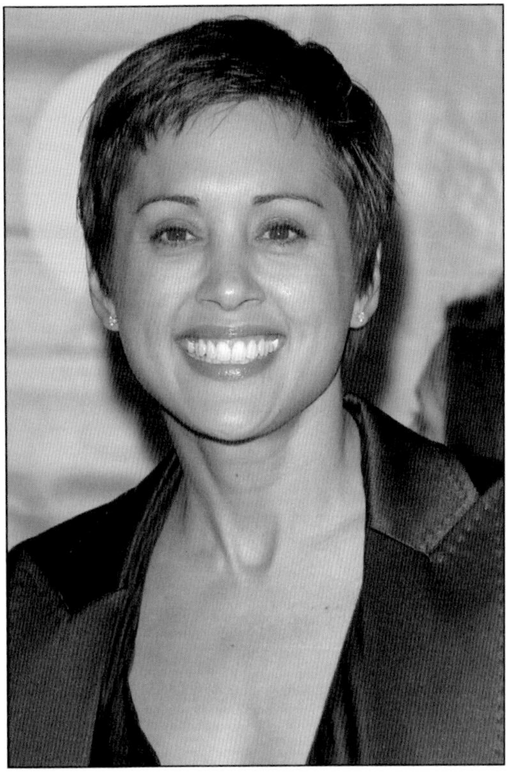

Actress Honey Labrador, seen here in 2003, has appeared in such films as *Strange Days* (1995) and *April's Shower* (2003), which she produced, and several episodes of the *Red Shoe Diaries*. She wrote, produced, and was host of the 2005 reality series *Xcess/ Access*. (Courtesy of Sthanlee B. Mirador.)

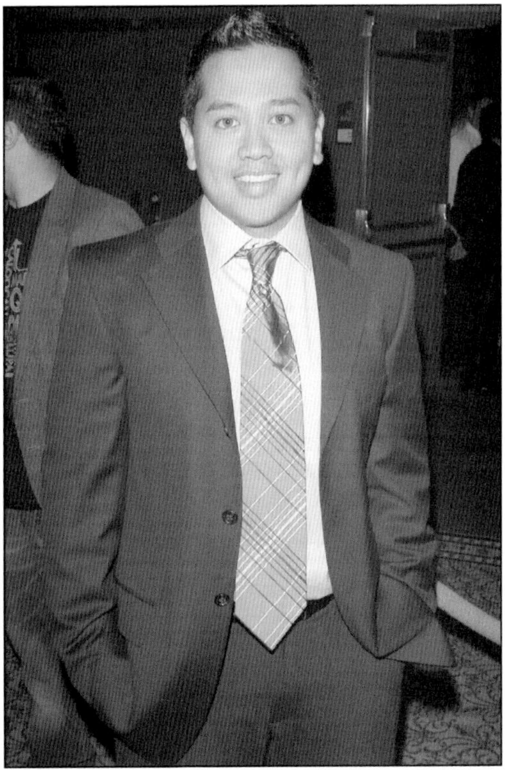

Rembrandt Flores, seen here in 2005, is a graduate of the University of California, Berkeley, and is the managing partner at Entertainment Fusion Group, L.A. He was formerly an associate producer for E! Entertainment Television Networks. (Courtesy of Sthanlee B. Mirador.)

Actress Giselle Toengi, seen here in 2007, studied at the Lee Strasberg School of Acting in New York and began her acting career at age 16. Her later credits include the feature film *A Year and a Day* (2005) and the series *Hokus Pokus*. (Courtesy of Sthanlee B. Mirador.)

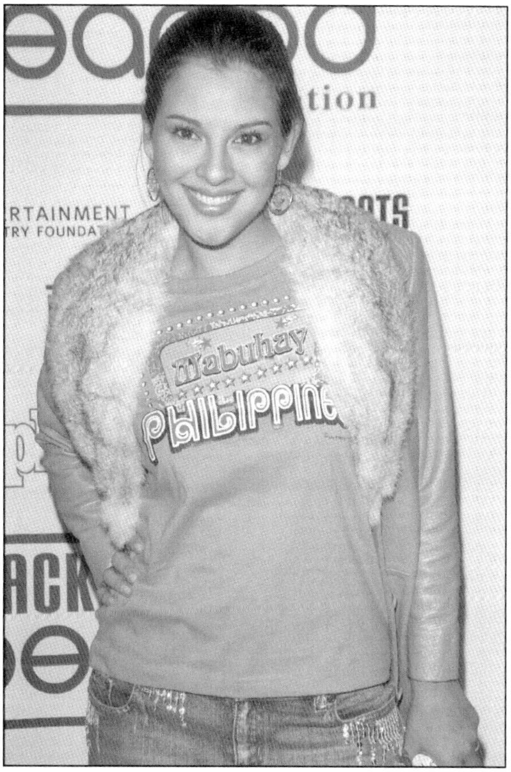

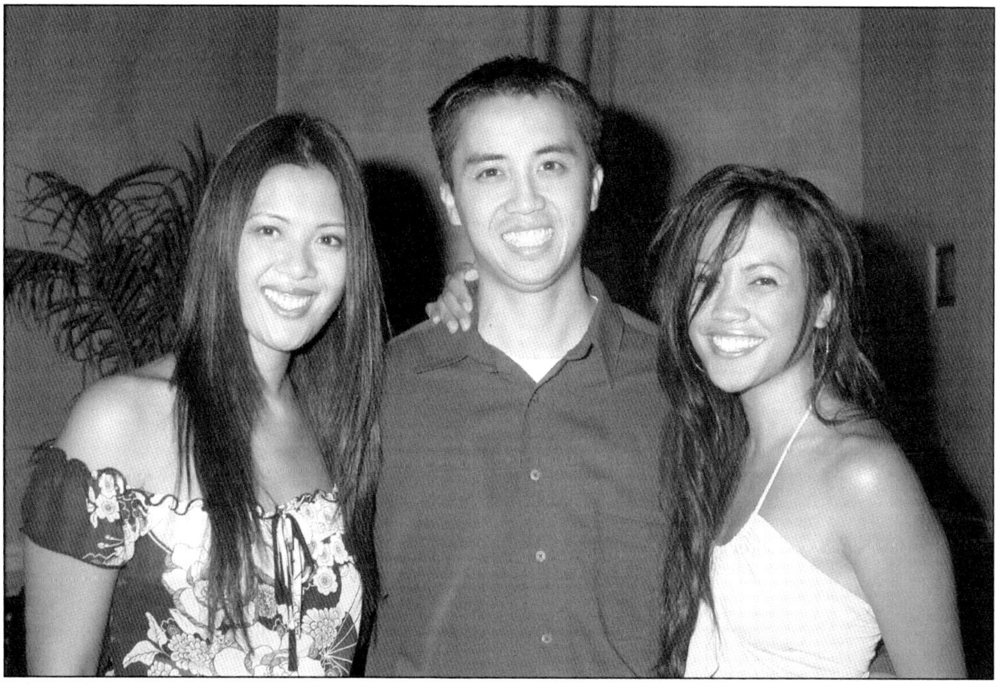

Filmmaker Patricio Ginelsa (center) is seen here with actress/comedienne Bernadette Balagtas (left) and actress Joy Bisco. Both actresses appeared in the film *The Debut*. (Courtesy of Sthanlee B. Mirador.)

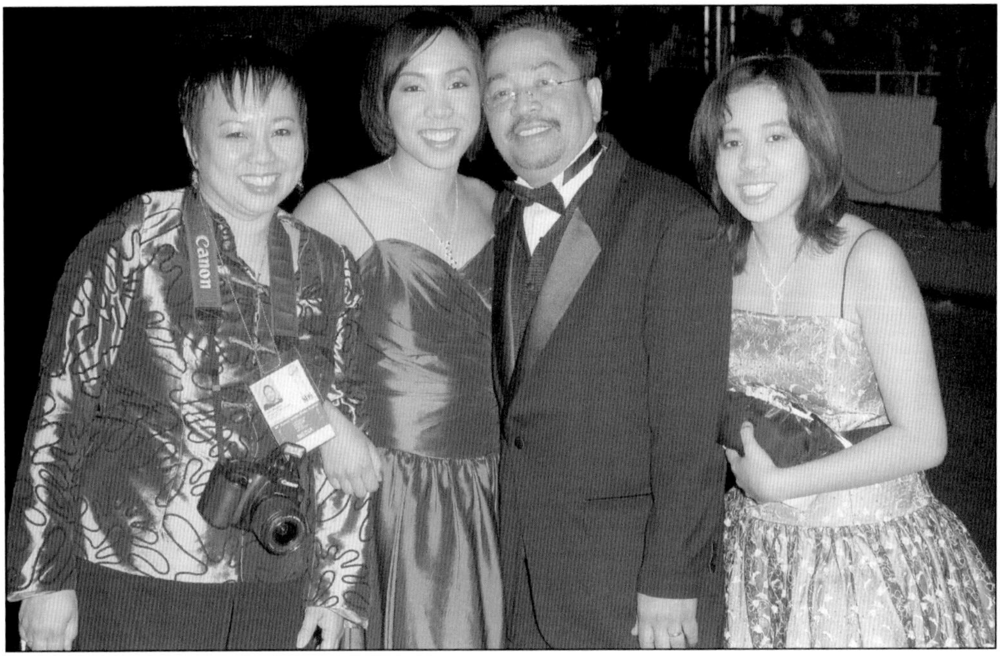

Hollywood columnist Janet Nepales (left) is shown with her family in 2007. She has been affiliated with both the *Philippine News* and the *Philippine Daily Inquirer.* (Courtesy of Sthanlee B. Mirador.)

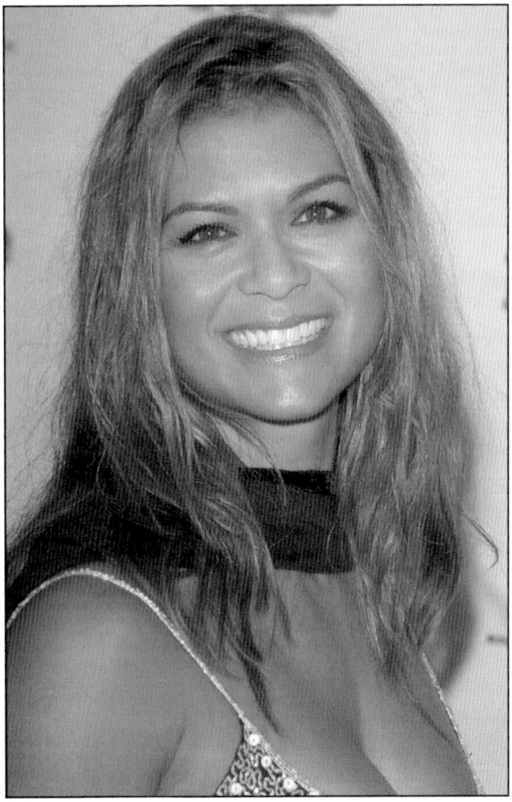

Born in Hollywood, Nia Peeples has performed as Liberace's opening act in Las Vegas on weekends and starred in such movies as *North Shore* (1987), *Deepstar Six* (1989), and *I Don't Buy Kisses Anymore* (1992). She has also been in the television movies *Swimsuit* (1989), *Sub Zero* (2005), and *Alpha Mom* (2006), as well as the television series *The Division*, *Barbershop*, and *The Young and the Restless.* (Courtesy of Sthanlee B. Mirador.)

Actor Reggie Lee showed up in 2007 at the premier of *Pirates of the Caribbean: At World's End*. Lee has appeared in *Prison Break* and in two of the *Pirates of the Caribbean* films, among many others. He toured nationally in the 1990s in the musicals *Heartstrings*, *Miss Saigon*, and *Carousel*. In 1997, he was awarded the Drama-Logue Critics Award for his performance in *F.O.B.* at East West Players. (Courtesy of Sthanlee B. Mirador.)

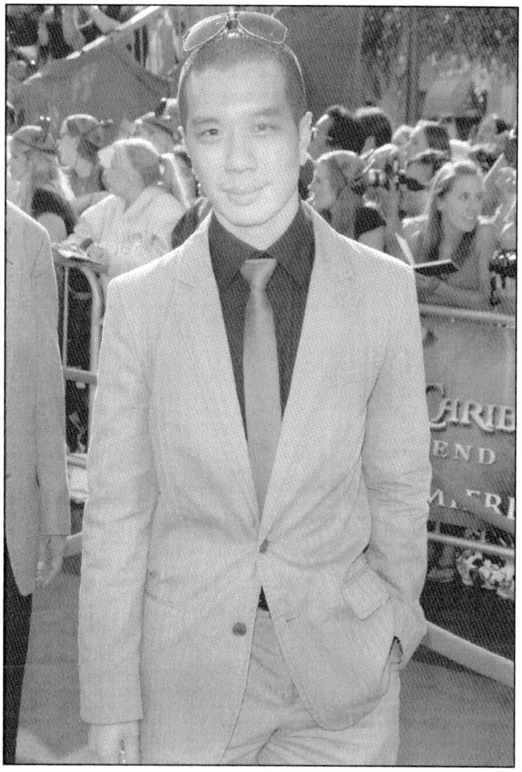

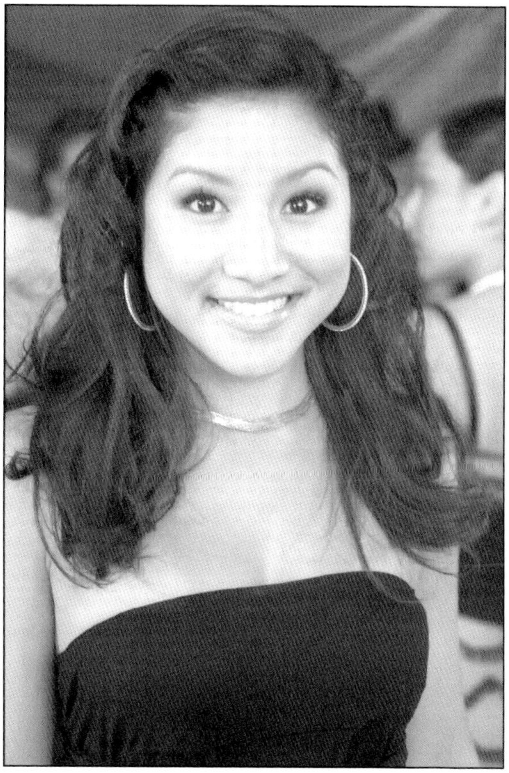

Singer Jasmine Trias, pictured here in 2006, registered a third-place finish as one of the finalists on the third season of *American Idol*. She has released two albums. (Courtesy of Sthanlee B. Mirador.)

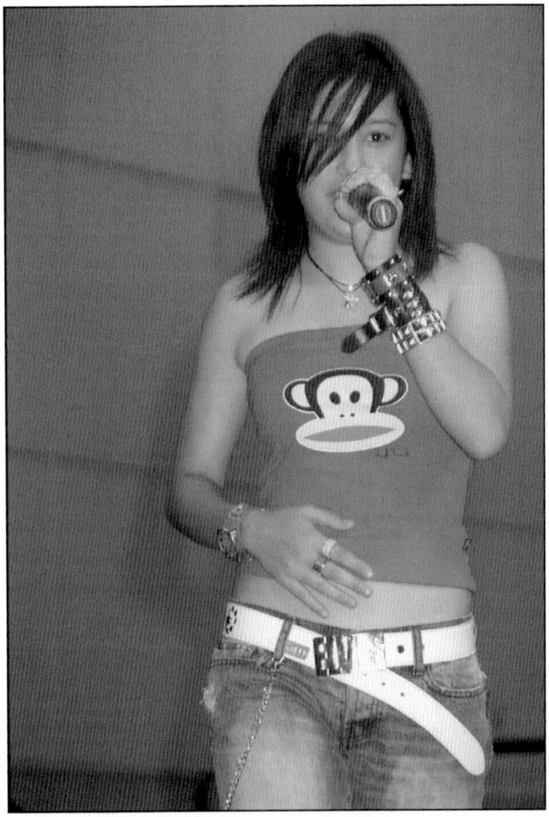

Actress and singer Lalaine Ann Vergara-Paras performs in 2001. Billed simply as Lalaine, she played the lead in the movie *Royal Kill*, starring Eric Roberts. Among many performing accomplishments, she has been featured on the Disney Channel, cast in the Broadway production of *Les Miserables*, featured on several television commercials, and has written several songs on her independent album. (Courtesy of Sthanlee B. Mirador.)

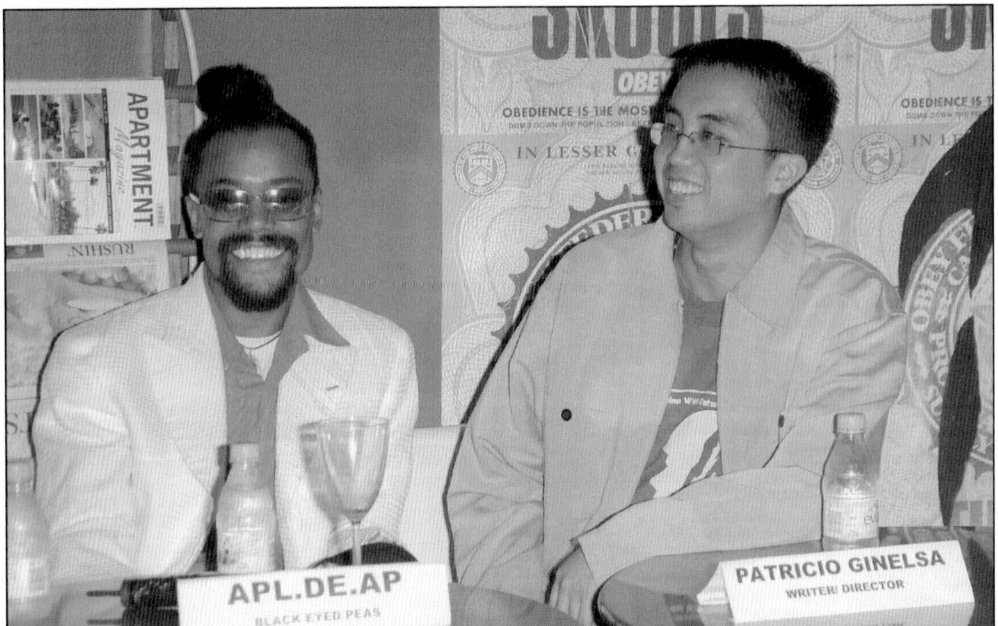

Allen Pineda Lindo, also known as apl.de.ap (left), of the Black Eyed Peas is seen with writer, director, and filmmaker Patricio Ginelsa in 2006. (Courtesy of Sthanlee B. Mirador.)

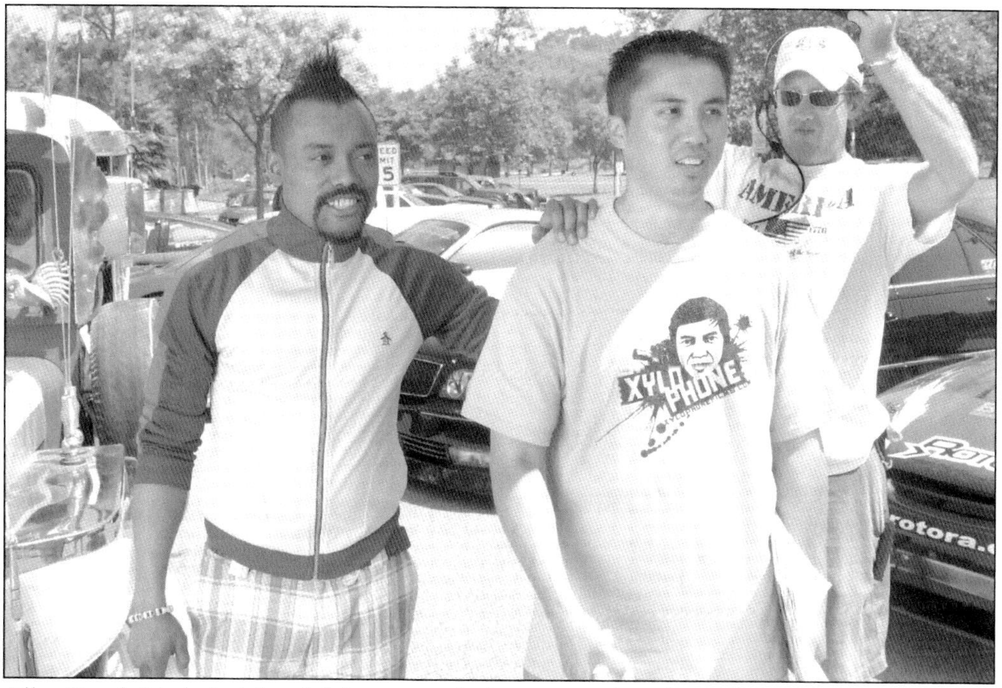

Allen Pineda Lindo (apl.de.ap), left, poses with the writer and producer of *Jeepney*, Patricio Ginelsa, on the film's set in 2006. (Courtesy of Sthanlee B. Mirador.)

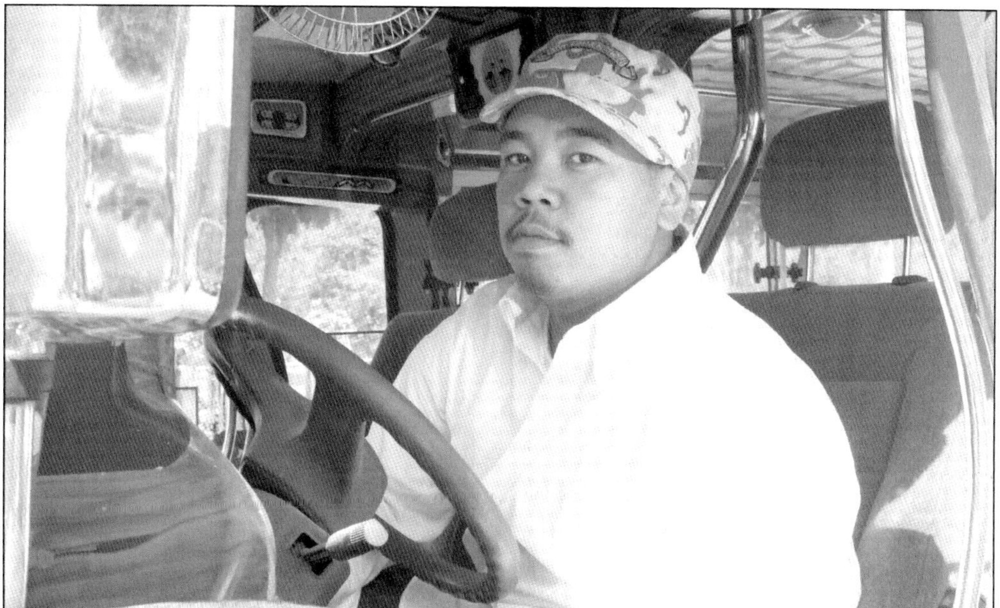
In 2006, deejay Rocky Rock sits behind the wheel of a "jeepney," best described as a multiple-fare Manila taxi, while filming *Jeepney*. Rock was the 2001 Guitar Center USA DJ champion, Linkin Park DJ champion, the main deejay for the 2004 Project Revolution tour, Philippines DMC champion 2005, and was featured on the Black Eyed Peas album *Monkey Business*. (Courtesy of Sthanlee B. Mirador.)

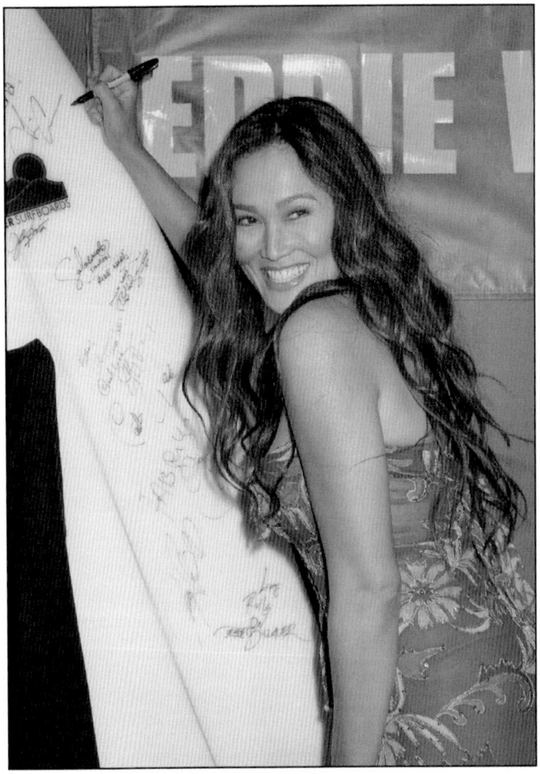

Actress and singer Tia Carrere autographs a surfboard at an event in 2002. (Courtesy of Sthanlee B. Mirador.)

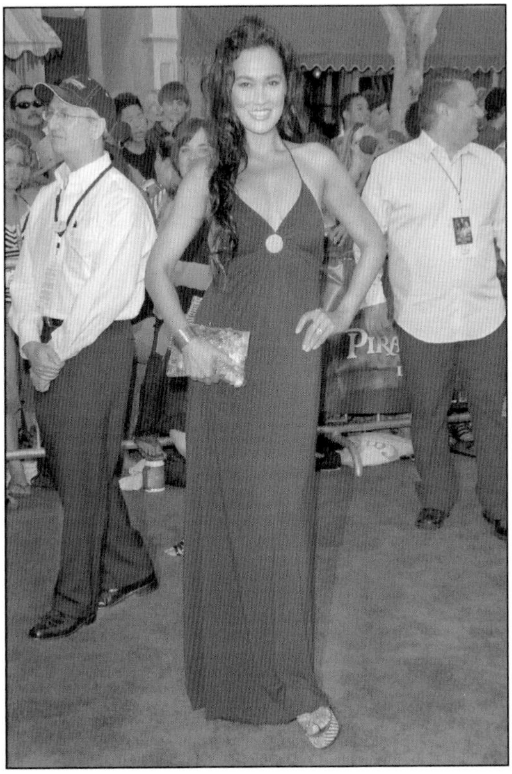

Tia Carrere poses on the red carpet at the premier of *Pirates of the Caribbean: At World's End*. (Courtesy of Sthanlee B. Mirador.)

Lou Diamond Phillips attended the 10th annual Screen Actors Guild Awards in 2002, which was held at the Shrine Auditorium in Los Angeles. (Courtesy of Sthanlee B. Mirador.)

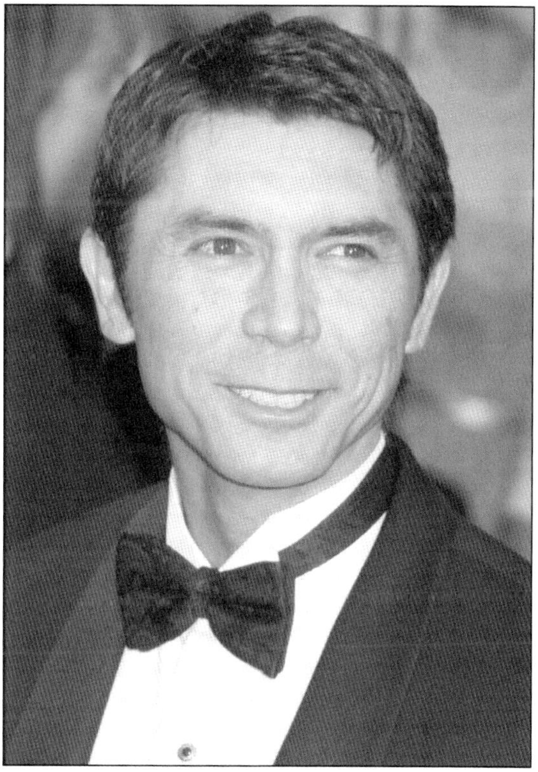

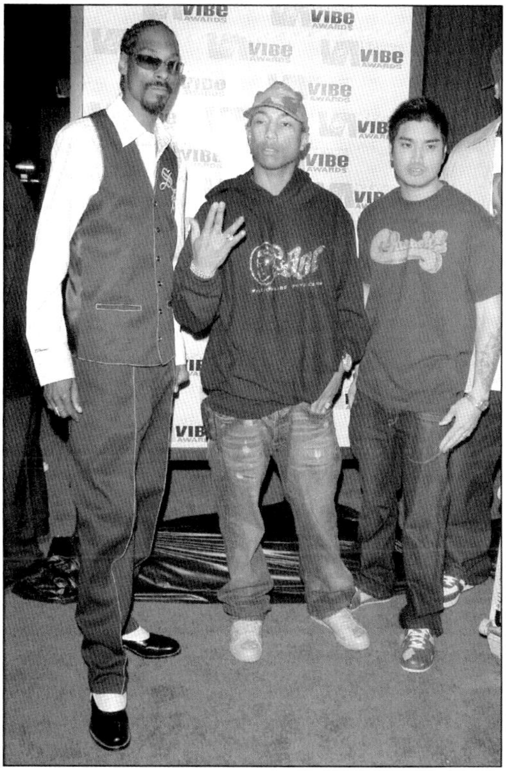

Charles "Chad" Hugo (right) is seen in 2002 with Snoop Dogg (left) and production partner Pharrell Williams. Hugo is an American Grammy Award–winning producer and, together with Williams, has produced several No. 1 hit tracks. (Courtesy of Sthanlee B. Mirador.)

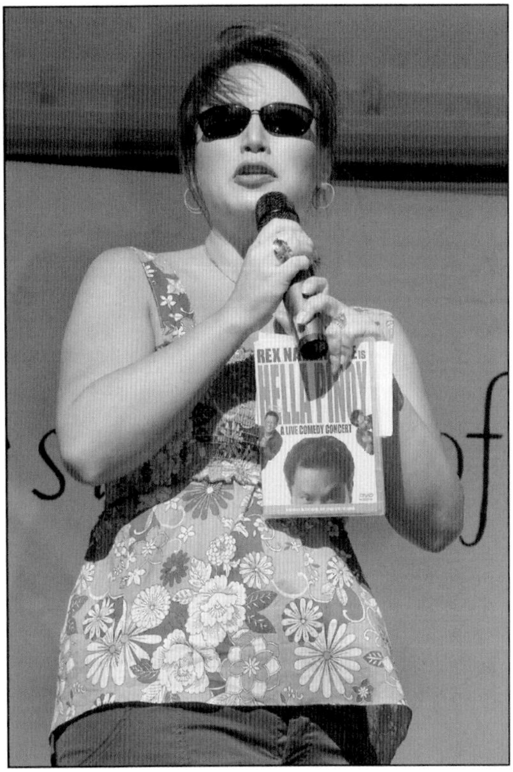

A health specialist and news reporter at the ABC affiliate in Los Angeles, Channel 7's Eyewitness News, Denise Dador is seen in 2002 promoting the *Hella Pinoy*, a live comedy concert. (Courtesy of Sthanlee B. Mirador.)

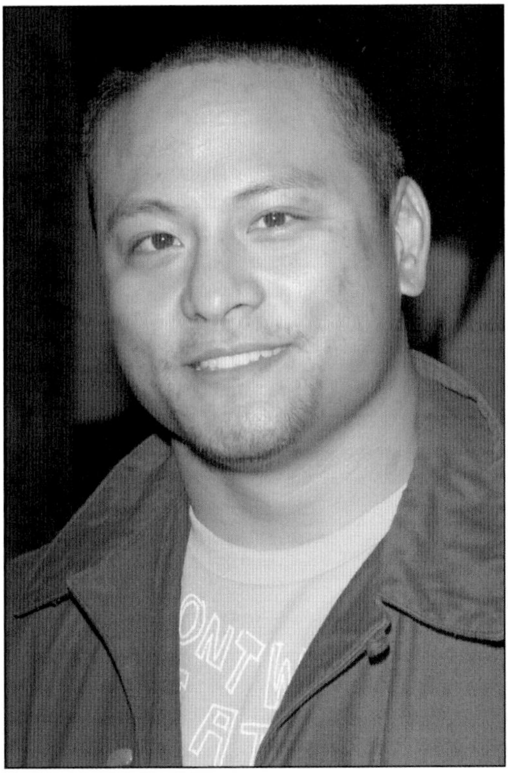

Martial artist Neal "Xingu" Rodil is best known as the "martial arts trainer to the stars." He appeared on episodes of the series *Absolutely True* and *Fashion House*. (Courtesy of Sthanlee B. Mirador.)

Actor and comedian Rob Schneider is best known as a regular on *Saturday Night Live* from 1989 to 1994. He is a writer, producer, and director and has been nominated for three Emmys for writing *Saturday Night Live*. He has also been nominated for four Razzie Awards, winning in 2006 for *Deuce Bigelow: European Gigolo*. (Courtesy of Sthanlee B. Mirador.)

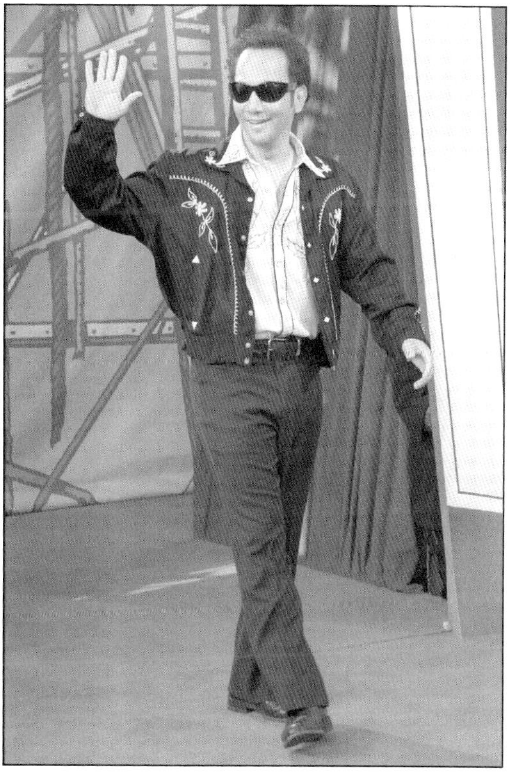

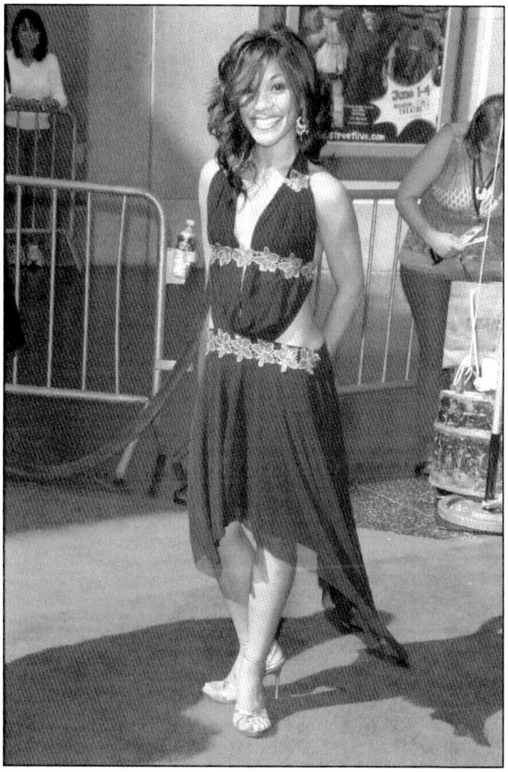

Dancer Melody Lacayanga is seen in 2007 on the red carpet for the Fox television show, *So You Think You Can Dance*. (Courtesy of Sthanlee B. Mirador.)

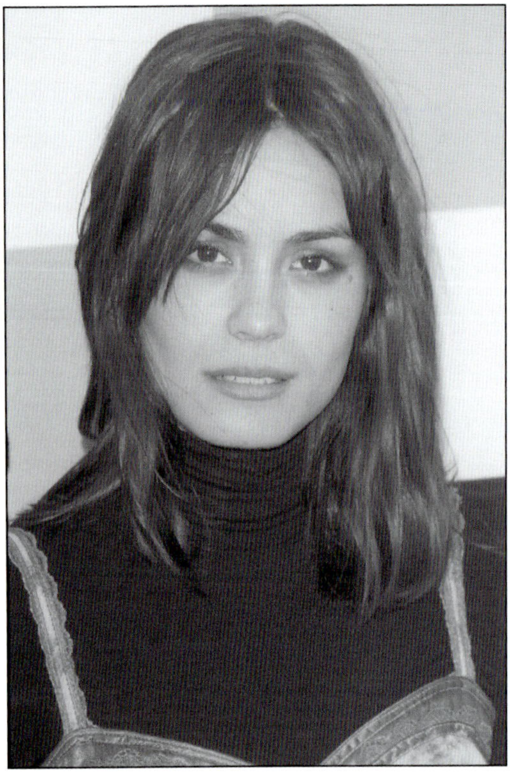

Actress Shannyn Sossamon, seen here in 2006, played the female lead, Lady Jocelyn, opposite Heath Ledger in the movie, *A Knight's Tale*, in 2001. She is an accomplished actress with several movie and television appearances to her credit, including regular roles on the series *Dirt* and *Moonlight*. (Courtesy of Sthanlee B. Mirador.)

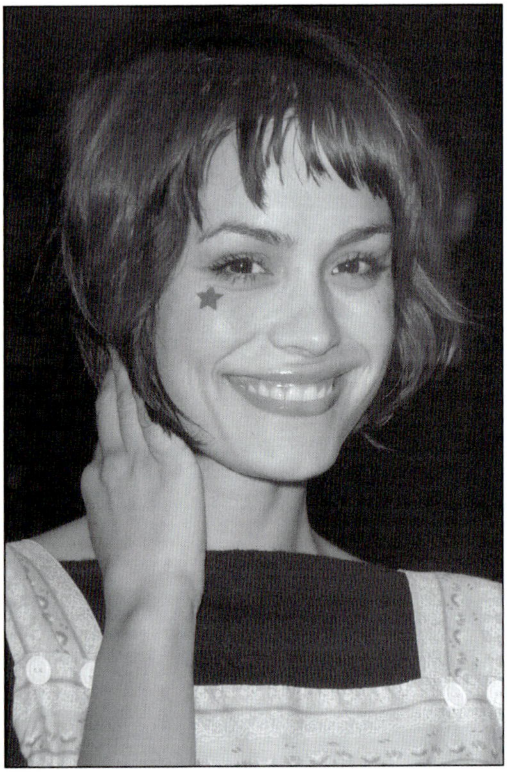

Shannyn Sossamon, seen here in 2005, came to Los Angeles at age 17 seeking a career in dance. She was also a deejay in local clubs. During one of her deejay jobs, she was approached about acting. (Courtesy of Sthanlee B. Mirador.)

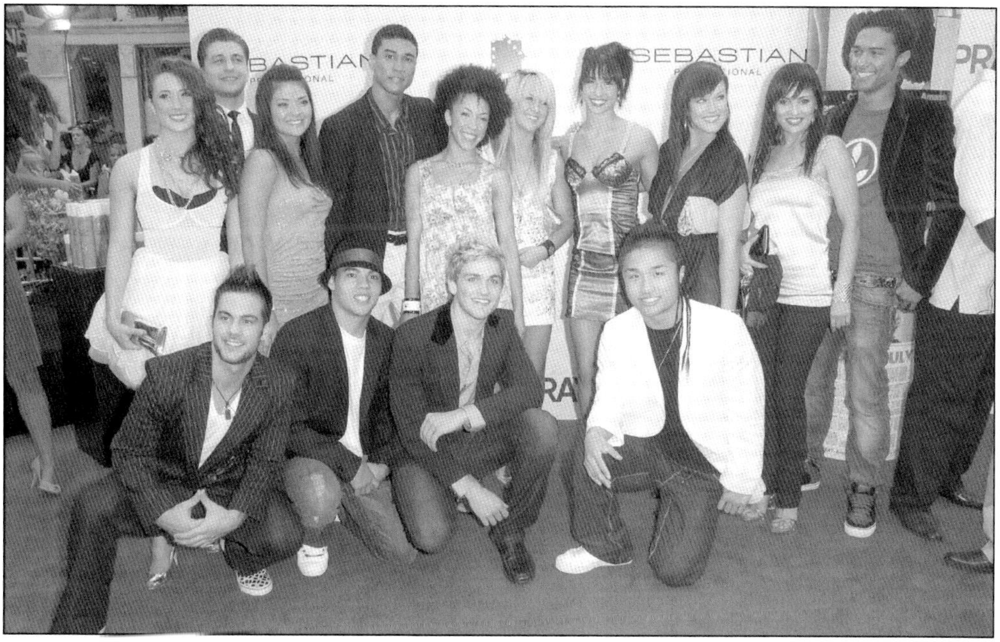

Dancer Dominic Sandoval (first row, second from left) is seen here in 2007 during the run of *So You Think You Can Dance*. He was a top 20 finalist on the third season. He began break dancing in 1999 before changing to hip-hop choreography and freestyle. (Courtesy of Sthanlee B. Mirador.)

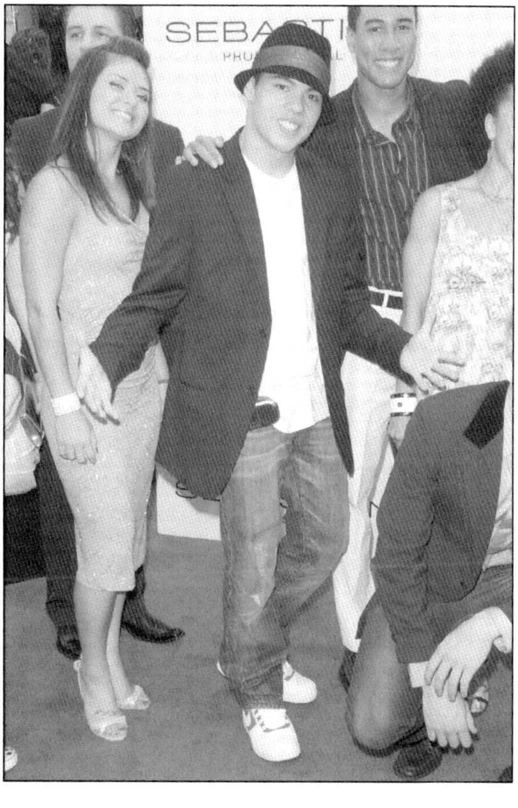

Dominic Sandoval (center) has diverse dance experiences, including performances at the Arco Arena in Sacramento, California, and at NBA and WNBA games as part of the halftime entertainment. (Courtesy of Sthanlee B. Mirador.)

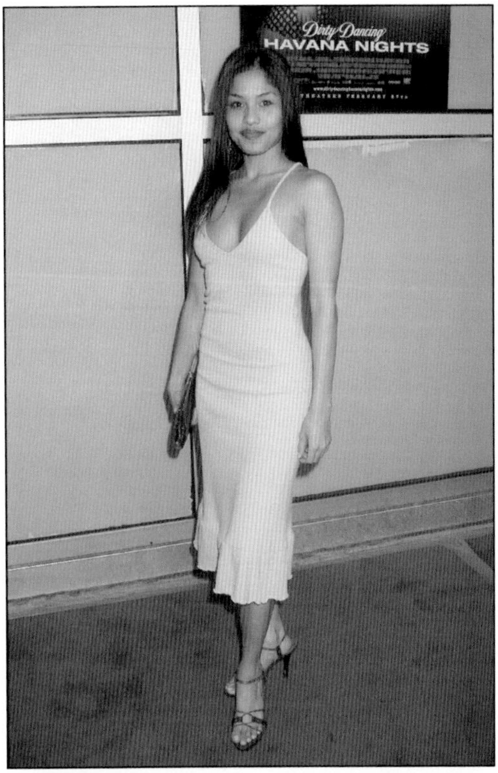

Melissa Howard, shown here in 2002, is a graduate of the University of South Florida with a degree in mass communications. She has become a reality show personality, actress, painter, comedienne, and writer. She was ranked no. 92 on *Maxim* magazine's "Hot 100 women of 2004." (Courtesy of Sthanlee B. Mirador.)

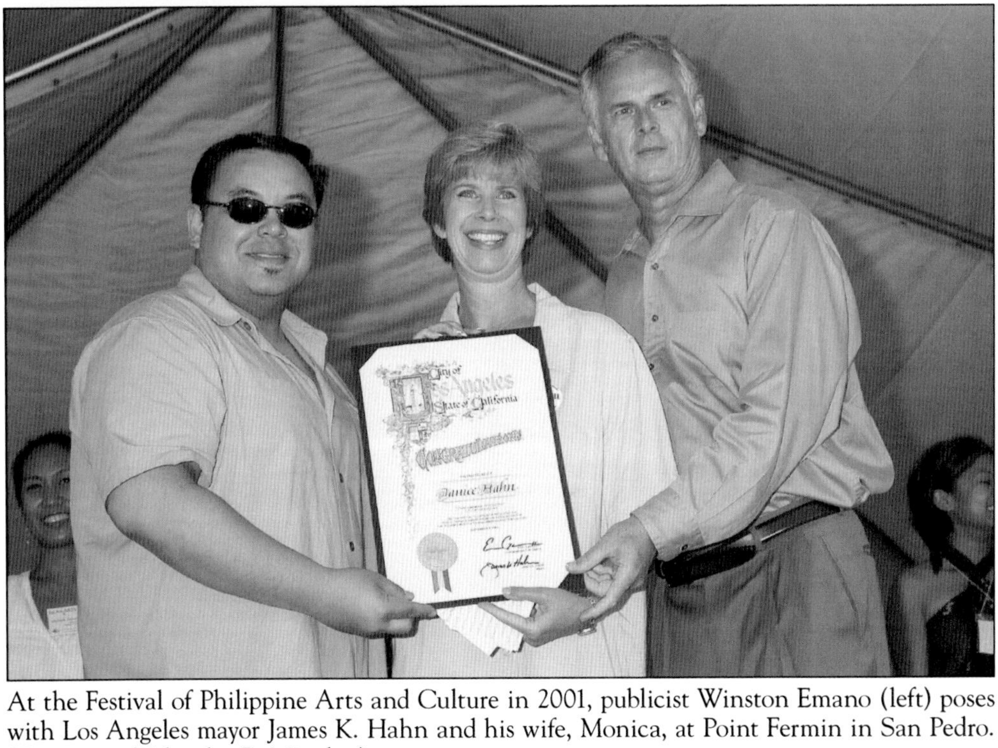

At the Festival of Philippine Arts and Culture in 2001, publicist Winston Emano (left) poses with Los Angeles mayor James K. Hahn and his wife, Monica, at Point Fermin in San Pedro. (Courtesy of Sthanlee B. Mirador.)

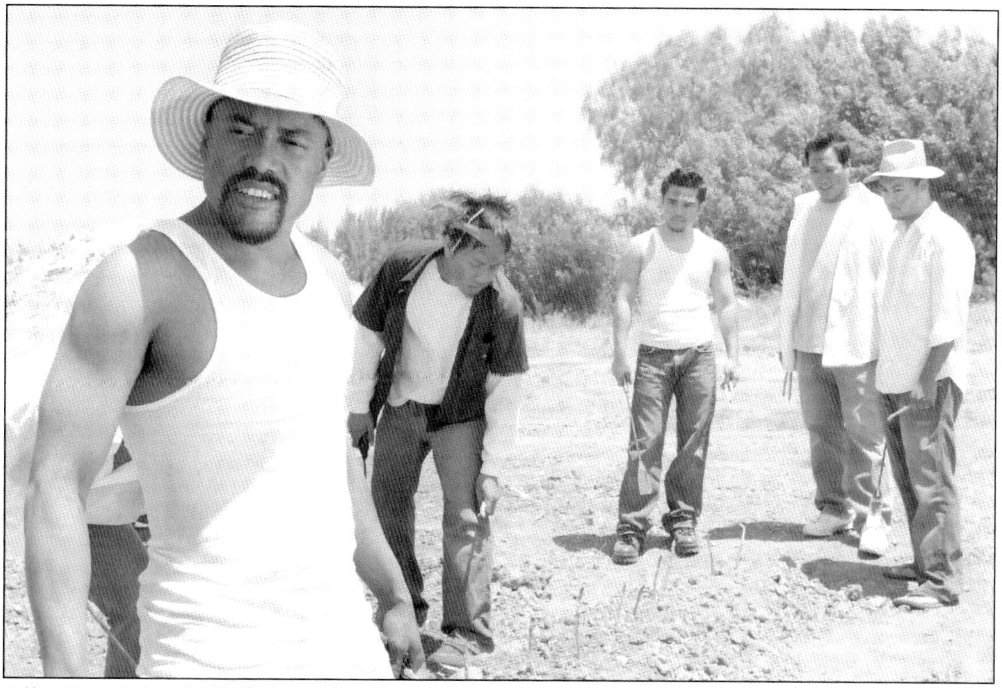

Allen Pineda Lindo (left) is seen here in the asparagus fields for the *Bebot (Generation One)* music video in 2006. (Courtesy of Sthanlee B. Mirador.)

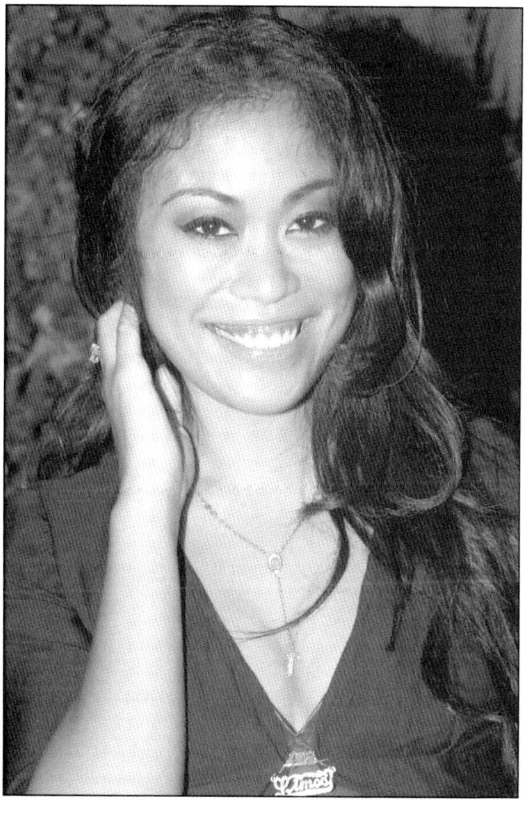

Actress Tiffany Limos made her acting debut in *Ken Park* in 2002. An accomplished flutist, harpist, and pianist, Limos modeled for the Ford agency in New York and sold two screenplays to Paramount Pictures at age 21. (Courtesy of Sthanlee B. Mirador.)

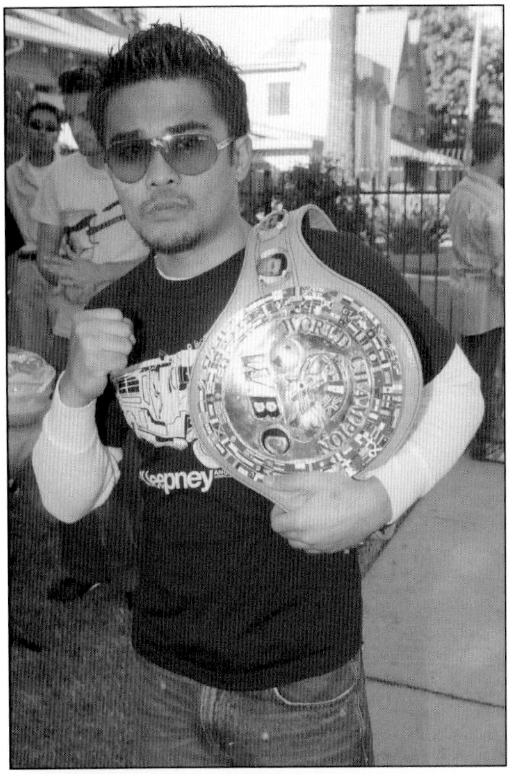

Professional boxer Brian Viloria is pictured on the *BEBOT* film set in 2006. In 1999, he won the U.S. championships, the national Golden Gloves, and the World Amateur Boxing championships. He is nicknamed "the Hawaiian" and "Pinoy Punch" at flyweight. In 2005, he dropped down to junior flyweight and won the WBC title. (Courtesy of Sthanlee B. Mirador.)

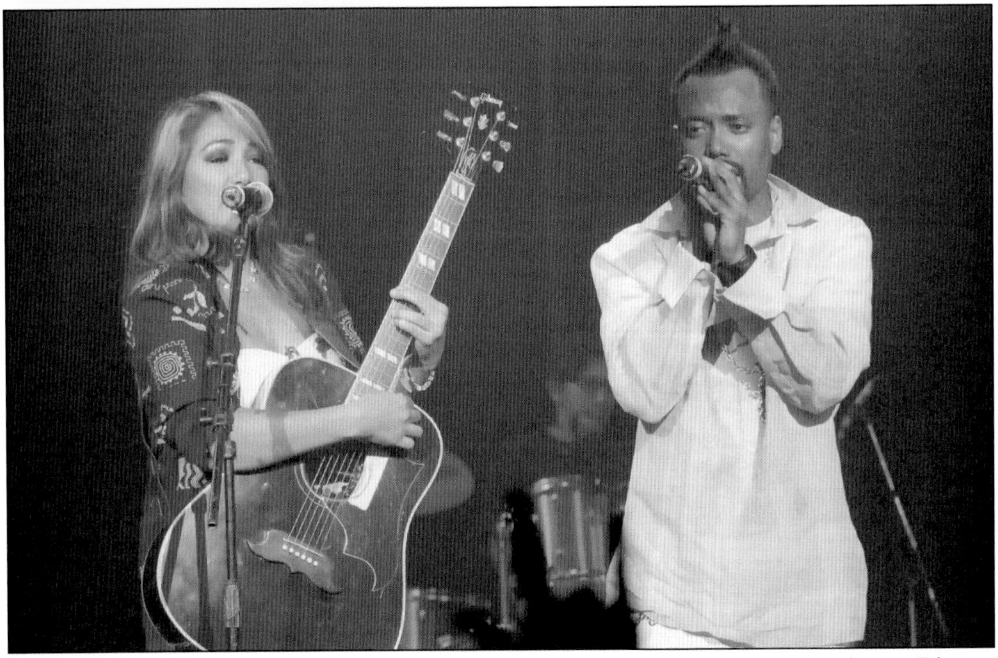

Lolita Carbon (left) and Allen Pineda of the Black Eyed Peas perform in 2006. Carbon, a Filipina folk singer, began singing at age 10, winning a best singer title on a live radio talent show. In 1976, she joined a folk duo, and in 1977, the duo became a trio and changed their name to ASIN. (Courtesy of Sthanlee B. Mirador.)

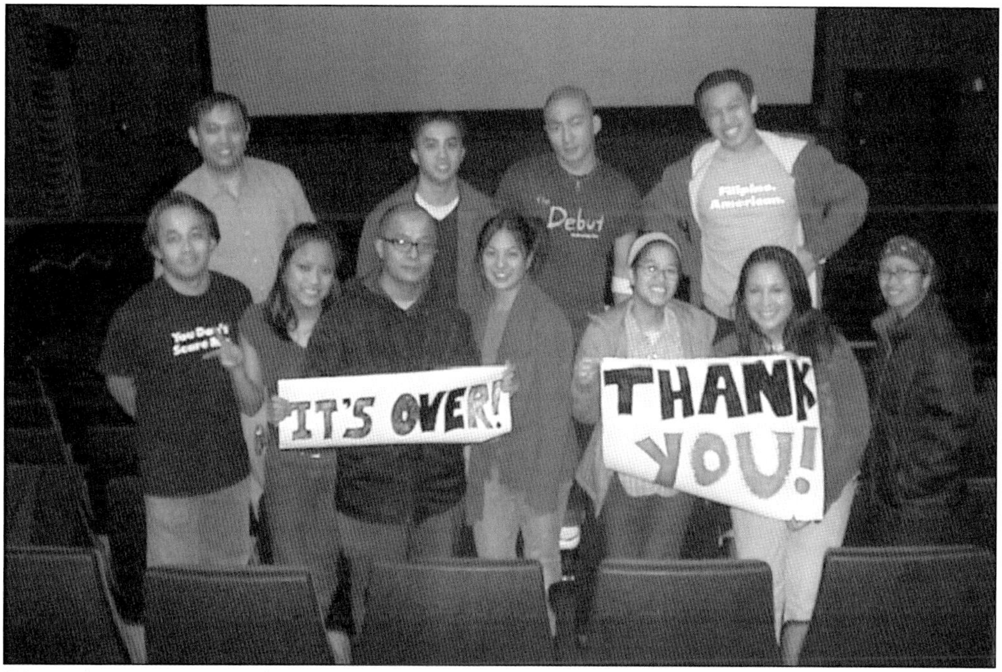

Filmmaker Patricio Ginelsa is seen with some of the cast of *The Debut* after its completion in 2006. (Courtesy of Patricio Ginelsa.)

Filmmaker Patricio Ginelsa is pictured in 2007 on Hollywood Boulevard. A graduate in cinema production from the University of Southern California, he is the founder of Kid Heroes Productions, a full-service production company that specializes in independent film and video projects. He also has worked on projects with the Black Eyed Peas and A&M Records (Universal Music). Some of his many accomplishments include *Lumpia, Bootleg Visuals*, the Black Eyed Peas' "The Apl Song," and many other projects. (Courtesy of Patricia Salumbides.)

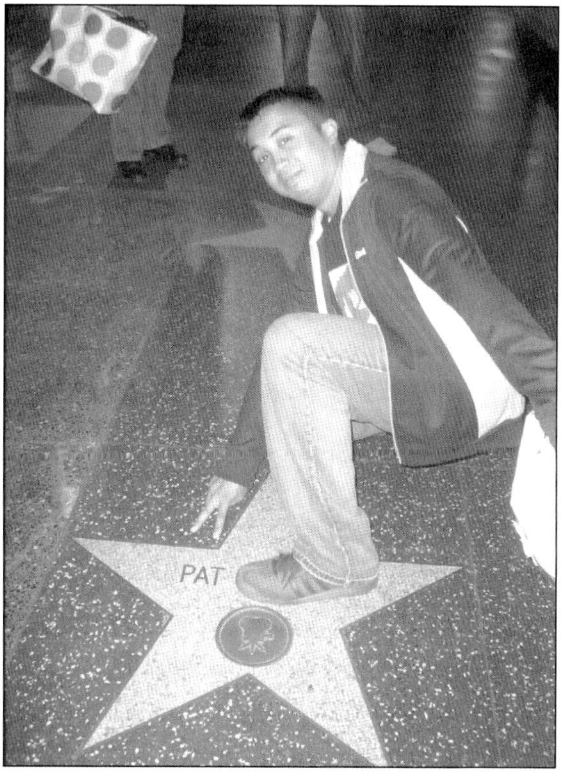

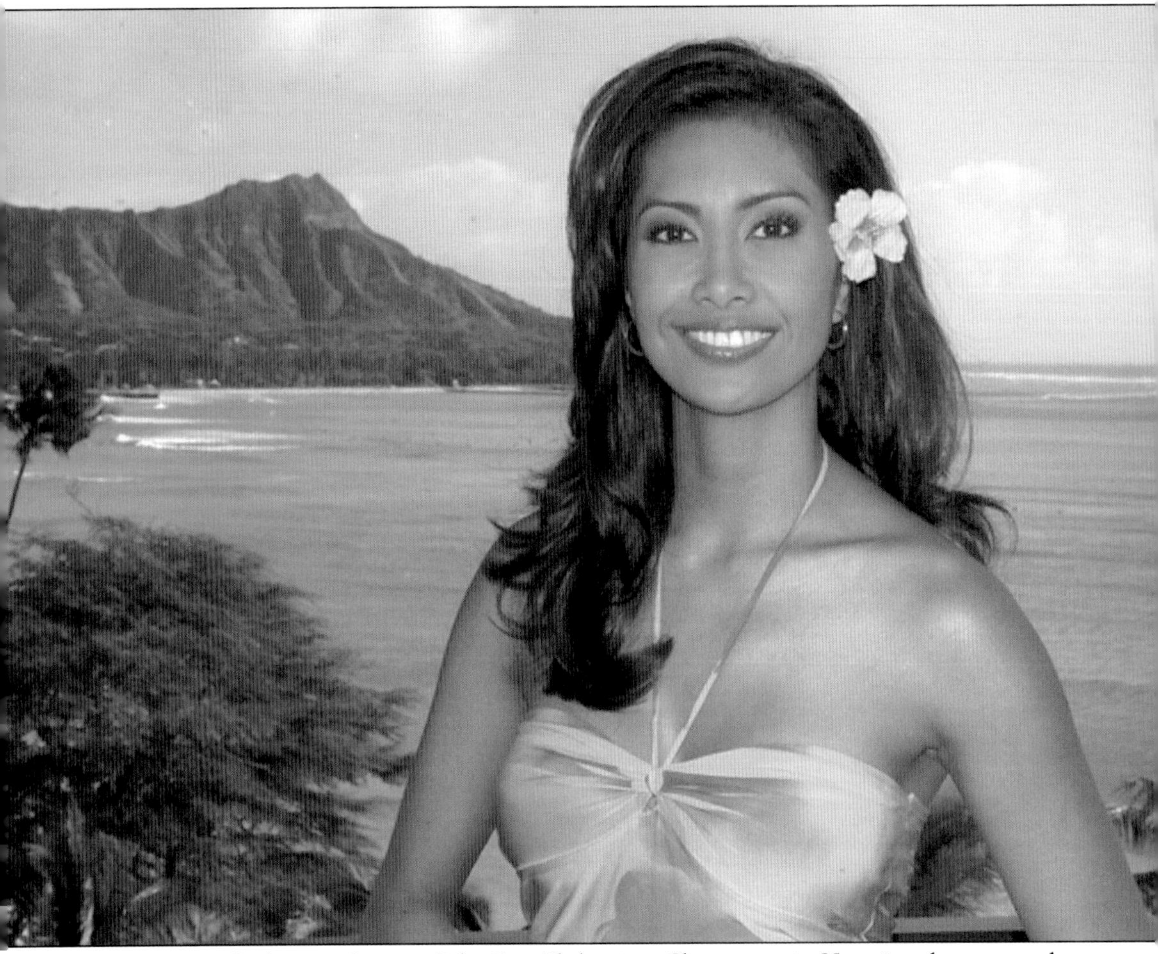

Maria Teresa Quiban was born in Cebu City, Philippines. She grew up in Hawaii and was an anchor and reporter from 1995 to 1998 at the NBC-TV affiliate in Honolulu, News 8. She relocated to Los Angeles from Honolulu in 1998 with her family, desirous of furthering her career in broadcast television. She was featured on the Orange County news channel from 1998 to 2000, when she became a news reporter at Fox 11 News/My 13 News in Los Angeles. Acknowledged by the Search to Involve Pilipino Americans (SIPA) organization, she was honored with the Gawad Manlilikha (creative arts) award in 2005. (Courtesy of Maria Teresa Quiban.)

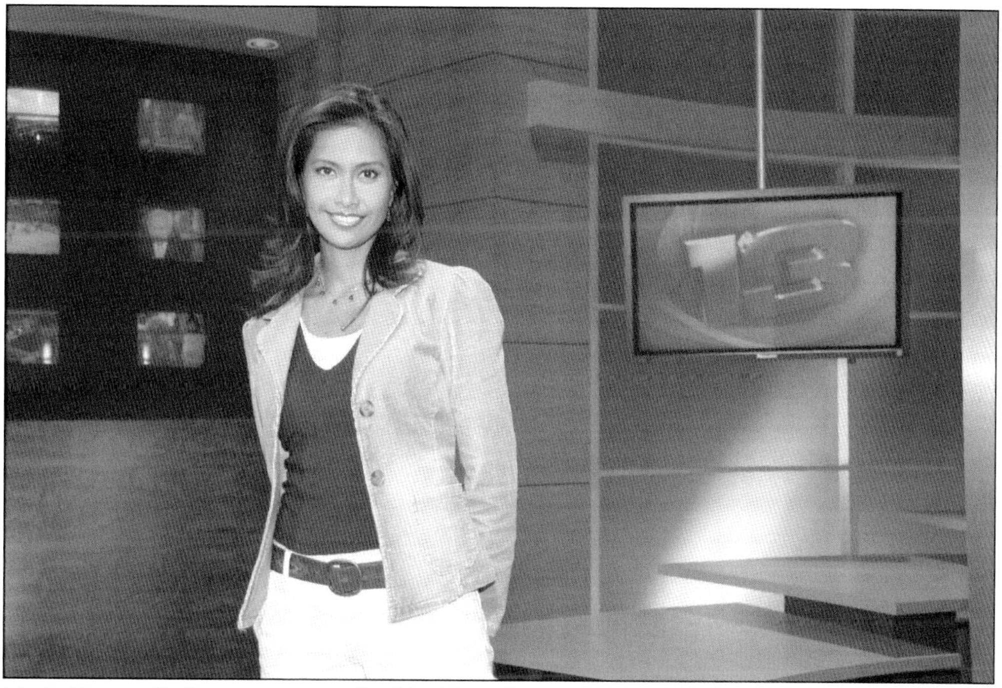

Maria Teresa Quiban is seen on the My 13 studio newsroom set. She is the weekday weather anchor and also serves as the weekend news anchor. At Fox 11 news, she was, at publication time, the weekend weather anchor and weekday fill-in anchor. (Courtesy of Celina Taganas-Duffy.)

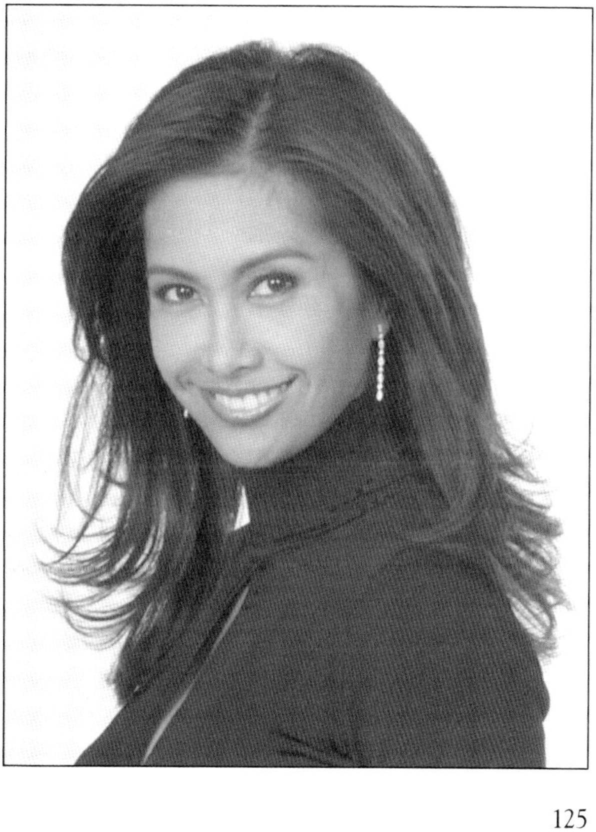

Maria Teresa Quiban represents the new generation of Filipinos in Hollywood today. She is highly acknowledged for and best recognized as a television news reporter, as well as for her roles as an actress. (Courtesy of Celina Taganas-Duffy)

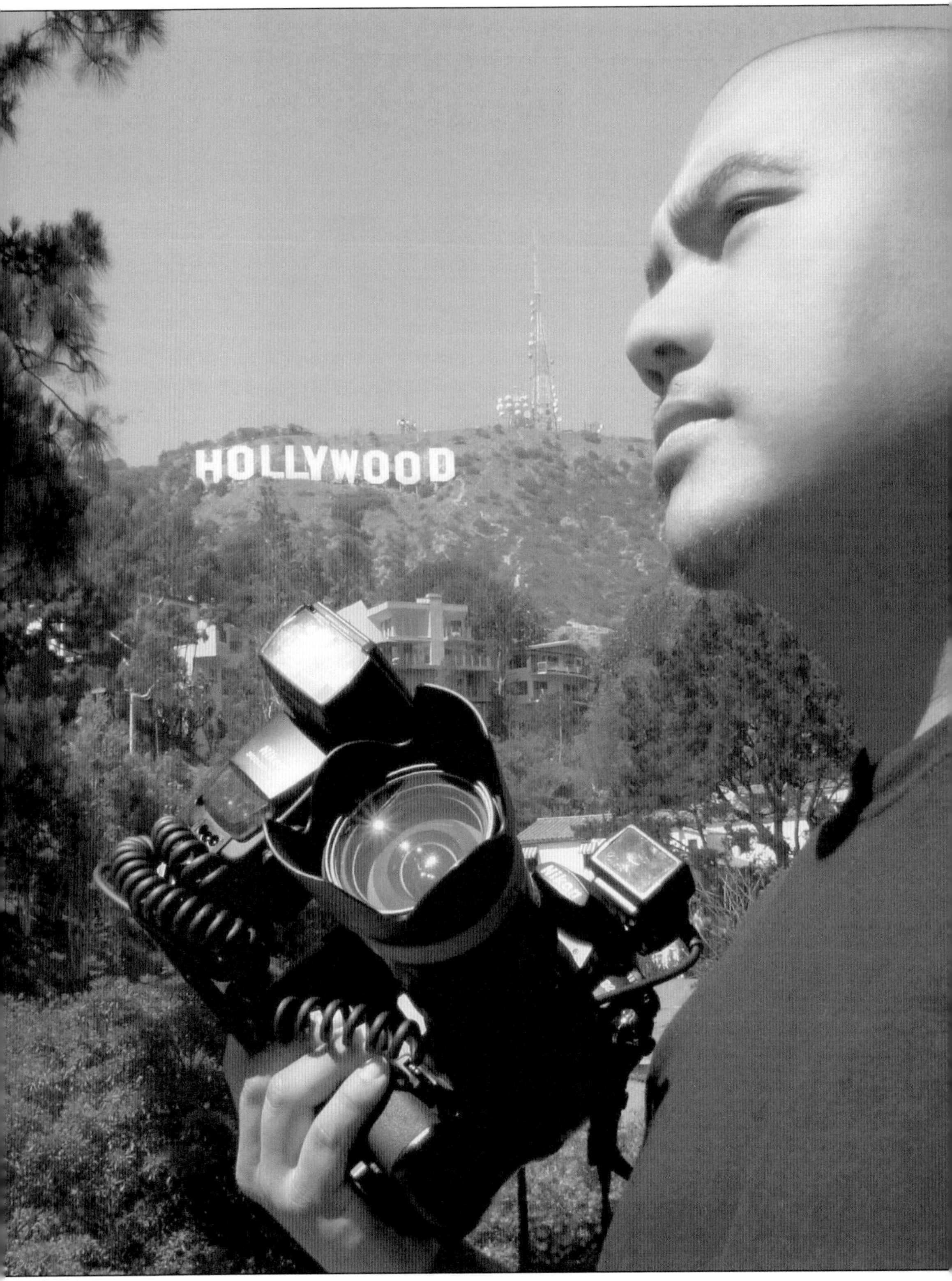
HOLLYWOOD

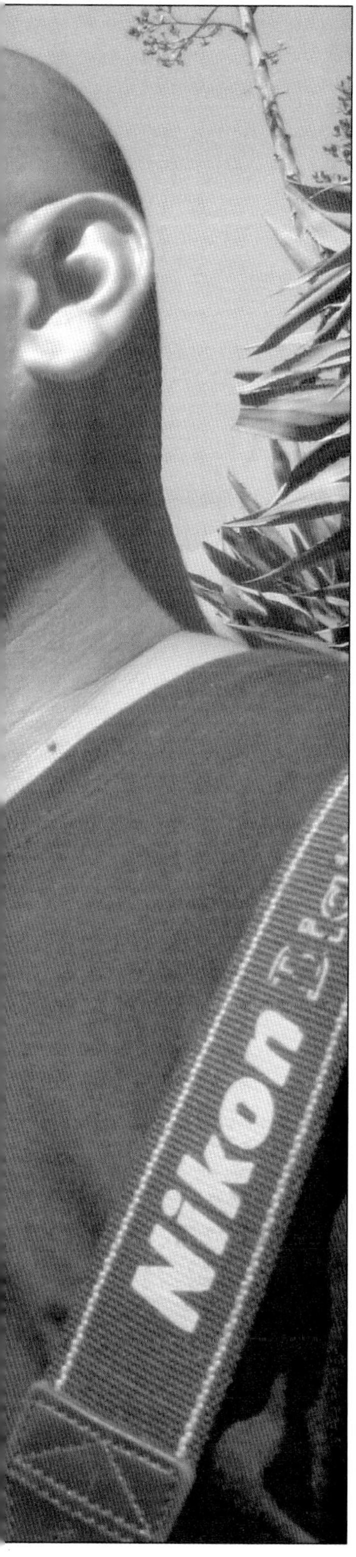

Pictured is Filipino American professional photographer Sthanlee B. Mirador. A graduate of the University of California, Irvine, Mirador's work includes photographic coverage of most major Hollywood events, including the Annual Academy Awards, Golden Globe Awards, Hollywood premiers, and celebrity events. His photographs are published around the world, and his work continues to promote the many talented and accomplished Filipinos in Hollywood today. (Courtesy of Peterson Gonzaga.)

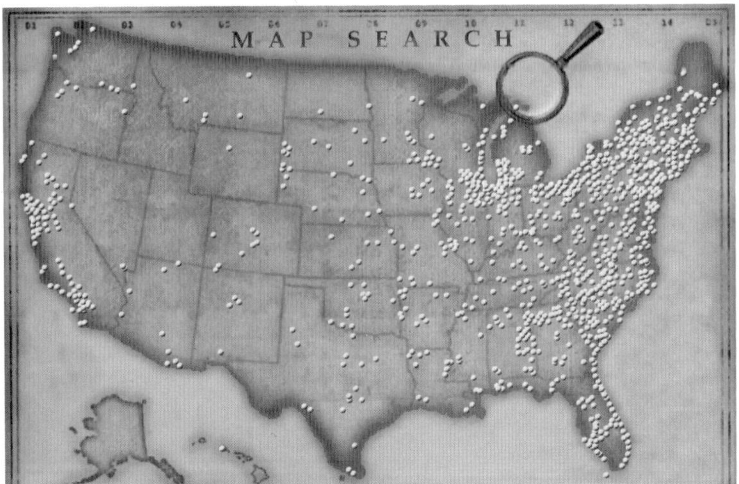
MAP SEARCH